100 Exercises for Showjumping

TRIAN
ACES LTD
nsurfaces.co.uk

100 Exercises for Showjumping

SARAH TUBBS

J.A.ALLEN

CONTENTS

PATHWAY
COACHING
EQUESTRIAN

INTRODUCTION

There are so many factors to riding a successful showjumping round that it can feel as if achieving it is a life's work – and it often is! As a rider and a coach I find I am always learning, and every encounter with someone else within the sport, whether experienced or not, can bring new ideas and thought processes that help to develop my understanding further.

In this book my aim was to try to address a broad spectrum of areas in which you can work your horse to help improve showjumping performance, from understanding the areas of flatwork that can help with the ride in the ring, to introducing a young horse to jumping, and a variety of basic exercises to develop any horse's rideability. As a coach educator as well as a coach, I have included tips for certain exercises to help coaches get the most out of them for their clients, although the tips will potentially be useful for anyone who helps you from the ground with your jumping.

I am also aware that not all riding environments are perfect, and that sometimes riders and coaches are building exercises with limited equipment or limited space. I have therefore created a range of exercises for small arenas, as well as providing an equipment list for every exercise, so that a quick glance will tell you whether you have enough poles or wings or both to build what you need for that particular exercise.

One item of kit that I repeatedly refer to is the 'half-round pole'. These are often available at builders' merchants and fencing companies at relatively low cost, and make excellent ground poles or place poles, as they don't roll underfoot if stood on, and the round profile on top is very forgiving, so they don't tend to lift up or break if a hoof lands on them. If you are using round poles as ground poles then investing in some form of pole holder, or making small wooden holders yourself, is worth doing to stop the poles rolling away if a foot touches them. These are particularly useful if you are doing polework on your own, as there is nothing more frustrating than having to stop riding the exercise to relocate all your poles when they get knocked!

Another essential piece of kit for coaches that is worth having for anyone building exercises at home is a tape measure. Whilst we would perhaps all like to think we can consistently walk a distance, there are days when it is easier than others! To be certain that you have built your distance accurately, it only takes a minute to put a tape measure on it, after you have paced it out, to be sure that it is correct. Every British Showjumping course is built using a tape measure for distances, and it can be a great help to know how your distances at home relate to those in the ring because you have built them accurately to a similar formula.

Safety cups are also a key piece of equipment for coaches and are well worth the investment, as these are designed to be used on the back bar element of any spread fence and will allow the pole to drop to the ground if a horse lands on it. In an ideal world, safety cups would be used on any spread fence used in training. If the number of these cups is limited, one located on the back bar of an oxer is better than none!

Most showjumping training now takes place on an artificial surface, but these still vary massively, and the nature of the surface can significantly impact upon both the horse's jump and its length of stride. For example, some waxed surfaces can ride a little holding and will shorten the stride, whereas a sand surface with something such as a grid-based underground watering system seems to encourage the stride to open; also deep surfaces shorten the stride generally, whilst firm surfaces often allow the stride to be longer. Building related distances is therefore something of an art form, and for all the distances listed in this book they can only ever be a guide, as the surface they are ridden on, as well as the location of the fences and the type of horse and rider combination training over them, can mean that some adjustment (even if it's only small) might be required to make it work well.

Another factor to bear in mind, whether coaching or riding, is the light. Bright daylight can reflect on the jumps or make it difficult for the rider to see easily, and early morning or late afternoon light as the sun rises or sets can make it difficult for both horse and rider to see the fence. This can mean that it becomes necessary to exclude a fence from a training session, or to change the direction in which it is jumped. Shadows can also cause an issue, as these can create a false groundline at a fence, or, when something such as Yorkshire boarding is used for indoor arena sides, the stripes between dark and light can cause horses to jump them or spook at them, which is worth bearing in mind when building jumping exercises.

If jumping under lights, ensure that the quality of light is sufficient for the horse to see the fence clearly (there is guidance from bodies such as Sport England on the minimum level of Lux for sporting arenas, which is helpful), and try to avoid lights mounted on the sides of the arena at fence height as these do not give good light coverage at ground level.

I have referred to the distances in the exercises primarily in imperial measurements as these are easier to explain and calculate (four yards equates to one canter stride for a horse, and two yards is the distance for take-off or landing, and these are easy to learn to pace out), but metric distances are also included.

I have referred to the horse throughout the book as male, for no other reason than my current horses are all geldings and it was less clumsy than a multiple pronoun!

GAIN

FLATWORK FOR JUMPING

Around 90 per cent of a showjumping track is ridden on the flat, and how your horse performs in the areas between the fences can significantly affect his performance over the jumps.

In terms of the development of the young horse, there are several exercises that can help with strengthening the hind leg and creating the suppleness and engagement required as the horse steps up the levels in his jumping; these are covered in this section. Other exercises in this section address the general rideability needed for a good showjumping round, as well as other areas that are key to the jumping exercises later in the book.

EXERCISE 1

The Scales of Training

All aspects of developing a horse are encompassed within the Scales of Training. Showjumping is made much easier by having a rideable horse for the areas between the fences, and this section aims to provide flatwork exercises that help to educate and improve your horse's way of going on the flat to improve his rideability to the fences.

Aim

The aim is to provide a description of the Scales of Training and explain how these can guide your work with your horse on the flat.

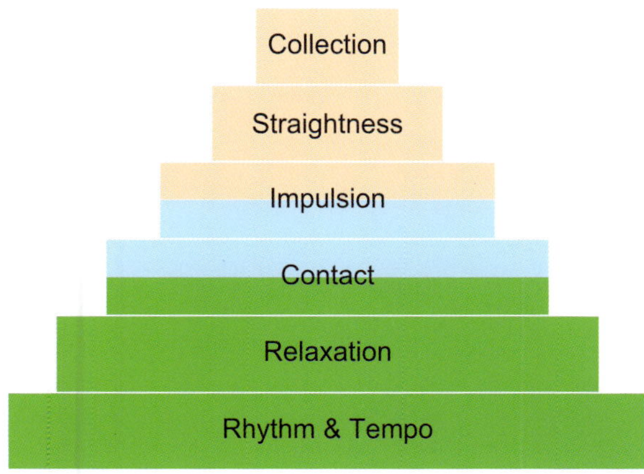

The scales of training.

The Principles of the Scales of Training

The Scales of Training originated in Germany and some of the meanings do not translate well into English, so I have tried to combine the two in the outline below.

Takt: Translates as 'rhythm and tempo'. The evenness of the horse's footfalls within a gait and the speed of those footfalls is the first and most essential building block. These two factors are a key judging element in dressage, and are essential to a good showjumping round.

Losgelassenheit: There is no direct English translation for this German word, and the usual interpretation is 'suppleness'; however, I think this can be misleading. The German 'Gelassenheit' translates as 'serenity', and 'gelassen' as 'calmly', so the 'suppleness' we refer to in English is really about your horse moving in a relaxed and calm manner, with no tension – it is sometimes interpreted as 'relaxation'. Although this comes after rhythm and tempo, it is hard to achieve a good rhythm when your horse is tense, so to some extent these two go hand in hand.

Anlehnung: This means 'rein contact'. As your horse develops in his balance, he should become able to stay consistently in a gentle rein contact whilst maintaining the other factors already mentioned. Often when the contact is not good, the rhythm and tempo can be affected, and relaxation is most definitely impacted – and these three elements work together as part of the initial training phase of your horse, where he is understanding and gaining confidence in what is being asked of him.

Schwung: This is a brilliant word that sounds like its meaning! We interpret it as 'impulsion', and combined with contact and the next element in the Scales of Training, it is part of the development of the horse's pushing power, which is fundamental to showjumping.

Geraderichtung: This is 'straightness'. This might sound simple to achieve, but its position so far up the Scales of Training reflects how difficult it is to achieve true straightness through turns as well as straight lines, and to have all four feet travelling correctly with the right amount of alignment through the head, neck and spine. All horses begin with some level of asymmetry, and then we add a rider (who may not be that symmetrical!) to the equation. Then add in all the other requirements of the Scales of Training, particularly impulsion, and perhaps it becomes more obvious why true straightness can be difficult to achieve. From the perspective of showjumping, this element can be hugely influential in the ability to take off in a balanced manner. It is also easier to judge the take-off point if the horse is straight on the approach.

Versammlung: This means 'collection'. Although the level of collection needed for showjumping is very different from that required for dressage, being able to shorten and lengthen the canter is essential at the higher levels, whilst maintaining impulsion, rhythm and straightness.

How to Ride It

- When you are schooling your horse, the Scales of Training are a great reference point and inspiration for those days when you need to find something to focus on in your training.
- Depending on the age of your horse and his level of training, review the appropriate aspects of the Scales of Training and see if you can identify which area could be worked on that day. As you work your horse, keep noticing which areas are working well or improving and where you can still work to improve, or add in the next level of the Scales of Training and see if you can maintain the other areas still – for example, can you add impulsion and maintain rhythm and tempo?
- Many of the exercises outlined in this book provide techniques that will improve performance in relation to the Scales of Training.

TIP: THE VALUE OF VIDEO

If you are not sure where your horse needs to improve in relation to the Scales of Training, it can be helpful to get a friend to video you riding in all three paces so that you can review it and think about the various aspects later, without time pressure or the distraction of being on your horse and addressing issues in that moment.

EXERCISE 2

The Half Halt

Aim

This is such a fundamental element of riding that it is almost certainly familiar; however, riding it well in relation to showjumping is worth practising, as the key is to be able to retain power whilst adjusting your horse's balance.

How to Ride It

- Riding a half halt is like changing down a gear in a car or on a bike, in that it should maintain or increase the power ratio but not change the pace (unless you use that change of gear to then accelerate!). By increasing engagement, it also allows the horse to lighten in the shoulders and take the weight more on to the hind legs, which helps with the balance on the approach to a fence.
- The half halt should therefore be ridden from the hind leg first, so close the lower leg before asking anything else so that the hind leg is stepping under the body and retaining energy.
- Think of then growing tall in your upper body and engaging your core muscles to ask the horse to momentarily come up through the shoulders, and think of a split-second pause in forward momentum before closing the leg and riding forwards again.
- If your horse does not react to your change in body position, you can slightly increase the pressure on the outside rein or both reins for a stride. Hopefully as your horse becomes accustomed to the sequence of aids you will need less rein aid, but if not, you can repeat the half-halt aids again until he understands what is being asked of him. Try to avoid a continuous pull to get the half halt as this is likely to lead to a tug of war with your horse, which doesn't tend to be won by the rider!
- Practise riding the half halt within the canter, and ride a few strides afterwards, noticing how the balance and power has improved as a result.
- When riding to a fence, try riding a half halt about six to eight strides before the jump to prepare your horse by gaining his attention and improving his balance and engagement in the canter. This is often further away from the jump than people think!

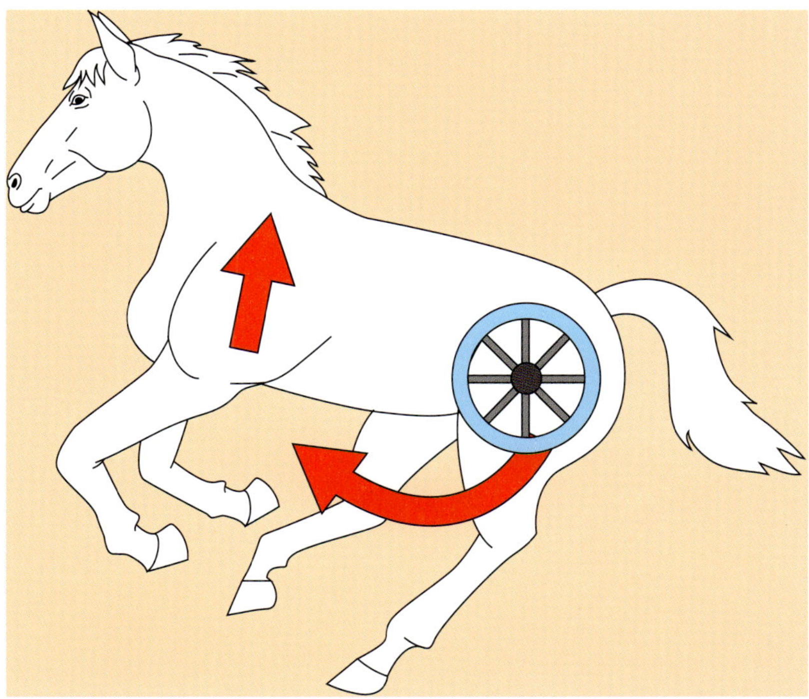

The half halt needs the hind leg to be engaged and creating power to help elevate the shoulders.

EXERCISE 3

Lengthening and Shortening the Stride

Aim

Although maintaining an even rhythm round a track of showjumps is a basic principle of a fluent round, there are often occasions when you will need to slightly lengthen or shorten the stride in a related distance as a result of the preceding jump. At the more advanced levels, the course-builder might also make the distance a little shorter or longer to challenge the adjustability of the horse and the effectiveness of the rider, so being able to adjust the length of stride without losing power or gaining speed is relevant at all levels.

How to Ride It

- It is much easier to shorten the canter round a turn because this is when the horse will naturally look to shorten his stride. So initially it will be easier to introduce this exercise by lengthening down the long sides of an arena and shortening on the short sides.
- To lengthen the canter, slightly lighten your seatbones and flex your hips towards the back of the saddle and your shoulders very slightly forwards, but keep your chest up (be careful not to drop down and forwards, as this will make the horse more likely to run on to the forehand). Close your leg to ask the horse to move forwards, but maintain a contact down the rein so that the energy is contained and the horse doesn't become flat and run on to his shoulders. The aim is to lengthen the stride, and not to get faster, shorter steps.
- To shorten the canter, sit tall in the saddle, close the leg to ride a half halt, and repeat as needed to contain the stride. Key to this is holding a tall upper body position with your core muscles engaged so that the rein aids are not needed too much. It is important that the stride shortens but the energy is not lost.
- Once you can achieve this, try changing it so that you create the lengthening on the short sides and the shortening on the long sides, which is slightly more challenging for the horse to achieve.

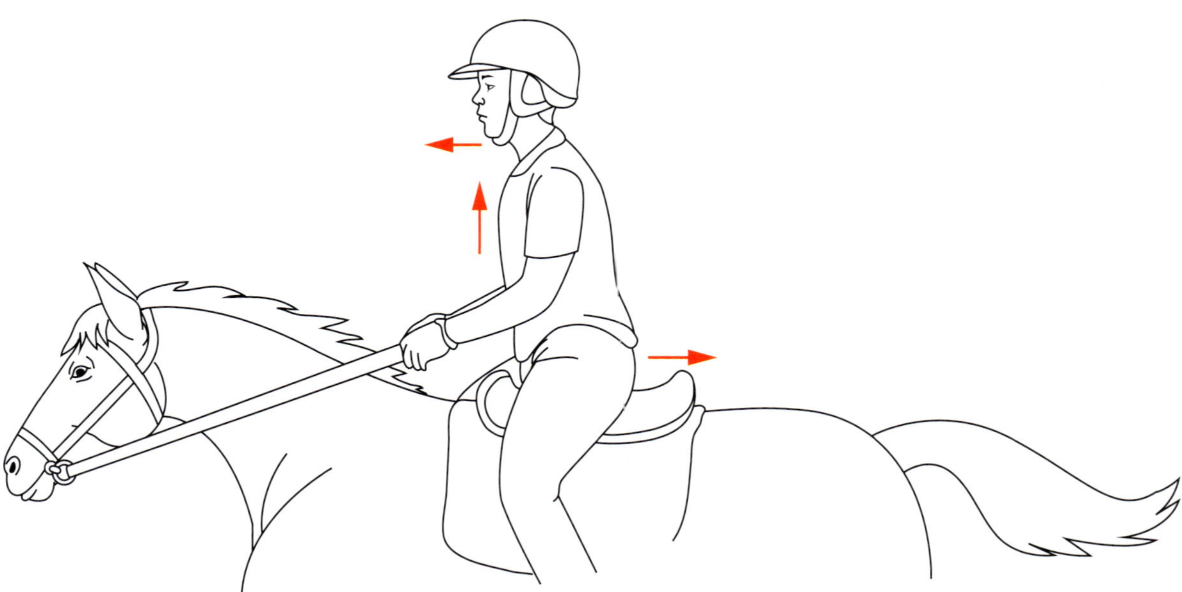

Lengthening the stride by slightly lightening your seatbones and flexing your hips towards the back of the saddle whilst keeping your chest up.

EXERCISE 4

Leg Yield in a Straight Line

Aim

Leg yield is a very useful exercise to train your showjumper not only to respond to the aids to move to the left or right without changing pace, but also to help train him to engage the hindquarters and improve the suppleness of the hind leg.

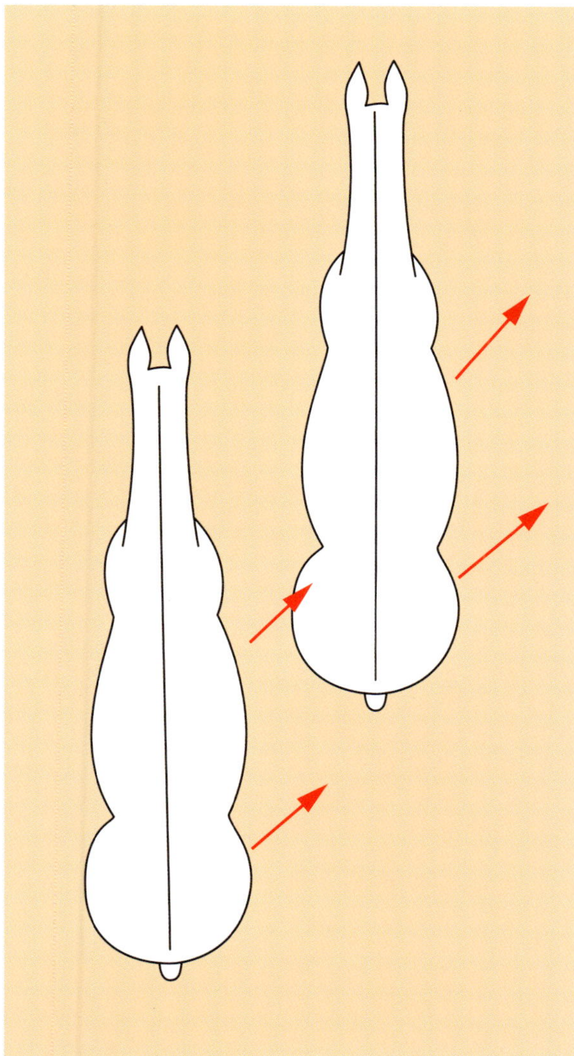

Leg yield from the three-quarter line to the track – your horse's body should stay in a straight line moving laterally so be careful to ensure the shoulders do not lead the way to the track.

How to Ride It

Leg yield from the three-quarter line to the track:

- Begin this exercise in walk and only progress through the paces once you and your horse are confident.
- The key to this being ridden successfully is to start by making your horse straight! So, when you turn on to the three-quarter line, ride the first part of it in a straight line (and if your horse starts to anticipate the leg yield, ride the three-quarter line straight a couple of times before trying the leg yield again).
- To give the aids to leg yield, have a very slight poll flexion (not neck bend) to the inside, and ensure that you control your horse's shoulder with your outside rein. Then use your inside leg slightly behind the girth to ask your horse to step over towards the track from the inside hind leg stepping across. Sit level in the saddle but have the feeling, if anything, of your weight being very slightly into the inside seatbone in preference to the outside.
- As you ride the movement, be careful that your horse does not begin to lead with the shoulders. This can feel more dramatic than the correct movement, but it means that the hind leg is not stepping across and so the movement is less beneficial for the suppling of the hind leg.

Leg yield from the track to the three-quarter line:

- This movement is slightly more challenging than the first one, as the wall usually draws the horse towards it, but it is probably the most useful one for showjumping purposes. Training your horse to move laterally from the outside aids allows you to straighten him easily to a fence out of a turn.
- As with the first exercise, start slowly and build up the pace.
- Ride the corner of the arena staying on the track. Flex your horse's poll very slightly to the outside (an indirect rein aid, where you bring your outside hand towards your horse's neck or slightly across the neck to the other side, can help to achieve

this flexion). Control the degree of bend and your horse's inside shoulder with your inside rein as a direct rein aid (taking the rein straight back towards your hip). Sit level in the saddle but have the feeling of your outside seatbone being fractionally more present than the inside seatbone (your weight is therefore marginally on the inside of the flexion), and use your outside leg just behind the girth to ask your horse to step away from the wall with his outside hind leg.

- Focus on the hind leg creating the movement across so that your horse's body stays parallel to the wall and doesn't fall in. Continue the movement towards the three-quarter line, then ride straight for the last two or three strides so that you can change the bend to ride the corner correctly.
- Once you are able to ride these movements confidently, try riding the leg yield from the track to the three-quarter line, aiming to achieve this by halfway up the long side, change the flexion and yield back out for the second half. This makes sure your horse is responding to your aids and not anticipating the movement. Once you are riding it in canter, keep your weight on the side of the leading leg to avoid getting an unintended flying change – though by this point your horse should be moving off the lateral leg aid more readily anyway.

EXERCISE 5

Leg Yield on the Circle

Aim

This version of leg yield is helpful to improve suppleness and balance, and it can be useful when working with forward-thinking horses: the circle element allows you to apply the lateral leg aids for the yield, but the horse is less able to rush forwards if he misunderstands this and thinks it is a forward aid, due to the fact that you are constantly turning.

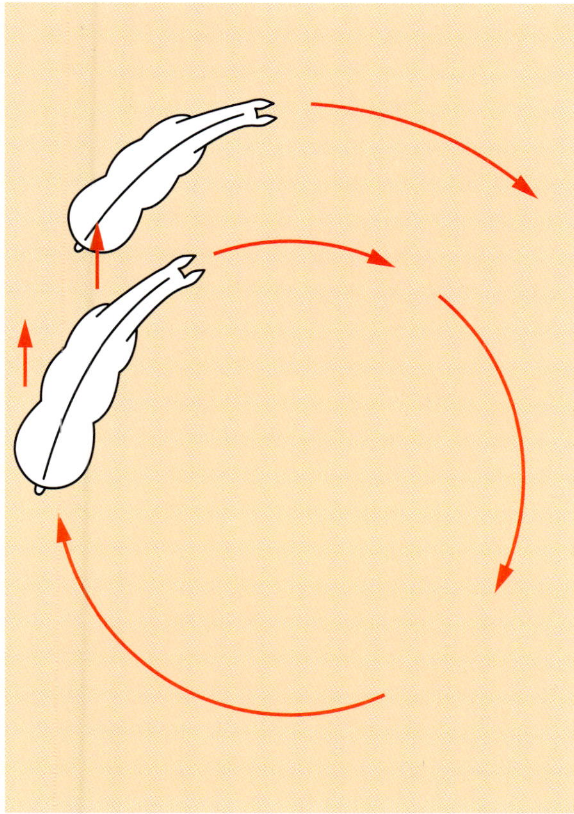

Leg yield in and out of a circle, keeping the alignment of the body the same.

How to Ride It

- Start by riding a large circle, ideally at least twenty metres. Establish that circle initially in walk, thinking of keeping an even bend through your horse's body.
- Then slightly straighten your horse's neck. Apply the outside leg just behind the girth and ask your horse to gradually decrease the size of the circle. Be careful that he doesn't fall on to the inside shoulder and lose balance, so keep the movement gradual to keep it as consistent as you can, with the whole body moving across in alignment as much as possible. Think of sitting evenly in the saddle, or fractionally into the outside seatbone, so you are not tempted to lean to the inside to help decrease the circle.
- Once your circle has decreased to around ten metres, create a small amount of poll flexion to the inside and start to ask your horse to step back out on to the larger circle by using your inside leg slightly behind the girth. Sit evenly in the saddle, thinking of only slightly more feeling into the inside seatbone. It is very easy here for the horse to fall out on to a bigger circle through the shoulder, which requires less suppleness than stepping out from the inside hind leg, so control the outside shoulder with the outside rein, and if necessary, ride a halt and ask the hind leg to step over, then continue the movement forwards again if you lose the shoulder too much. Thinking of the hind leg almost leading the way back out of the circle can help to get the correct feeling, even though we are actually aiming for it to be in alignment with the shoulders.
- As you ride this in canter, you will feel how useful this training will become for turns, shortening with engagement, and jump-off technique, as your horse responds to moving off the lateral aid to change direction and maintains his power and engagement of the hind leg through the movement.

EXERCISE 6

Leg Yield on a Diagonal Line

Aim

Riding leg yield across the diagonal in trot before asking for the canter transition is a very useful way to set up your horse's body for a correct strike-off and a more engaged transition. This exercise can therefore be useful for horses that find one leading leg harder to achieve than the other, and for horses that need to learn to stay balanced and engaged in the transition, rather than running on to the forehand.

How to Ride It

- You can begin this exercise in walk whilst you and your horse become familiar with it. Start by riding the turn on to the diagonal line – for example, using the arena markers you might ride the diagonal M-X-K.
- Once your horse is on the diagonal line and has taken a couple of paces towards K, apply a little outside rein pressure as a half halt to control the new outside shoulder (this will be the outside rein when you have changed the rein – so if you are riding the diagonal to change the rein from right to left the outside rein will become the right rein for the leg yield) and at the same time, apply your inside leg just behind the girth.

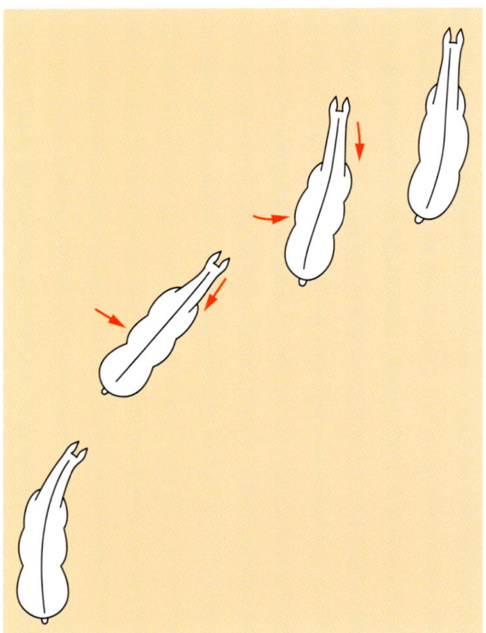

Applying the new inside leg and supporting with the new outside rein creates a movement into leg yield on the diagonal.

- Keep your seatbones level in the saddle but have fractionally more feeling into the new inside seatbone towards the inside of the bend and ask your horse to fractionally flex at the poll towards the inside. You do *not* want neck bend as this will cause your horse to lose balance and fall on to the outside shoulder.
- Gradually over a few steps, ask your horse to move his body over from your inside leg aid, so that he moves from being on the diagonal line heading towards the corner marker, to being parallel to the long side whilst moving laterally towards the corner.
- Think of applying the leg and rein aids on and off, ideally as the outside front foot is landing, so that your inside leg supports the movement across whilst you control the outside shoulder and foreleg. However, the most important thing is to give your horse the opportunity to respond to your aids by applying them on and off rather than holding the aids on without a release of pressure.
- Once you have mastered this on both reins in walk, repeat the exercise in trot.
- To introduce the canter, think of completing the leg yield as you reach the track at the end of the diagonal line, at which point your horse will be in the correct position for the canter strike-off. As you meet the track, apply your canter aids so that you are in canter before you ride into the corner.

TIP: ACHIEVING THE CORRECT STRIKE-OFF IN CANTER

If you still struggle a little with the correct canter strike-off, a slightly raised pole just after the marker as you head into the corner can help achieve the transition correctly. Raising it slightly higher on the inside helps to elevate the inside shoulder and hind leg and therefore encourages your horse to strike off into canter with the correct, outside hind leg.

EXERCISE 7

Shoulder In and Shoulder Fore

Aim

Both these movements are useful to help improve suppleness and engagement. Shoulder fore is less of an angle than shoulder in, and so is a good way of introducing this movement to your horse.

How to Ride It

- It can be helpful to start by riding a ten-metre circle in the corner of the arena just before the long side. This will put your horse's body in the same alignment as he will need for shoulder fore.
- Riding the circle, sit level but be aware of your inside seatbone having fractionally more pressure, seeking an even bend through your horse's body, so a slight inside flexion, controlling the bend through the outside rein, with the inside leg just behind the girth to engage the inside hind leg, and the outside leg slightly further back ready to control the hind leg from stepping out if needed. Your shoulders will be in alignment with your horse's shoulders, so slightly turned to the inside.
- As you complete the circle, position yourself and your horse as if you are about to start another circle. Then as your horse's inside forefoot leaves the track to start the circle, change your shoulder positioning to align it with the long side of the arena (so you will have a rotation in your upper body, with a fraction more weight remaining in the inside seatbone but your hips staying level), apply your inside leg (ideally as the inside hind leg leaves the ground) to encourage your horse to keep the hind legs towards the wall and maintain the neck and body positioning on this line – but by changing your shoulder alignment you are now continuing the bend in the body but riding up the long side rather than on a circle.
- If the angle in your horse's body is just enough that both front feet have left the track but all four feet are on slightly different tracks, then this is shoulder fore. Once the outside foreleg has left the track enough to be lined up with the inside hind leg, your horse will be working on three tracks (inside fore on one track, inside hind and outside fore on a second track, and outside hind on the third track), which is shoulder in. Shoulder in requires quite a high degree of suppleness and engagement, so build up to it by developing shoulder fore first.
- Always complete the exercise by straightening up your horse's body before you ride the turn so that there is a differentiation between the exercise and riding the corner, and your horse doesn't fall into the turn out of the shoulder in.

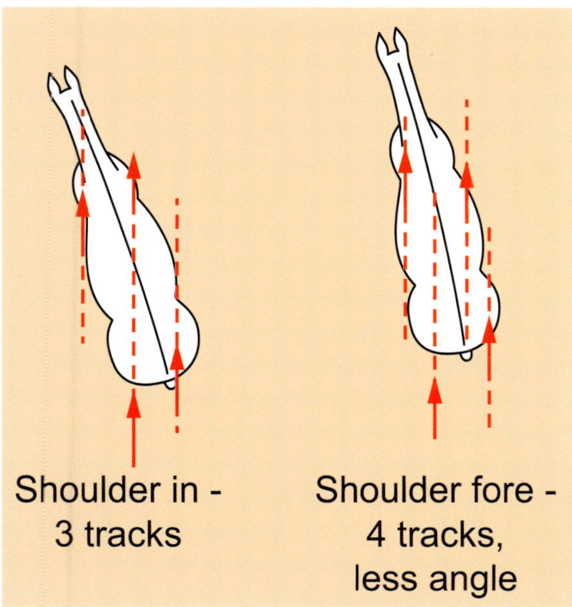

Shoulder in is on three tracks – the inside foreleg being on one, then the inside hind and outside fore on another, and the outside hind on the third track. Shoulder fore is on less of an angle and therefore all four feet should be on slightly different tracks.

COACHES' TIP: STAND HEAD ON TO THIS EXERCISE

Try to stand head on to this exercise – that is, at the end of the long side – so that you can give your rider feedback on the angle of the horse (four tracks as opposed to three tracks).

EXERCISE 8

Travers

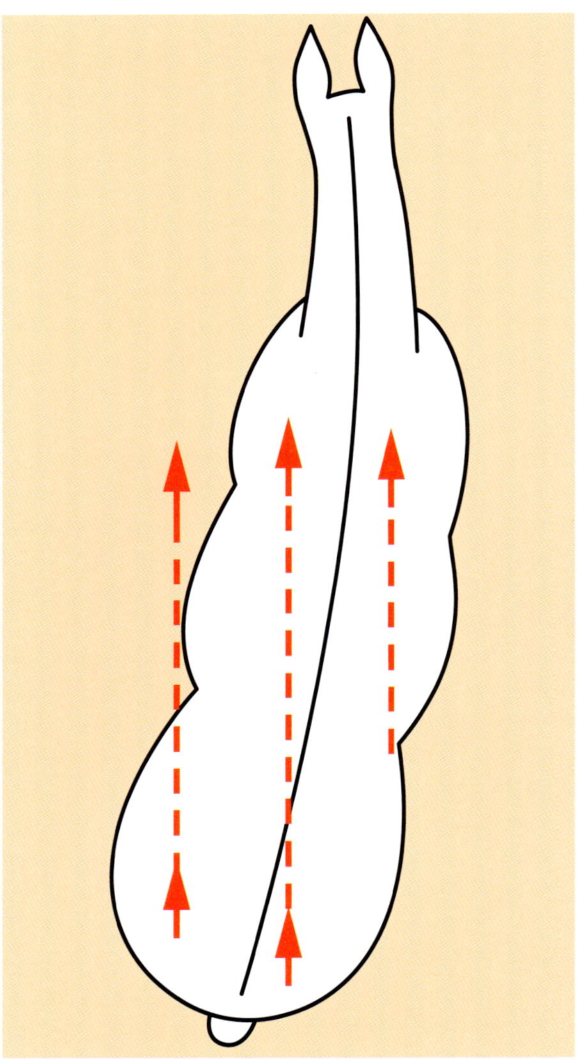

In this exercise, the horse is on three tracks: his inside hind on an inside track, then the outside hind and inside fore on the same track, and the outside fore on a separate, outside track.

Aim

Travers is a good exercise for developing the suppleness and power of the hind limbs. It is effectively a movement of the hindquarters on to the inside track, and so requires suppleness through the body to allow the hind legs to be carried to the inside whilst maintaining inside bend. Once the hind legs are in this position, they are having to step under the body more and have a higher degree of flexion to support the movement, so developing strength and suppleness.

How to Ride It

- As with shoulder in, it can be helpful to ride a ten-metre circle preceding this movement, as it sets up the horse's body for the correct positioning.
- Position yourself on the circle with your seatbones level but with fractionally more weight in the inside seatbone; then as you get towards the end of the circle, maintain the slight inside flexion and apply your outside leg behind the girth to stop the circle being fully completed – that is, leave the inside hind leg on the inside track, which is the last step before completing the circle.
- Square your shoulders in the direction of travel and keep applying your outside leg when needed to maintain positioning (ideally when the outside hind leg is about to leave the ground). Maintain the inside flexion. To achieve correct travers, your horse should be on three tracks – the inside hind leg on the first track, the inside foreleg and outside hind leg on the second track, and the outside foreleg on the third, outer, track.
- To develop the exercise more, try riding shoulder in (Exercise 7) to half-way up the long side, then ride a ten-metre circle, and continue up the remainder of the long side in travers. This allows you to work suppleness in two directions, and the circle helps to set up the second movement.

EXERCISE 9

Renvers

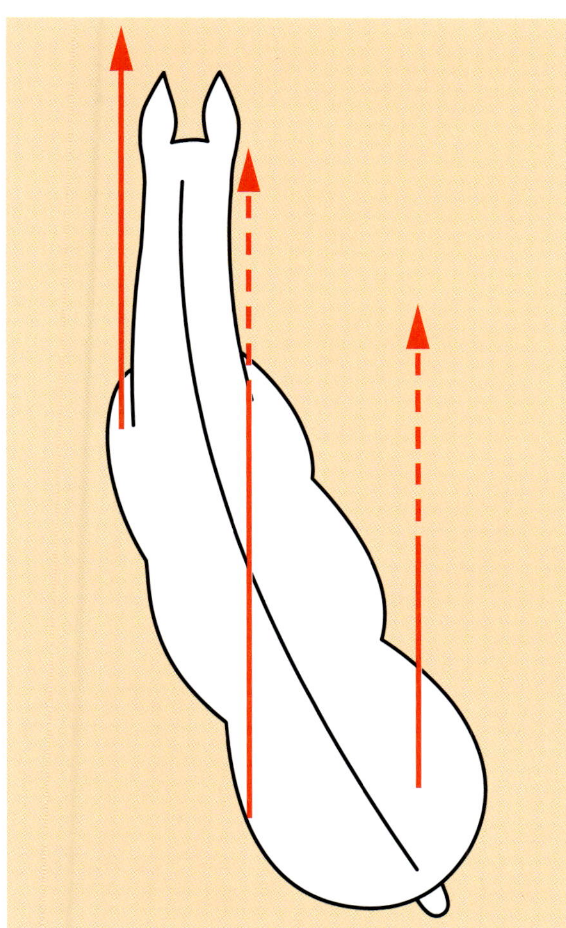

In this exercise, the horse's head and shoulders are away from the track, his outside hind leg has remained on the track and is now to the inside of the bend, the outside hind and inside fore are on the same track and the inside foreleg is on the track furthest away from the wall and is to the outside of the bend.

Aim

This movement is another good exercise to increase the suppleness and engagement of the hind legs. It can also be useful in a collecting-ring environment to work the opposite bend when a change of rein is not possible.

How to Ride It

- This movement is basically travers (*see* Exercise 8), but with the horse's body moving in the opposite direction. The quarters are positioned towards the wall, with the shoulders on an inner track and the flexion is marginally towards the wall. The wall helps to control the hind leg from stepping too far across and losing engagement.
- You can either move the shoulders off the track to create the positioning for renvers, or start on an inside track and move the hind leg towards the wall to commence the movement.
- Ride renvers by maintaining a slight flexion at the poll (be careful not to get too much neck bend) towards the wall using an indirect rein on the side nearest the wall (the 'inside rein' as it is to the inside of the flexion). Your outside rein (furthest from the wall) controls the degree of bend, but your outside leg is key to maintaining the position by applying it near the girth to control the positioning of the outside foreleg, and moving behind the girth as needed to control the outside hind leg and keep the inside hind leg on the track.
- Keep yourself level in your hips and looking in the direction of travel, with a fraction more feel towards the inside seatbone, but without leaning in that direction.
- Complete the exercise by moving the shoulders back to the track to ride straight.

EXERCISE 10

Turn on the Haunches

Aim

This exercise is really useful to sharpen up a lazier horse, get them moving off the aids and engaging from the hind leg.

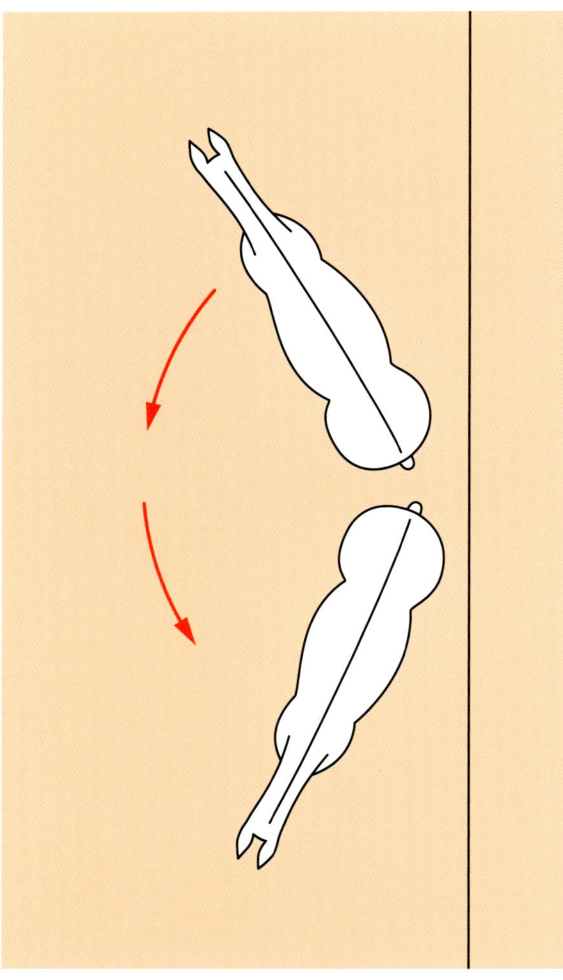

In this exercise, the hind legs stay in (or near) the same place and the front legs move around to change direction.

How to Ride It

- Start by riding this from walk, and ideally use the arena wall or fence to help you.
- Ride a half-halt transition parallel to the wall, so that you almost come to a halt. Put your weight fractionally more in your inside seatbone, keeping your hips and shoulders level, and open the inside rein very slightly to guide your horse (for true turn on the haunches a slight indirect rein to create poll flexion to the inside as a precursor to the pirouette is more correct, but for showjumping the priority is the movement off the outside aid and engagement of the hind leg, rather than training the collection for a pirouette, so less bend is, to my mind, acceptable).
- Look in the direction you want to go and apply your outside leg beside the girth to ask your horse to move his front legs round, whilst using a half halt on the outside rein as needed to keep his hind legs on the track and stop him stepping forwards out of the movement (although when starting you can make the movement less 'on the spot' and gradually reduce the space you ride it in).
- Turn on the haunches is completed when you and your horse are facing back the way you came, having moved round in effect on a half circle.
- To improve power and impulsion, I use this movement to change the rein in canter, which adds power to the transition as your horse will push off into canter from a more sitting and engaged hind leg.
- Canter to the half-way point on the long side of the arena. Ride a direct transition to walk if you can and almost halt, then move your horse round the turn on the haunches in walk, before changing the bend upon the return to the track and immediately striking off into canter. The more quickly you can get the transition, turn and return to canter, the more you will be developing the quickness of your horse's reactions, and the better the push from the hind leg into canter too.

EXERCISE 11

Reinback

Aim

Reinback when performed well is beneficial for developing your horse's core strength, as well as helping to move his weight on to his hind legs to aid his power and engagement.

How to Ride It

- Reinback should be a fluent movement from the halt, and similarly after the reinback into a forward step, whether walk, trot or canter.
- Introduce this from walk, firstly riding forwards into a halt transition.
- Sitting level, lighten the seatbones slightly and bring your legs back clearly behind the girth. Keep your ribcage lifted as you do so and your head up, so you are not collapsing forwards.
- As you close both legs on your horse, resist gently down the rein. This movement is not created by pulling back, so if you are struggling to get the steps back, an assistant on the floor standing in front of your horse can help by gently tapping the shoulder or leg to encourage a backward step. As soon as you achieve a backward step, soften the aids from the rein and leg for a moment before repeating the aids for additional steps.
- As soon as you have completed the number of steps of reinback that you want, change your weight aid back into your seatbones and ride forwards out of the movement. The last step of reinback and the first step of walk should be fluent and in a rhythm.
- As your horse's confidence and understanding of the movement increases, you can progress through to canter, riding reinback and straight out of it into canter as the next step.

For this exercise, lighten your seatbones slightly but keep your ribcage lifted and bring your legs back to give the aid for the movement, alongside a slight pressure and release on the reins for each step.

TIPS: TEACHING REINBACK

If you don't have someone to help you from the ground to teach your horse how to reinback, you can also introduce it in hand yourself and use the voice command 'back'. Standing in front of your horse, touch him on the chest (don't try and push him back!) and give the voice command, praising him when he makes a step backwards. If this is still difficult to achieve, a light touch with a dressage whip on his leg to encourage him to pick it up (think of it like a fly tickling the leg) can help to create the idea of the movement.

If your horse doesn't move back in a straight line under saddle, use the leg in a backward position on that side to try to correct it; and again, an assistant on the ground standing near the shoulder on the side the horse is moving towards can help to train him to improve his straightness.

EXERCISE 12

Canter Shallow Loop

Aim

This exercise is designed to increase suppleness and balance in the canter. From a jumping perspective we are not seeking a particularly deep loop, just the principle of moving on to a curving line and back to the track while maintaining balance and rhythm.

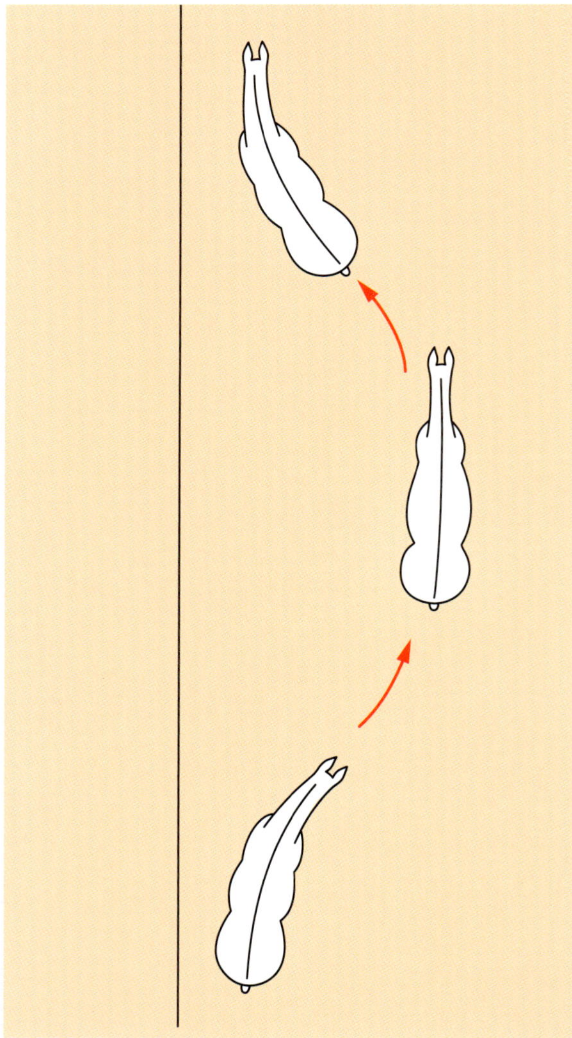

Riding a canter shallow loop means leaving the track, changing the bend briefly, then returning to the original bend as you return to the track. If your horse changes leg, try the exercise first without so much change of bend and ensure you keep your weight in the seatbone on the side of the leading leg.

How to Ride It

- Key to riding this successfully is maintaining your weight over the leading leg, so if you are in right canter, keep your weight slightly more in the right seatbone whilst keeping your hips level.
- From the corner of the arena turn the horse slightly off the track to create a loop no more than five metres in from the outside track. As you approach the mid-point of the curve, gently create a slight bend to the inside whilst keeping your weight over the leading leg so that you don't cause your horse to try to change legs. This is where you are asking for the most suppleness and balance from your horse, so keep the curve very slight to begin with and you can increase the challenge with a deeper curve as your horse develops strength and suppleness.
- As you leave the curve to return to the track, return to the original direction of bend to ride away from the line through the corner.

TIPS: TEACHING THE HORSE NOT TO CHANGE CANTER LEAD

If your horse tries to change lead at the mid-point of the shallow loop don't punish him for something that will be useful elsewhere! Instead, when trying this exercise again, maintain the same bend throughout the loop initially, and then gradually straighten the neck out mid-loop until he understands that your aids are not requesting a change. Once he is confident in the exercise then the slight change of bend mid-loop can be reintroduced.

EXERCISE 13

Flying Changes

Aim

While several of the other exercises outlined in this section address the development of strength and suppleness of the hind leg, the flying change requires this engagement and suppleness but is also integral to a fluent jumping round as your horse steps up the levels. This exercise outlines how to ride the flying change, and also gives a couple of tips and exercises to help to develop the change.

How to Ride It

- Some horses find performing a flying change very easy, usually as a result of the energy and balance they have in their canter, where others take more time to organise their legs and to develop the strength and elevation to perform it well.
- To ride for a change, the easiest route is to simply ride a change of direction across the middle of the arena, where it is clear to your horse that there is a change of rein. Think of sitting tall, and then create a change of bend across the middle, whilst switching weight gently to the new inside seatbone and applying the new inside leg to ask for the change. If needed, you can add the new outside leg behind the girth to ensure the outside hind steps through. Be careful to keep your shoulders level as you ask for the change – often riders throw their shoulders in the new direction of travel, but this can make the hips move the opposite way as a counterbalance and therefore confuses the aids.
- A simple way to help your horse achieve the slight elevation to aid the change of leg is to place a small vertical, raised pole or cavaletti across the centre of the arena. Apply the aids for the change of leg a stride before the step over, particularly applying the new inside leg to start to create the new bend on the approach. If your horse does not give you the flying change, then ride the first corner with inside bend – therefore maintaining the correct bend (in effect riding counter canter) – before riding a transition back to trot to change the lead. This helps to make it more evident to your horse what you are asking for, as it will be more difficult for him to keep his balance through the corner on the incorrect leg, and so may help you to then obtain the correct lead afterwards.
- Using a little leg yield to a fence located on the diagonal can also help to create the change (*see* Exercise 84). Creating leg yield by riding to line up with the outside of the fence and then yielding back to the centre begins to create suppleness in the new direction of travel on landing, and so can help to set up your horse more effectively for a change of lead over the fence.

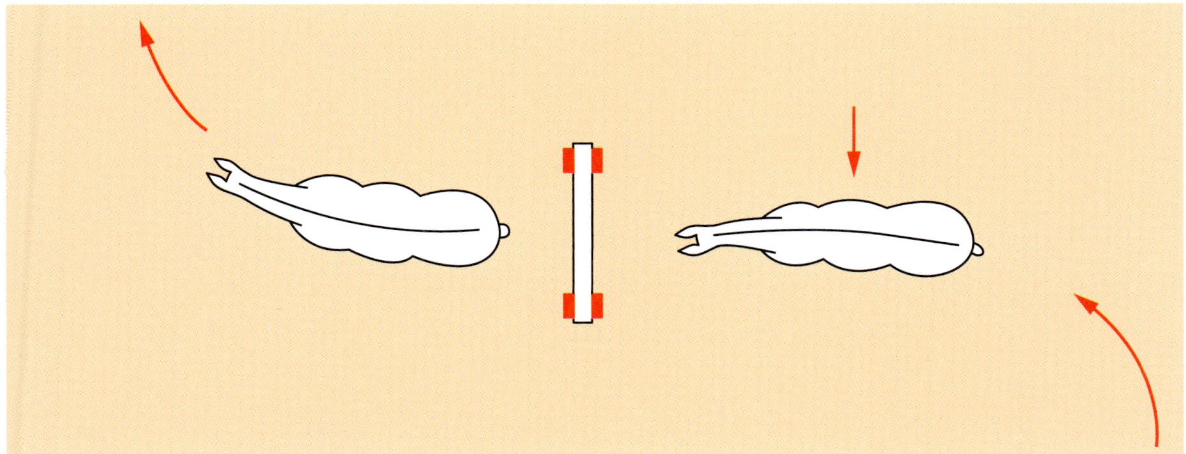

Using a raised pole to help create the flying change, apply the outside leg on the last stride or two of the approach to help set up the suppleness in the new direction of travel and aid the change.

POLEWORK EXERCISES

Polework exercises have a multitude of uses, from rehabilitation work that encourages the horse to use his body more correctly, to suppleness exercises that provide variety for dressage horses, as well as developing strength, balance and co-ordination in the showjumper, and helping to train the rider to judge distance and maintain balance.

In this section you will find a variety of exercises, from a basic introduction to polework to more complex exercises, including tasks that combine flatwork movements from the previous section with poles or cavaletti.

EXERCISE 14

Introductory Polework Exercise

Aim

This is a basic exercise to introduce your horse to polework if you have not done this before.

Set-Up

Equipment:

- A minimum of three poles or half-round poles
- Six pole pods or other pole holder if possible (if using round poles)

Start with a single pole, secured with pole pods or the arena surface, if using a round pole, so that it doesn't roll.

As you progress through the exercise and you and your horse become confident in it, add two more poles (avoid having just two poles together as these can end up being jumped as one unit!). The distance between the poles should be 3ft 6in (0.9m) for ponies, to 4ft 6in (1.2m) for horses.

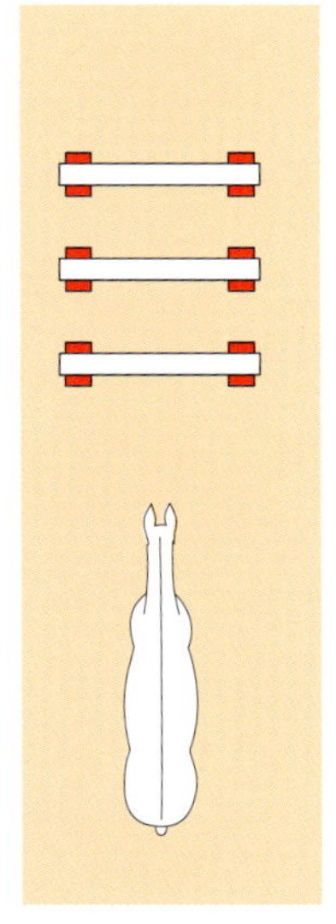
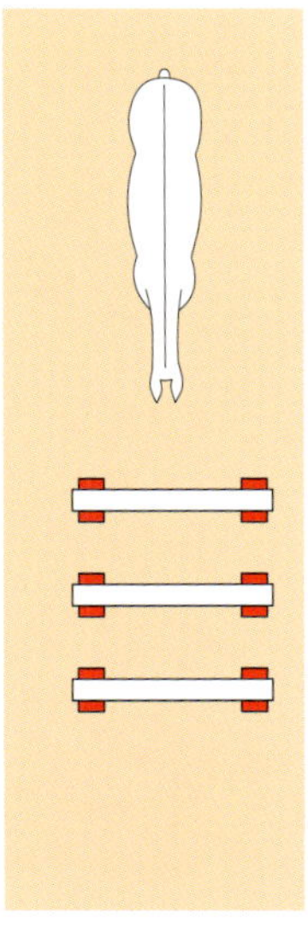

Introduce polework with a single pole, then increase to three poles. Do not use two poles on their own as these can end up being jumped together!

If you have enough poles, you can set up the same exercise on both long sides of an arena.

It can be the same set-up for a canter exercise, but increase the distance between the poles, making it about 9ft (2.75m); shorten this to about 7ft (2m) for small ponies, and extend it up to 10ft (3m) for a large or big-striding horse.

How to Ride It

- Start the exercise in walk. Focus on keeping your eyes on the line you intend to ride, and maintaining straightness. It is important that you don't look down at the pole as you approach the last few strides as your horse is likely to then wonder what you are looking at! He will have already assessed the pole and be looking forwards beyond it by the time you are taking the last stride to it.
- Ride the pole a few times in walk and then progress to a trot approach, still focusing on looking ahead and riding straight.
- Once your horse is confident approaching the single pole in trot on both reins, add in the other two poles and repeat the exercise.
- On the first attempt at this, completing this part of the exercise is likely to have taxed your horse's brain and body enough. However, when you return to the exercise, if you and your horse are confident to do so, you can progress after the trot work to start to canter over single poles and then build up to three poles as described in the set-up above.

TIPS FOR OVERCOMING HESITATION

If your horse hesitates at any point, keep your eyes up and close your legs to encourage him forwards. Try not to turn away from the pole even if you have come to a halt. Give your horse time to look and think about the question, but without the option to move away from it. If you have an assistant, they can walk over the pole in front of you (but be careful they are at a safe distance so the horse doesn't stand on them!), or if that doesn't work or it isn't safe to do with your horse, you can ask them to carefully create a box of poles around you, which means that your horse will be stepping over a pole if he goes backwards or sideways as well as forwards. Usually at this point he will opt for going forwards over the original pole, but have a hand on a neckstrap if you have one as it can be a bigger step when he does decide to go!

EXERCISE 15

Straightness Exercise

Aim

To work on straightness and control of pace over and between sets of poles.

Set-Up

Equipment:

- A minimum of six poles or half-round poles
- Twelve pole pods or other pole holder if possible (if using round poles)
- Two additional poles, or these can be replaced by lines in the sand or cones or fillers if no more poles are available, as these are for guidance only to help with straightness and the accuracy of the transitions

Set up the exercise as in the diagram, but introduce it with a single pole at each end the first time if the poles are raised and your horse is unfamiliar with these. Once he is familiar with these, add the other two poles at each end (never use just two poles – use one or three upwards). The poles should be 3ft 6in (0.9m) apart for a small pony, and 4ft 6in (1.2m) for a horse. There should be enough space between the two sets of trot poles to ride transitions in between: about 18yd (16.5m) should be comfortable to allow this, but it can be less if necessary – leave enough room to ride a turn comfortably after the poles!

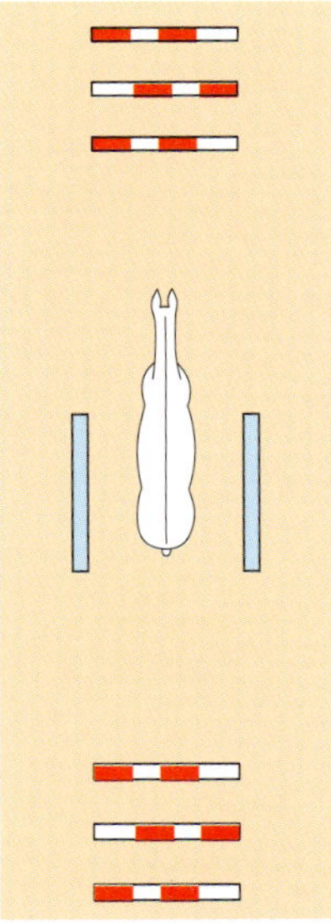

Tramlines between sets of poles can help work on straightness, and can also be used to work on obedience through accurate transitions between the sets of poles.

It can be the same set-up for a canter exercise, but increase the distance between the poles, making it about 9ft (2.75m); shorten this to about 7ft (2.13m) for small ponies, and increase it to 10ft (3.05m) for a large or big-striding horse.

How to Ride It

- Begin in trot and focus on riding a good rhythm and in a straight line over both sets of poles with a balanced turn before and after the poles.
- When you and your horse are confident with this exercise, introduce a trot-walk-trot transition after the first set of poles and before the second set of poles. You should still be focusing on straightness! To increase the level of challenge progress to trot-halt-trot transitions.
- For the canter version, progress as above and ride any of the transitions in between, although the one I prefer is canter-walk-canter, as it keeps some forward momentum but reduces the risk of flattening that can occur in canter-trot-canter transitions. You might need a little more room between both sets of poles for the canter work.
- Try to ride your transitions between the guideline poles or markers for better accuracy and organisation.

TIPS ON HOW YOU RIDE YOUR TRANSITIONS

Be aware of how you ride your transitions: your horse should respond to you growing taller in your body in the downward transition, and creating resistance there through your core, rather than just pulling the reins. Ensure that your lower leg stays underneath your body to help keep the hind leg stepping under in the downward as well as the upward transitions.

Short, quick rein aids are more effective than a holding pull, and with the addition of an effective body position, you should be able to achieve a point at which you hardly need to touch the rein to create a downward transition, as the aids will come from you sitting tall and tightening your core muscles.

When you are able to achieve a responsive transition, try riding just a half halt and continuing to the second set of poles. Notice the change in your horse's balance and preparation as the hind leg comes underneath and the shoulders lift in the half halt. This is a very useful tool in the ring!

EXERCISE 16

Shallow Loop Exercise

Aim

This exercise helps to create suppleness and obedience on both reins by riding the shallow loop round the cones, and trains the rider to plan ahead and prepare correctly so as to also achieve straightness over the trot poles in between.

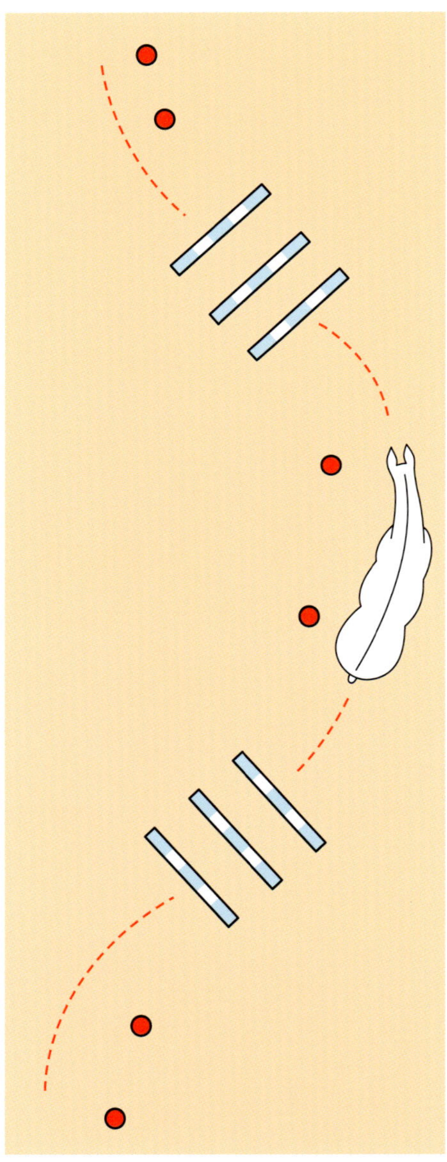

Use cones to help create an accurate shallow loop.

Set-Up

Equipment:

- Six cones or other small, safe object such as pole pods
- Six poles or half-round poles
- Twelve pole pods or other pole holder if possible (if using round poles)

Set up the exercise as in the diagram but introduce it with a single pole the first time, especially if the poles are raised and your horse is unfamiliar with these. Once he is familiar with these add the other two poles on each side (never use just two trot poles – use one or three upwards). The poles should be 3ft 6in (0.9m) apart for a small pony, or 4ft 6in (1.22m) for a horse.

How to Ride It

- Your primary focus should be on steering your horse with your legs and looking and planning ahead.
- Especially with young or inexperienced horses, try to use an opening rein to guide them (taking the hand away from the neck in the direction of travel), rather than pulling on the inside rein to execute the turns.
- Think of using the inside leg to help engage the horse's inside leg through the turn and aid suppleness, then apply the outside aids to help straighten up for the poles. The aids switch sides for the middle loop and switch back for the final corner.
- If you are not getting straight for the poles, make sure your horse's ears are in line with his shoulders so you have not got too much neck bend and think about using the outside leg and hand to straighten him more if needed.

> **TIP: THINK AHEAD!**
>
> It is much easier to ride this exercise if you can be looking four or five strides ahead of yourself so you can plan the line!

EXERCISE 17

X!

Aim

This is a simple trot-pole exercise that can be used in different ways to improve the use of the rider's legs to steer.

Set-Up

Equipment:

- One pair of wings
- Twelve half-round poles, or round poles
- 24 pole pods or other pole holder if possible (if using round poles)

The easiest location for this exercise is on the centre line of the arena. At X set up two wings, approximately pole distance apart (10ft or 3m).

The first of each set of trot poles should be situated roughly parallel to the wing on that side but a few paces away. Try to put each set of poles in a similar location as in the diagram. The poles should be 3ft 6in to 4ft 6in (0.91–1.22m) apart depending on whether you are building for a pony or a horse.

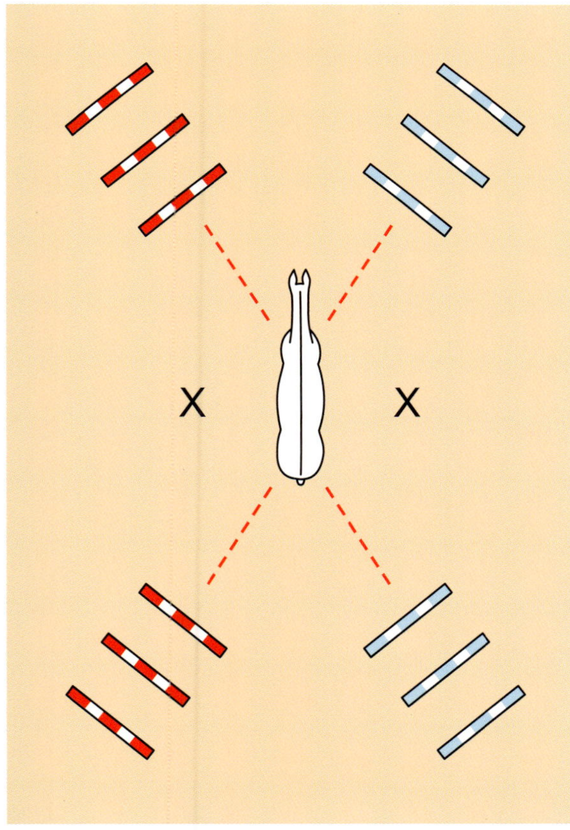

This versatile pole exercise allows you to work straightness through the centre of the exercise and provide variations over the poles, including diagonal lines and dog leg lines.

How to Ride It

- Start by simply riding up the centre line between the wings, trying to stay central to the gap. If you like, you can test your horse's obedience and your accuracy by adding a transition directly between the wings.
- There are then several options with the trot poles:
  - You can ride a straight diagonal line across both sets, riding through the wings on an angle, if you have managed to get the line to work in your set-up!
  - You can ride one set of poles and then ride a dog-leg line to get straight and ride through your wings and up the centre line.
  - You can reverse this and ride up the centre line, through the wings and then turn to a set of poles.
  - You can ride to one set of poles, then change the bend through the wings and ride to the other set on the same side of the arena.
- For all these options, think about creating the turn through your leg aids more than your hands and keep looking a few strides in front of where you are so that you can plan your lines accurately and be prepared for each change of direction.

EXERCISE 18

Figure-of-Eight Exercise

Aim

For this trot-pole exercise the aim is to be able to ride supple and accurate turns in a good rhythm with control of pace throughout.

Set-Up

Equipment:

- Twelve poles or half-round poles
- 24 pole pods or other pole holder if possible (if using round poles)
- Four cones or similar markers if available

Set up the exercise as in the diagram. Try to keep the angle of the curve relatively gentle, placing three poles on the curve as shown to create a figure-of-eight.

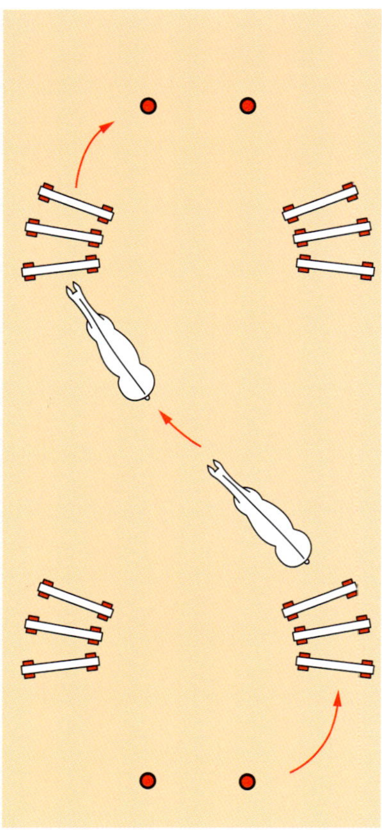

This figure-of-eight exercise demands suppleness and frequent changes of bend. Cones can help control the line.

To help with accuracy use cones or similar markers to help keep the horse and rider out on the correct curve between the poles at each end.

The trot poles should be placed 3ft 6in (0.9m) apart for a small pony, and 4ft 6in (1.22m) for a horse, the distance between each pole measured from the middle of each pole. To help create the curve, the inside of the poles will be a bit closer together and the outside a bit further apart.

How to Ride It

- Establish a steady, rhythmical trot and begin by riding past the cones to the first curving line of poles.
- Make sure you are looking and planning ahead and using your legs to help guide your horse over the middle of the poles.
- If you are starting on the right rein you will have used your inside (right) leg to help engage the inside hind leg for bend and suppleness. As you come over the last trot pole and start to ride the figure-of-eight, introduce your left leg to engage what will now become the inside (left) hind leg. Control the horse's outside shoulder with your outside rein, and be ready to use the outside leg behind the girth if the horse's quarters move out.
- Ride the exercise a few times, thinking about creating smooth lines and changes of direction with a soft, opening inside rein and accurate lines over the middle of the poles.
- The challenge can be increased for more experienced riders by asking them to collect the trot and ride the inside of the curve, or open the trot and ride the outside of the curve over the poles, or to mix it between the two, so ride the forward outside line for one set of poles and the collected inside line for the next.

> **TIPS: HOW TO PREVENT YOUR HORSE RUSHING**
>
> If you find your horse rushing over the poles or across the middle of the figure-of-eight, add a transition to walk, or even halt, in the middle of the figure-of-eight and then proceed back into trot and to the next set of poles.

EXERCISE 19

The Dog-Bone Exercise

Aim

This is a trot-pole exercise designed to improve suppleness and enable the rider to practise looking and planning ahead and using their legs to direct the horse and create bend.

Set-Up

Equipment:

- Eight poles or half-round poles
- Sixteen pole pods or other pole holder if possible (if using round poles)
- Four cones or similar safe markers

Set up the exercise as in the diagram. You can make the curve as steep as you like (within reason!) but be aware that an increased bend will be more difficult to ride. The curve should bend out towards the outside of the arena – for smaller arenas such as 20 × 40m, the poles could curve away from the long side. For arenas of 30m diameter or more the exercise will fit comfortably across the width. Place the cones so that the line from the poles continues out but leaving enough room to change direction around them.

The trot poles should be placed 3ft 6in (0.9m) apart for a small pony, and 4ft 6in (1.22m) apart for a horse, the distance between each pole measured from the middle of each pole. To create the curve, the inside of the poles will be slightly closer together and the outside further apart.

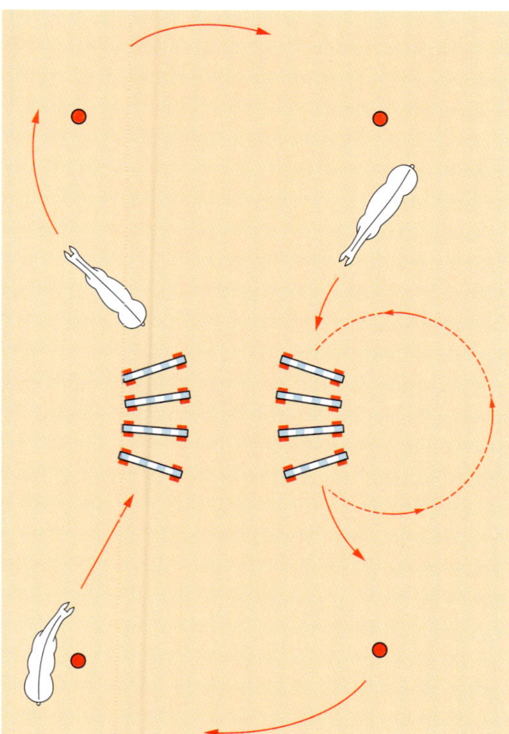

This exercise demands more suppleness and flexibility of the hind leg by using poles on a curving line.

How to Ride It

- If there is space to do so, you can start by approaching from outside the exercise and ride the first curve over the poles as part of a circle without changing direction. Once this has been achieved on both reins in balance and in a good rhythm, then move on to the next stage.
- Now approach the curving poles either from your circle or from outside the marker cones, but once you have completed the first set of poles, change the bend to ride round the outside of the two cones and approach the second set of poles, changing the bend as you approach them.
- Make sure you are looking and planning ahead. Control the outside shoulder with your outside rein and use your legs to help guide your horse's body. The more prepared you are for each change of direction, the more fluent your ride through the exercise will become.
- Once you have practised the exercise in one direction, change the rein and approach from the other direction.

> ## COACHES' TIP: HELPING THE RIDER TO ADDRESS BALANCE
>
> The key observation area for this exercise is around the change of direction at the cones – the horse may fall in or out at this point, and it is more likely to happen here than over the poles where the rider has something more to 'aim for'. This exercise provides a good opportunity to help the rider address balance when changing direction, which can also relate to riding a course of fences later.

EXERCISE 20

The Helix

Aim

The Helix is a good exercise to improve the rider's use of leg aids for direction and create suppleness on both reins for horse and rider!

Set-Up

Equipment:

- Four cones or other small, safe object such as pole pods
- Twelve poles or half-round poles (it can be eight poles, in which case make two sets of single poles if you lack poles or space)
- 24 pole pods or other pole holder if possible (if using round poles)

Set up the exercise as in the diagram, but if the poles are raised on pole pods and this is the first time your horse has seen these, then introduce the exercise with a single pole first. The poles should be 3ft 6in (0.9m) apart for a small pony, and 4ft 6in (1.22m) apart for a horse.

For smaller arenas you can use single poles at one end of the exercise and make the turn a little tighter at that end if needed.

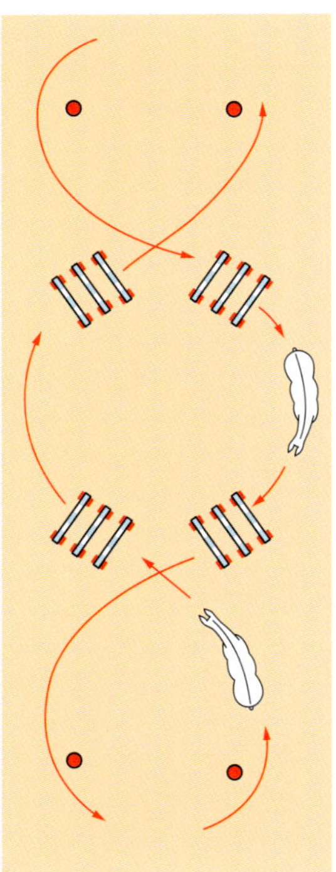

Use cones to help keep the shape of the helix at each end and think of directing your horse through the changes of bend with your legs.

How to Ride It

- Your primary focus should be on steering your horse with your legs and looking and planning ahead.
- Use the inside leg to engage the inside hind leg of the horse and create suppleness round the cones. If the horse drifts out, use your outside leg just behind the girth and close the outside rein. Try to use an opening inside rein to turn, rather than pulling on the inside rein, as pulling can create too much neck bend and cause the horse to drift out more.
- Once out of the turn round the cones, try to ride straight over the centre of the poles without the horse moving left or right.
- As you are completing the first set of poles, start to apply the new inside leg for the change of bend, and work to create suppleness through the curve to then get straight for the second set of poles. (It is likely that it will be easier to do this in one direction than in the other.)
- Complete the first half of the Helix by riding a loop back round the second set of cones, and then complete the exercise by riding over the two sets of poles on the other side of the arena.

TIP: RIDING A HALF HELIX

To make the exercise easier you can ride a 'Half Helix' first, in which case ride the first two sets of poles, but at the cones continue up the long side to the beginning again, rather than looping back to work up the other side of the arena.

Coaches' tip: This exercise can be ridden as a 'Half Helix' with two riders – one each side – but they must be capable of looking and planning ahead to avoid each other where the tracks overlap near the cones. It is a good challenge for more advanced riders, but make the rules clear as to what to do if they do get near each other!

EXERCISE 21

Using Angled Poles

Aim

Using poles raised on just one side allows the rider to work on their horse's suppleness. Raising the inside of the poles on a curve creates engagement of the inside hind leg by lifting it higher, and is also useful to stop the horse from falling in if that is what he tends to do. Raising poles on the outside of the curve moves the horse's weight on to the inside hind leg whilst increasing flexion of the outside hind leg, and is useful for horses that swing their quarters out. Raising them on alternate sides helps to keep the same level of elevation on both sides of the body.

Set-Up

Equipment:

- A minimum of three poles
- Three pole pods or other pole holder (alternatively jump wings or blocks on a low setting can be used)

Place at least three poles on either a straight or a curving line with the middle point set at 3ft 6in (0.9m) apart for a small pony, and 4ft 6in (1.22m) for a horse. When using a curving line, the inside line should be slightly shorter and the outside line slightly wider so it can be used by a pony and a horse at the same time, with the pony travelling on the inside line and the horse the middle or outside line. Raise one end of the pole with a block, pod or wing so that it is slightly off the ground. Keep the raised side consistent for a curving line – that is, all the poles raised on the inside, or all of them on the outside.

The same exercise can also be set up for canter, with a distance of about 9ft to 10ft for horses (2.75m to 3.05m) and from 7ft (2.13m upwards) for ponies on the middle of the curving line and angled in the same way as the trot poles so that shorter-striding horses and ponies can take the inside line.

How to Ride It

Riding the straight line:

- If you are using angled poles on a straight line, it is generally best to raise each end alternately so that you help activate both hind legs equally and therefore help keep the horse straight.
- Focus on channelling the horse straight with your legs and keep your eye on the line afterwards. If the horse is not holding a straight line, widen your hands and keep a gentle, even pressure on both reins to help create a channel for him to step forwards into.

Riding the curving line:

- The key to riding any curving line accurately is to be looking ahead round the curve and using your legs to guide the horse round.
- Slightly open the inside rein to invite the horse round the turn, and use the inside leg if he moves in, although more frequently he is likely to drift out, in which case the outside leg is needed to hold the central line.
- Begin by riding the exercise in trot on both reins. If the horse has a tendency to fall in one way and to drift out the other, it can be helpful to have two sets of poles, one set raised to the inside and one set to the outside, that can then be ridden on either rein to help address the issues evenly.
- Once the horse is confident working through the exercise in trot, you can try the same exercise with canter poles.

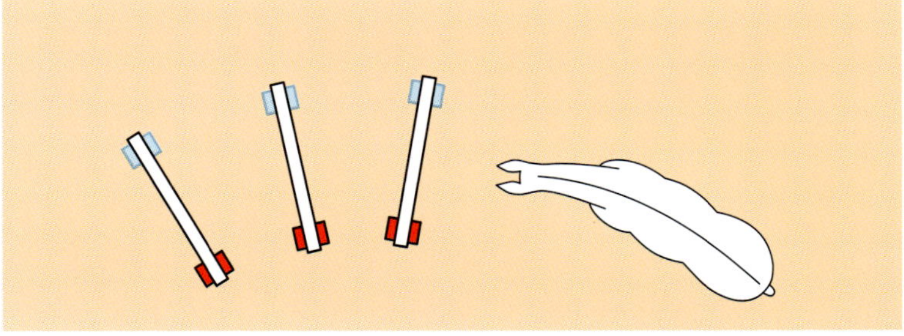

When using angled poles, raising them on the inside (red) elevates the inside hind leg and the inside shoulder to help prevent the horse falling in. Raising them on the outside (blue) elevates the outside hind leg and shoulder and helps control the hindquarters from swinging out.

EXERCISE 22

Canter Half Circle

Aim

This exercise is designed to help train the rider to look and plan ahead for accuracy, and to direct the horse with their legs, rather than pulling the inside rein to turn. It also improves the engagement of the horse's hind leg through the turn, and helps maintain rhythm and balance. With a central cavaletti there is an additional element of control required for the second half of the circle.

Set-Up

Equipment:

- A minimum of seven poles or half-round poles
- Fourteen pole pods or other pole holders if possible (if using round poles)
- To increase the challenge, replace the middle pole with a cavaletti

Set up the exercise as in the diagram, but introduce it with a single pole the first time if the poles are raised and the horse is unfamiliar with these. Once he is familiar with them, set up the rest of the exercise. The tighter you make the curve the more challenging it is, so to start with make it as gentle a curve as possible.

The poles can be set up for trot to begin with, in which case they should be placed 3ft 6in (0.9m) apart for a small pony, and 4ft 6in (1.22m) for a horse, measured from the middle of each pole. As these poles are in a curved line the outside distance will be a little longer than this, and the inside will be a little shorter. For canter, the distance for small ponies will be around 7 to 8ft on the middle line (2.13m to 2.44m) and for horses around 9ft (2.74m) but can be up to 10ft (3.05m). However, bear in mind that because the horse is always turning, it is likely that his stride will be shorter than if the poles were in a straight line. If necessary, adjust the distance in order to create a round, balanced stride pattern for your horse – he doesn't want to be reaching to make the distance for each pole.

How to Ride It

- Establish a quality trot or canter before approaching the poles, and ride a half halt five or six strides before the poles to improve the horse's balance and gain his attention for the task ahead.

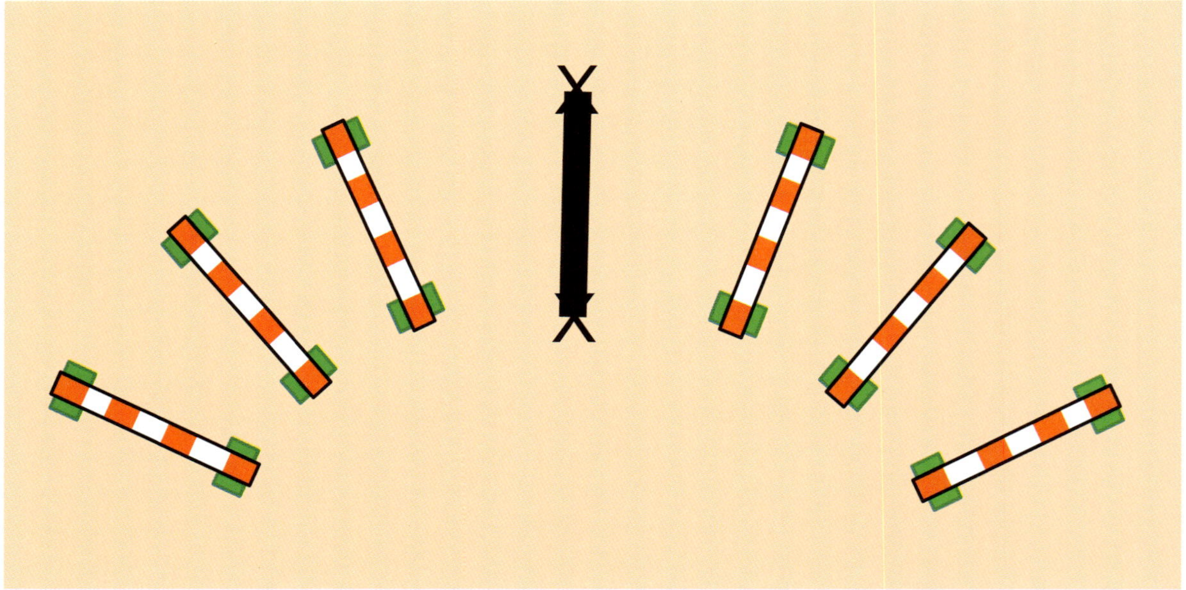

This exercise can be used with just poles, or add cavaletti. It challenges the rider to be accurate throughout the turn, as the horse will usually drift out as the line progresses.

- Your primary focus should be on steering the horse with your legs and looking and planning ahead.
- If additional help is needed to guide a young or inexperienced horse round the curve, try to use an opening rein (taking the hand away from the neck in the direction of travel), rather than a direct (pulling) inside rein, as a direct rein aid is likely to encourage the horse to bend too much and fall out through the shoulder.
- Focus on maintaining the same line all the way through the curve – if you are in the middle of the first pole you need to be in the middle of the last pole too!
- To increase elevation in the stride and work on control and regulation of pace, add in a cavaletti in place of the central pole. This will demand greater flexion in the horse's limbs, and can also create forward momentum that is then controlled by the poles on the second half of the circle.
  For greater intensity of workload, add in more cavaletti – but be aware that this is then very hard work for the horse, so you should limit the number of repetitions you ask of him.

TIPS: CREATING GREATER IMPULSION AND ELEVATION IN THE STRIDE

Looking round to the last pole on the circle helps maintain accuracy through the line.

Thinking outside the 'jumping' box, this exercise is useful to increase the quality of the paces for dressage horses by demanding greater engagement in the pace; riders can also use the inside line to work towards collection, or the outside line to lengthen the stride. For dressage horses I tend to build a shorter distance, such as 8ft (2.45m) canter poles, as they require elevation more than maintaining an open stride in this instance.

It is also a good preparatory exercise before tackling the flying change, as it creates greater impulsion and elevation in the stride, which aids the change.

Coaches' tip: If the horse is lacking power through the turn to a fence, this exercise can help generate an energetic canter, which can then link in to a fence afterwards – it can also help riders to find and maintain rhythm through the turn and to a fence.

EXERCISE 23

Flying Change with Cavaletti

Aim

This set-up helps to create the canter quality needed to generate a good flying change through the engagement of the hind leg.

Set-Up

Equipment:

- Six poles or half-round poles and one cavaletti
- Twelve pole pods or other pole holder if possible (if using round poles)

Set up the exercise as in the diagram, but if the horse is not familiar with cavaletti, then work a circle over a single cavaletti with no poles first until he is comfortable and confident with it.

The poles should be between 7ft (small pony) and 10ft (horse) apart, measuring from the middle of each pole. As this is quite a demanding exercise, start at about 9ft (2.75m) for horses, and adjust as necessary after this. A shorter distance between the poles helps keep the horse's balance more 'uphill', which will help with a successful flying change.

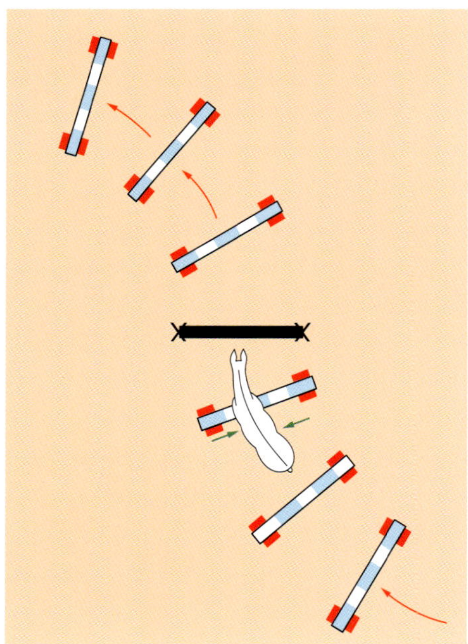

To help generate the flying change over the cavaletti, start to apply the new inside leg by the girth just before the cavaletti to indicate the change of direction, and have the new outside leg slightly behind the girth if needed to help activate the outside hind leg for the change.

How to Ride It

- It might be helpful to ride the line in trot first to get a feel for steering through the line accurately using your legs.
- Whilst practising in trot, be aware of transferring your weight into the new inside seatbone over the cavaletti (keep your shoulders and hips level and just think of the point of the new seatbone becoming heavier) and switching your aids from, say, left bend to right bend, with the new inside leg by the girth, and the outside leg more behind the girth.
- Ride the same exercise in canter, focusing on applying the current outside leg (which will become the new inside leg) by the girth just before the cavaletti, and transferring weight into the new inside seatbone at take-off to help generate the flying change. If the change doesn't happen over the cavaletti just maintain the same aids as it is likely to then happen over the three canter poles after the cavaletti.
- To work the flying change in the other direction, change the poles to create the curve the other way.

TIPS: CREATING A CORRECT FLYING CHANGE

This exercise can be useful for dressage horses to help them achieve a correct, or 'true', flying change, as it makes the hind legs more active and creates a little elevation in the step where the change happens.

If the horse moves in more one way, or is more reluctant to change one way, using one or two guide rails on the cavaletti or on the poles on the approach or landing can help to assist the body position and train him on how to be more balanced in that direction (*see* Exercise 89).

EXERCISE 24

Control and Accuracy Clock Face

Aim

This 'clock face' exercise challenges riders to maintain an accurate line between the poles and to attain a consistent speed and stride length in order to have the same number of strides between each of the poles.

Set-Up

Equipment:

- Four round poles or half-round poles
- Eight pole pods or other pole holder if possible (if using round poles)

Set up the exercise as in the diagram. The easiest way to get the four poles the same distance apart is to walk out the distance from the centre of the circle to the end of each pole.

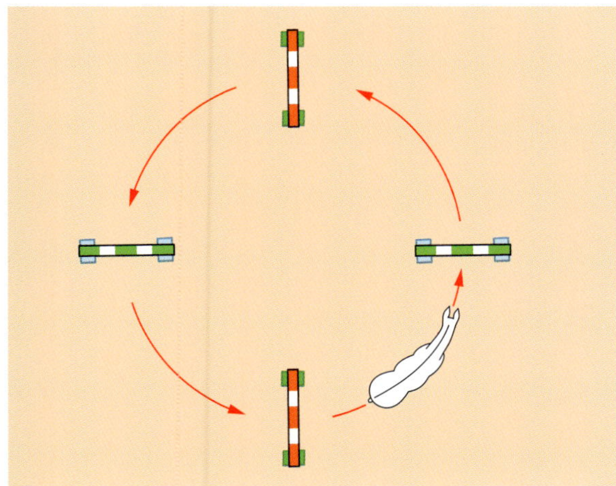

The clock face exercise demands accuracy from the rider looking and planning ahead, with the aim being to get the same number of strides between each pole.

How to Ride It

- Begin in trot and focus on riding a good rhythm and an accurate line round the circle so that your horse takes the same number of strides between each pole.
- When you and your horse are confident with this, ride the same exercise in canter, aiming to keep each distance and number of strides between the poles the same.
- Keep your shoulders level, making sure you don't lean in, and keep looking ahead round the turn, so your focus is three or four strides ahead towards the next pole.
- A good rhythm and consistent length of stride are key, as is riding the same line each time. It sounds easy but can take some practice to achieve!
- Depending on how big you are able to make your circle in the arena, slightly larger circles provide the option to make some of the poles into small jumps or cavaletti – for example at three o'clock and nine o'clock – to make the exercise more challenging, as the number of strides and the accuracy of the line should remain the same (provided the fences are just 'step-overs' of 20in (50cm) or similar).

TIP: HAVE THE SAME NUMBER OF STRIDES BETWEEN THE POLES

The aim is to have the same number of strides between the poles – to do this it might help to count out loud, or you could ask someone on the ground do so, if you struggle with this. Often riders accidentally count the stride over the pole as well, which leads to confusion – try using the word 'and' for the stride over the poles and then count the strides, so you would be counting '*and* one, two, three, four' to help avoid this.

EXERCISE 25

Related Distance Curving Line

Aim

This exercise can be ridden in trot but is designed to be worked through in canter to replicate the line that is often seen in competition with three fences on a curve.

Set-Up

Equipment:

- Three cavaletti or three pairs of wings (if these are to be made into jumps later)
- Six to nine half-round poles, or round poles (depending on if you're using cavaletti or not)
- Twelve to eighteen pole pods or other pole holder if possible (if using round poles)

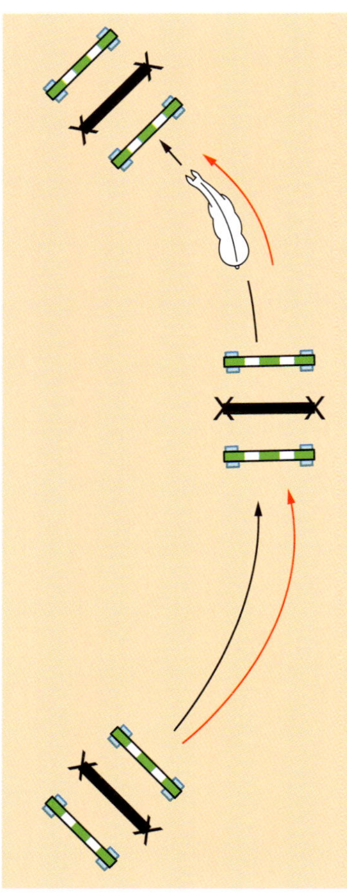

For this curving related line, ride the wider line shown in red for four strides between the poles, then ride the middle line, shown in black, once the poles are removed and you are riding cavaletti to cavaletti, taking four strides between each one

The middle element of this curve should be located at or near the track on the long side of the arena. Create a related distance on the curve between each set of poles. For example, from one cavaletti to the next, four strides would be about 18yd (16.5m) for horses, and 16 to 17yd (14.6 to 15.5m) for ponies, then increase by a maximum of 2yd (1.8m) for two fences, although with the curving line it can be adapted a little by changing the shape of the curve to suit the horse.

Each cavaletti or set of wings should have a pole placed on each side of it on a distance of between 7ft (2.13m) for a pony, and 10ft (3.05m) for a horse, depending on the length of their stride as well as the dimensions of the arena. I would normally start at 9ft for horses (2.75m) and adjust as necessary.

How to Ride It

- If you want to get a feel for the line first, you can ride it in trot with the canter poles in place.
- You can then ride the three canter poles on the wall on their own to complete your warm-up and to check that the distances work well. Ride this in both directions.
- Now add in the other sets of poles. You can ride one set to the middle set first, riding straight after the middle set, before linking all three later in the session.
- Ride the curve a little wider than you would to your fences so that you can add four strides in between each combination of canter poles.
- Be aware that the wall can affect your line by drawing the horse towards it, or, if it has banners or mirrors for example, it can push the horse inwards.
- Once you can ride this successfully in both directions, you can take away the poles and work over the cavaletti, or build fences and ride the line as you would encounter it in competition. Be aware that the second distance will almost certainly ride shorter as inevitably you gain momentum riding through the line.

EXERCISE 26

Straightness and Control Exercise

Aim

This exercise helps to get the horse listening to your aids and responding quickly to them, within a set framework that aids straightness.

Set-Up

Equipment:

- 24 poles or half-round poles, or 21 poles and the option of one to three cavalletti
- 24 pole pods or other pole holder if possible (if using round poles) for the trot and canter poles

Set up the exercise as in the diagram, but if including cavaletti it might be appropriate, depending on horse/rider experience, to include only one at first. Ensure that there is enough space to be able to turn between the tramline corners in trot, so a small gap is required at least!

Set the trot poles at the top so they are 3ft 6in (0.9m) apart for a small pony, and 4ft 6in (1.22m) for a horse.

Put the tramlines (depicted in blue) to guide straightness at least one pace – 1yd (0.9m) – away from the trot poles; for very novice horses, or those who are not familiar with tramlines, make it nearer 3yd (2.75m).

The canter poles on the long sides of the exercise should be placed about 8 to 9ft (2.45 to 2.75m) apart, though this can be reduced to about 7ft (2.13m) for ponies and extended to about 10ft (3.05m) apart for longer-striding horses. Given the 'control' nature of this exercise, including tight turns and transitions, it might be more comfortable for horse and rider to start over a shorter distance and lengthen it if it is needed later, or if you want to increase the challenge by demanding a bigger canter more quickly after the turn.

If you are also adding in the cavaletti, the set-up will depend on the size of the space you are using, but it can be set on a one-stride canter distance of 7yd (6.4m) for horses, or 6 to 6.5yd (5.5 to 5.9m) for ponies, on a curving line (or straight if your arena is big enough); or it can be a small line of bounces to engage the hind leg and if your arena is smaller – start on a low setting (such as a raised canter pole) at 3 to 3.5yd (2.7 to 3.2m).

This exercise requires accuracy and control to complete the full circuit., with tramlines to dictate the line and aid straightness.

How to Ride It

- Start by riding the trot poles on the short side of the arena on their own, focusing on the quality of the turn before and after the tramlines, and noticing where your horse achieves straightness and where it needs improvement. Do this exercise on both reins.
- Introduce the canter-pole exercise on its own down the long side of the arena, focusing on the same thing and riding a transition to trot at the end of the line. Ride the canter poles towards the end of the arena where the trot poles are.
- Now ride the canter poles, make a trot transition afterwards as soon as possible, and then ride a

turn between the tramlines and over the trot poles. Repeat this on both reins.

- The challenge can then be increased so that you canter the first set of canter poles, ride trot over the trot poles, and ride the canter transition afterwards to canter over the second set of canter poles.
- To complete the circuit, add in the cavaletti or final set of canter poles at the bottom after the second set of canter poles, so that you are riding a complete loop incorporating trot and canter.
- To progress the exercise and to further the challenge the canter poles can be turned into a small jump on one side or both by moving in two poles to create a groundline either side of a small vertical.

TIP: LOOK AND PLAN AHEAD

Make sure you are looking and planning ahead throughout this exercise, and focus on using more outside aids to turn, especially outside leg, rather than putting pressure on the inside rein. If you find that the horse falls out of the shoulder through the turns, make sure that you are maintaining a good contact with the outside rein, and start to indicate that you are going to turn by using your outside leg a little before the turn.

For the downward transitions, see how much you can achieve by sitting tall and using half halts to make the transition as light as possible in terms of rein aids. As your horse becomes familiar with what you are asking, this becomes easier – you might need to be firm and clear at first, especially if the horse is enthusiastic!

EXERCISE 27

Serpentine and Leg Yield Version 1

Aim

This is a relatively simple exercise that can be built in a narrower arena; in effect it is two exercises in one. I particularly like this set-up for leg yield as it helps to control the shoulder from falling out because of the location of the poles, so the quality of the leg yield tends to be more correct.

Set-Up

Equipment:

- Nine poles or half-round poles
- 18 pole pods or other pole holder if possible (if using round poles)

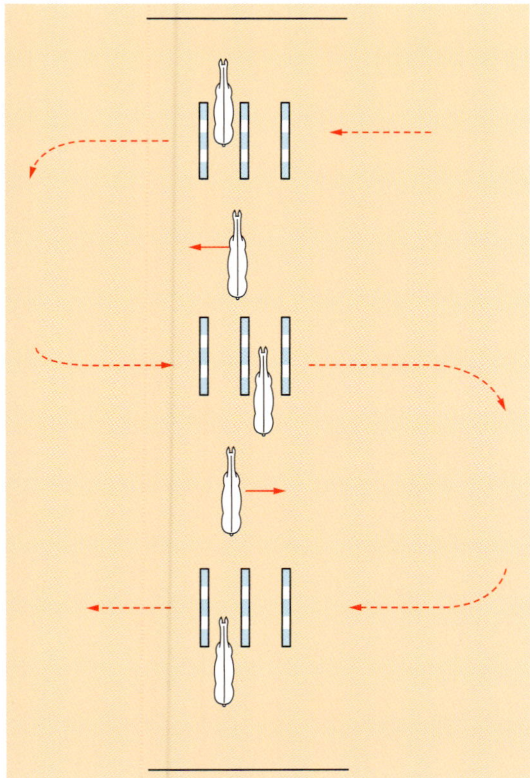

This exercise uses the serpentine of poles to warm up, and you can then leg yield in and out of the middle of them: the poles help control the shoulder and straightness of the leg yield. Leave enough room at either end of the arena to ride your turn!

Build the three sets of trot poles on the centre line of the arena approximately the same distance apart but allowing room at either end to turn after the poles (so that you can ride between them and not hit the wall at the end!). The trot poles should be 3ft 6in (0.9m) apart for a small pony, and 4ft 6in (1.22m) apart for a horse.

How to Ride It

- The warm-up exercise is to ride the trot-pole serpentine. Depending on how much room you have, you can add an extra loop at either end without the poles. Focus on creating the same degree of suppleness and bend on each rein before ensuring you are straight for the poles across the centre.
- The second exercise is to work up between the poles, effectively riding the centre line.
- Start by riding between the gap on one side – for example the right-hand side – then leg yield off the right leg to ride straight between the gap on the left-hand side, and then leg yield off the left leg to return to the right-hand side again. You can then switch reins and/or switch which channel you ride through to vary it. The exercise is easiest ridden in trot, although it could be ridden in canter once you are finding it straightforward to perform.
- Focus on keeping your horse's neck straight and your hips and shoulders level. Apply the new inside leg just behind the girth to ask for the step across, and control the outside shoulder with the outside rein, but keep everything smooth, rhythmical and balanced, and take care not to use the rein to make the movement across.

TIP: KEEP THE HORSE STRAIGHT

With leg yield don't go for too much movement across, but focus on keeping the horse straight and almost think of the hind leg leading. This isn't strictly correct, but the tendency is for the horse to fall on to and therefore lead with the outside shoulder to reduce the need to engage the hind legs. By focusing on keeping the front end straight and moving the hind legs over, often this results in a straighter and more correct movement.

EXERCISE 28

Serpentine and Leg Yield Version 2

Aim

This exercise uses the serpentine from the previous exercise (27) but relocates the leg yield to make it easier to ride in canter, and provides options to add cavaletti and fences to it for a more complete training session.

Set-Up

Equipment:

- 21 poles or half-round poles (cavaletti can be used in the canter bounce curve and serpentine)
- Ten wings or jump blocks
- 30 pole pods or other pole holder if possible (if using round poles)

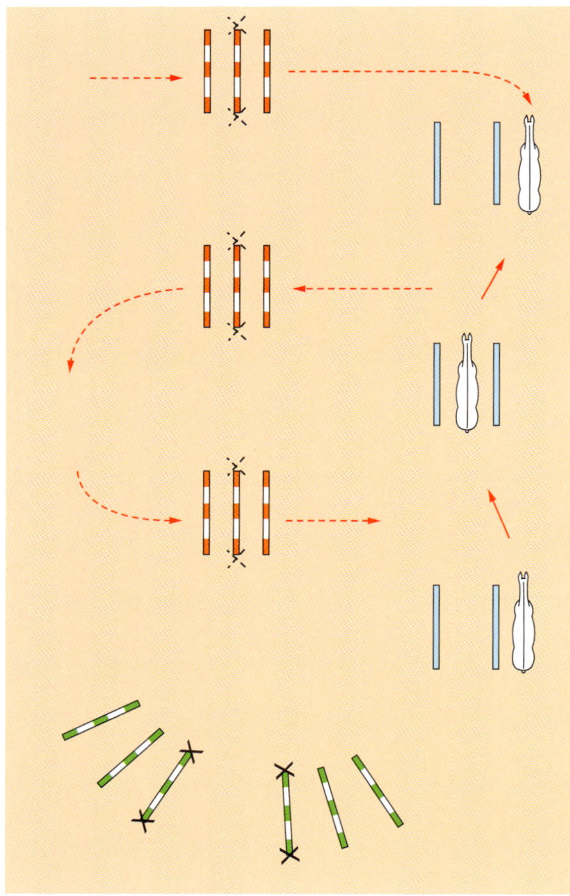

This is an extended version of the leg yield exercise, which has more room to create canter leg yield, and the trot pole serpentine can be developed into canter poles or fences as the session progresses.

First make the tramlines on one long side of the arena near the three-quarter line, placing each pair of poles about two to three paces apart – 6 to 9ft (1.83 to 2.74m) – to give sufficient room to work through them. Leave as much space as you can between each set of poles so you can leg yield in and out – ideally at least 36ft (11m).

Next set up your trot-pole serpentine so that the lines of approach or departure fit between the tramlines you have just set out. Add wings beside the middle trot pole on each loop of the serpentine if you want to build these into fences later. The trot poles should be 3ft 6in (0.9m) apart for a small pony, and 4ft 6in (1.22m) apart for a horse.

Finally, build your canter poles on the curve if you have space to do so – these should be lined up so that you can come out of the tramlines and ride to the curving line of canter bounces, and vice versa. The canter poles should be placed about 9ft (2.7m) apart measuring from the middle of the poles for the bounces, but can be 7ft (2.13m) apart for shorter-striding ponies and up to 10ft (3.05m) for longer-striding horses; if you add a second set of bounces, make a minimum one-stride distance between each set: this would be 7yd (6.4m) for horses and about 6 to 6.5yd (5.5 to 5.9m) for ponies (a distance with more strides between is more forgiving in terms of accuracy and stride). Wings can be placed beside the last element of the first set and the first element of the second set to make small step-overs on a one-stride distance later in the session (increase the distance if you decide to make these fences bigger).

How to Ride It

- Start by riding the trot-pole serpentine exercise, using your legs to make sure the horse is supple round the turns and through the change of bend, then working on sitting level and straight to ride to and from the trot poles with the leg aids helping to maintain straightness. The rhythm should be the same throughout.
- The next exercise is to leg yield into and out of the tunnel of poles. It may be helpful to start

this exercise in walk, but it can be ridden in any pace once mastered. Start by riding close to the outside of the first set of poles. Create a small amount of outside bend, controlling the other shoulder with a little direct rein. Keep your hips and shoulders level and apply the outside leg just behind the girth to ask the horse to move over towards the middle of the tunnel of tramlines. Ride straight between the second set of tramlines, then flex the poll slightly to the inside and apply the inside leg just behind the girth to ask the horse to leg yield back out past the last set of tramlines, controlling the shoulder with the outside rein.

- The trot-pole serpentine and leg-yield exercise can then be linked together.
- For the canter work, you can begin with the canter leg yield in and out of the tramlines, keeping your weight fractionally more to the side of the leading leg (but not leaning!).
- Then go round the outside of the main exercise and ride just to the canter bounces. As these are on a curve, keep looking and planning ahead. You are more likely to need to keep using the outside leg to maintain the curve, as horses tend to move on to the outside shoulder as they progress through the exercise and make the distance longer as a result.
- You can progress the exercise in the following ways:
  - Canter the leg-yield exercise either before or after the canter bounces.
  - Make the trot-pole serpentine into small fences and ride these in canter.
  - Make the canter bounces into two small fences on a distance so they can be ridden on their own or linked to any of the other exercises listed above.

EXERCISE 29

Obedience and Engagement Using Reinback

Aim

This exercise can help to work on your horse's obedience as he needs to make a downward transition after the first set of poles, and then move back into trot before the second set. Forward-thinking horses will find the first element more challenging, and less forward-thinking horses will need to respond promptly to the aids for the transition up to trot to complete the second set of poles.

The curving line through the exercise requires a little more balance to achieve suppleness through the curves and straightness between and over the poles.

The reinback exercise between the tramlines encourages the horse to engage his core and hindquarters to improve his elevation and power.

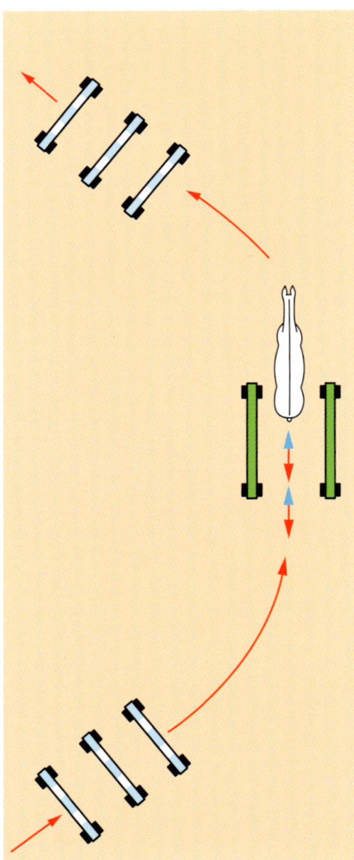

The tramlines in this exercise aid straightness of the reinback and can be used independently of the trot poles or linked to one or both sets.

Set-Up

Equipment:

- Eight poles or half-round poles
- Twelve pole pods or other pole holder if possible (if using round poles)

Set up the exercise as in the diagram, but if the poles are raised on pole pods and this is the first time your horse has seen these, then introduce the exercise with a single pole first. The poles should be 3ft 6in (0.9m) apart for a small pony, and 4ft 6in (1.22m) apart for a horse.

The exercise can be built in a straight line (as in Exercise 15), or with the poles offset from the tramlines as in the diagram. The latter set-up makes it slightly easier to avoid the horse locking on to both sets of poles down the straight line, but requires you to get him straight for the transition in the middle.

How to Ride It

- Introduce the horse to the exercise by simply riding over the poles, through the curve to the tramlines, then curving back to the other set of poles. Focus on keeping the horse straight for each pole section.
- Add a halt transition between the tramlines before proceeding back to trot to the second set of trot poles. Focus on keeping the hind leg engaged through the transition, and the horse's body straight between the tramlines.
- To complete the exercise, ride the first set of trot poles, then ride a halt transition at the end of the tramlines before riding a reinback for three to five steps between them. To do this, slightly lighten your seatbones, keeping your chest and head up, move both legs behind the girth and apply gentle pressure down the rein and with your legs. It can help if the horse has performed this in hand and is familiar with a voice command. As the horse takes a step back, slightly release the pressure and then repeat for the next step until you have achieved the number of steps you want. Then return your weight to your seatbones and close the leg by the girth to move forwards – ideally the last step of reinback and the first step into trot should be fluent and in the same rhythm, so without a pause in between, but this can take practice to achieve! Finish the exercise by trotting over the second set of trot poles.
- The exercise can be ridden on both reins. Repeat a few times each way to improve accuracy, straightness and obedience.

EXERCISE 30

Turn on the Haunches with Poles

Aim

This is a useful exercise for horses that need to be more energetic and engaged. This exercise also helps improve response to the outside aids to aid the turn.

Set-Up

Equipment:

- Six poles or half-round poles
- Four pole pods or other pole holder if possible (if using round poles)

Set up the exercise as in the diagram. You can progress this exercise to a small fence if you want, in which case place wings beside the two poles that you will be working over. You can also create this with three or more trot poles in place of the single ground pole.

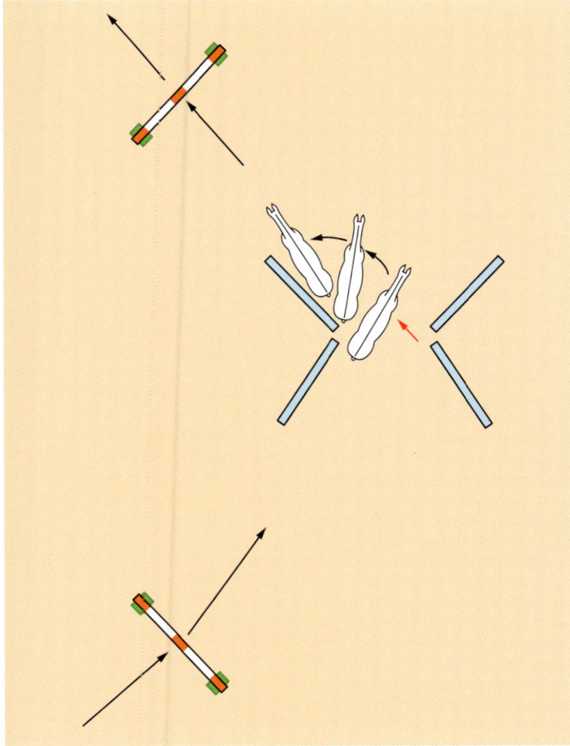

The poles in the centre of the exercise help guide the degree of turn on the haunches. Apply the outside leg near the girth to create the turn.

Ensure the angled rails are at a relatively open angle and approximately the same distance from the two ground poles you will work over.

How to Ride It

- This exercise can be ridden in walk first, or commence in trot depending on the horse.
- Approach the first pole out of the turn – for example on the right rein. Ride a straight line over the pole, and ride a halt at the apex of the angled poles, ideally with the horse's hind leg near the apex.
- Put your weight into your seatbone nearest the direction of travel (from an initial right rein approach this will be your left seatbone).
- Open the inside rein slightly to indicate the direction you will be moving in, and apply your outside leg near the girth to bring the shoulders round the apex of poles to face the second ground pole. (Be careful to turn the horse with your leg, and not by pulling on the inside rein.) Use the outside rein to stop the horse walking forwards – although with a novice horse a turn about the haunches is fine so a little movement is not a problem; then progress the challenge with a more advanced horse by making him move round without stepping forwards to do so. Ride out of the exercise over the second pole.
- The same exercise can be performed in canter, and it can also be progressed to a pivot (or 'lead') turn by riding a half halt instead of a halt, and using a little outside flexion to help with the turn, otherwise still applying the same aids. Small fences instead of ground poles can be used at this point too, provided there is enough space to do so.

TIPS FOR GREATER CHALLENGE AND COLLECTION

Coaches' tip: I have suggested an opening inside rein here for turn on the haunches as this leads more readily into the pivot turn, which uses more outside bend for jumping purposes (see Exercise 63). However, for greater challenge and collection (depending on what you want to achieve) you can ask the rider to use an indirect or direct rein aid to create inside flexion in this movement, so moving nearer to riding a pirouette.

INTRODUCING YOUR HORSE TO JUMPING

Many of the exercises already outlined in this book will develop your horse to help him succeed as a showjumper, and these exercises link into them, but are more specifically designed to help with introducing a young horse to jumping under saddle (loose jumping is addressed in Chapter 7 Gridwork, as this usually takes the form of a basic grid).

It is important with any young horse to give him time to understand the questions you are asking of him, and to be aware of where he is in his development both mentally and physically, so that you avoid pushing him too much before he is ready.

Jumping work requires the horse to use his muscles in a different way and so should be built up gradually. Whilst repetition is helpful for the horse to understand the exercises set, the amount of repetition will need to be carefully gauged for each individual horse so that he doesn't become fatigued. It can be much harder to assess this with a hot, forward-thinking horse, so err on the side of caution where possible, as there is an element of mental as well as physical fatigue to consider.

EXERCISE 31

Introducing Wings and Poles

Aim

This is a basic plan to get the horse going confidently, straight and in balance between sets of wings.

Set-Up

Equipment:

- A minimum of one standard pole
- Pole pods to secure the poles if available
- A minimum of two jump wings

Start by setting out the two wings the right distance apart to fit a pole, and remove any cups. Secure one pole between the wings either with pole pods or block it in with arena surface (so the pole doesn't roll if the horse catches it with a hoof). If the horse can

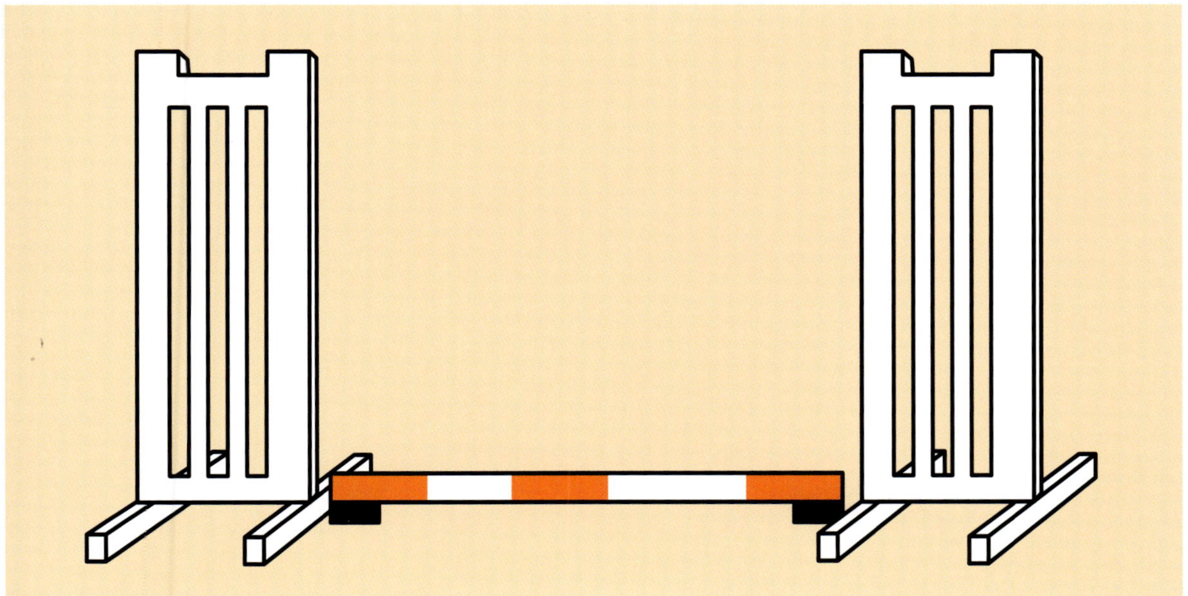

You can introduce a horse to showjumps by beginning with poles located between sets of wings.

be difficult to steer, add tramlines before and after the wings at least 9ft (2.7m) away from the wings and approximately the same distance apart from each other.

How to Ride It

- It is important to focus on looking and planning ahead, so look for the line to the pole early and then as you get nearer, look up and ahead to plan the ride away.
- Give the young horse as much time as possible to be straight and to see what he is approaching. Start the exercise in walk or trot depending on how confident he is, and where he is at in terms of his training. Slower paces make it easier to control direction, so if in doubt, start slow and build up the pace once the horse is confident in what he is being asked to do.
- Once you have crossed the pole, ensure you ride a straight line afterwards – establish these principles now and it is much easier to ride round a course later!
- If you have space and more jumps available to you, this exercise can be built into a little 'course' of poles. Introduce each one individually and then link them together, keeping the lines smooth and easy with no tight turns.

TIPS ON KEEPING THE HORSE STRAIGHT

If the horse struggles to hold a straight line, you can introduce tramlines as outlined above. It can also help to open both hands away from the neck to create a funnel effect to help channel the horse straighter (rather than correcting with one hand and then the other) – keep a connection down both reins evenly, and use both legs evenly to ride him forwards into the channel created by the wide hands.

Some young horses will look or hesitate at a pole, perhaps because it is a different colour or has different wings. If this happens, keep your eyes up at all times looking where you want to go next, because looking at the pole as well might suggest to your horse that you agree there is something to look at and worry about!

Try never to turn out of a 'fence' so there is never a side-door option! If it is a jump (as later on) it can always be dismantled if you have someone to help you, so that you can walk over it. It might take a little patience, but once your horse has crossed it once there is usually no problem with it after that.

EXERCISE 32

Introducing a Fence

Aim

This section provides a plan to introduce the horse to jumping through a balanced trot approach, making the take-off point comfortable and the jump easy to achieve.

Set-Up

Equipment:

- A minimum of two standard poles and one half-round or additional standard pole
- Pole pods if available to secure the poles
- A minimum of two jump wings and cups

This exercise can be varied depending on the temperament of the horse and which set-up therefore works best for him.

Option 1: Put three trot poles 3ft 6in (0.9m) apart for a small pony and 4ft 6in (1.22m) apart for a horse, either raising and securing them with pole pods, using half-round poles that don't roll, or blocking in the poles with the arena surface to ensure they don't roll. In a straight line directly after the trot poles set up the two wings at pole distance apart on a distance of 8ft (2.44m). Reduce this distance slightly for smaller ponies to about 7ft (2.13m), and extend it to 9ft (2.74m) for bigger-striding horses: the idea is to keep the stride length for the pony or horse comfortable and rounded, and not let it become long and flat.

Option 2: Set up one place pole, secured as the trot poles in option 1, in line with the wings at the same distance as outlined above – that is, 8ft (2.44m), or adjusted to suit the horse.

The first option is useful to maintain energy and rhythm to the fence, so can help those that need a little more impulsion from the hind leg, and it can keep a more forward-thinking horse in a good rhythm. However, for horses that are not so confident with the exercise, or that rush too much even with the trot poles in place, option 2 will be easier. For those

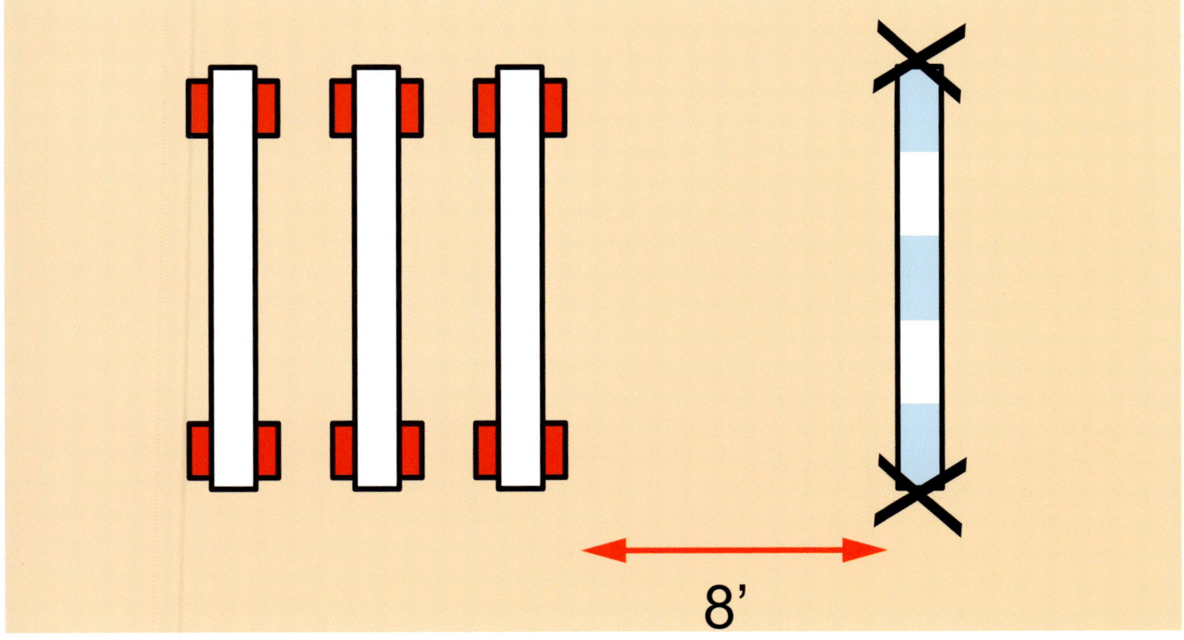

This is a basic grid to introduce a balanced trot to a fence. You can use three trot poles before the fence or a single pole, depending on your horse and what will suit him best.

tempted to rush, the initial approach can be in walk, and then proceed to trot near the place pole using option 2.

Once you have ridden the exercise and you and the horse are confident riding through the wings, add in a small vertical.

How to Ride It

- For both options 1 and 2, begin by riding straight on the approach and over the pole(s) in trot, maintaining the straightness through the jump wings and when riding away afterwards.
- Once this is achieved comfortably, a pole can be added between the wings, secured with a pole pod or the arena surface. At this point you can introduce the idea of a canter transition at, or just after the wings, as the jump will be a similar effect, so getting the horse to think forward at this point can help.
- Add in a second pole to create a small fence. I prefer to start with a very small vertical as it equates to more of a raised canter pole, rather than introducing a cross-pole at this stage. Forward-thinking horses are likely to step into canter in the space between the place pole and the small 'step-over' fence. Allow them to do this, and canter away after the fence. If your horse is not already stepping into canter, add a little leg pressure in the gap between the place pole and the step-over, and focus on riding the canter away from the jump.
- As the horse's confidence builds, the step-over can be increased in height, keeping everything simple and calm, and repeating the exercise in the same way.

EXERCISE 33

Introducing More Fences

Aim

This set-up introduces the horse to jumping a few fences linked together, using a trot approach that helps maintain straightness, balance and confidence.

Set-Up

Equipment:

- A minimum of six standard poles and three half-rounds or additional standard poles
- Pole pods to secure the poles, if available and using round poles
- A minimum of six jump wings and cups

Create a basic course such as in the diagram, keeping the fences small to start with and putting a place pole about 8ft (2.44m) before each fence. (Reduce the distance slightly for smaller ponies to about 7ft (2.13m), and extend it to 9ft (2.74m) for bigger-striding horses and as the fence height increases if needed.)

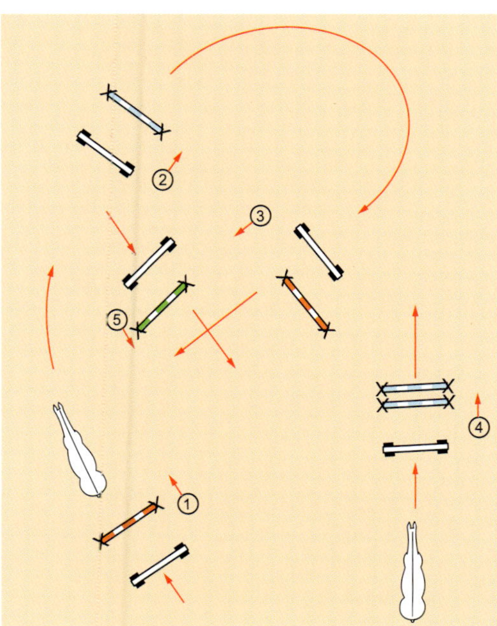

This is a suggested basic course plan for riding round a sequence of fences in trot, with place poles to help with accuracy and build confidence at each fence.

How to Ride It

- The idea with this exercise is to be able to trot and pop a series of fences in a calm manner, working on straightness and balance.
- Begin with a single fence with a place pole, ensure a straight approach, close the leg if needed in the space between the place pole and the small fence to encourage forward momentum, and ride canter away from the fence for a few strides before resuming trot.
- Repeat with each individual fence, ensuring the horse is confidently approaching it before moving on to the next one.
- Once each fence has been jumped individually, start to link them together, landing in canter and riding a few strides before returning to trot to approach the next fence. Keep everything simple and flowing, with no tight turns or short related distances at this stage.

TIP: CONSOLIDATE THE HORSE'S TRAINING

If the horse gets strong and you are struggling to bring him back to trot consistently to approach the next fence, add a circle to help bring him back to trot, or add walk transitions after each fence and then proceed back into trot. Just because you had a course in mind doesn't mean you have to complete it immediately – it is better to ensure that each fence consolidates what you are working on and training the horse to do, rather than insisting on getting to each fence in the course regardless of how the horse is in his balance, rhythm and straightness.

When taking a horse to a new venue this approach can be helpful as well, even if you have been introducing canter to fences. By approaching in trot, it is easier to control direction and so it is easier to avoid a run-out when the horse is introduced to new fences and a new location where he might not be as confident as he is at home. Adding some place poles, if available, can help with confidence as these will be a familiar exercise, although trotting and popping most of the fences without a place pole is often more practical in this scenario.

EXERCISE 34

Adding in Canter

Aim

This exercise introduces cantering into a jump using a controlled approach to aid balance and develop confidence.

Set-Up

Equipment:

- Two sets of wings
- A minimum of five poles, or four poles and one half-round pole
- Pole pods if available for round ground poles

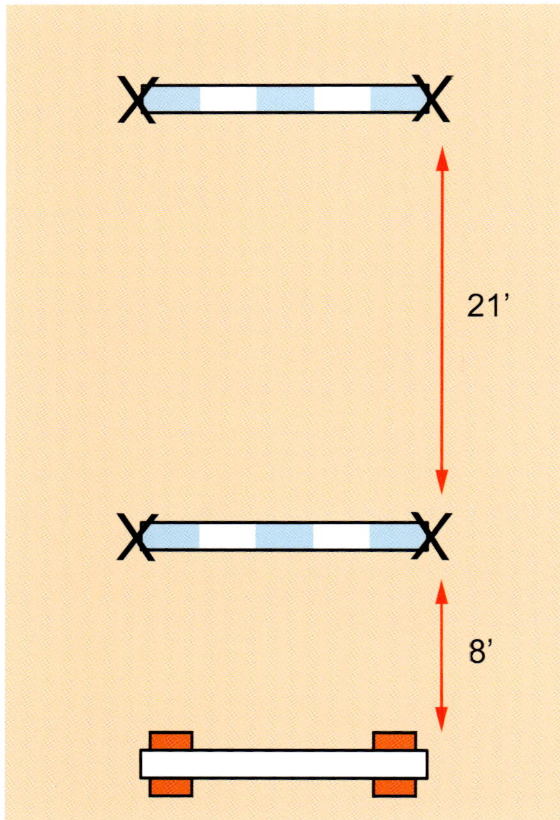

This is a basic grid set-up to start to introduce canter to a fence. You may need to adjust the distance slightly to make it comfortable for your horse as it should feel easy at this stage in their training, and the distance can be affected by factors such as your horse's confidence, forwardness, height and balance. Assess it before you add the second fence, and make the distance shorter if your horse is not taking you forward confidently.

Set up one place pole, secured with pole pods or the arena surface if it is a round pole, then add a small fence directly after the place pole on a distance of 8ft (2.45m).

The second element to this exercise can be set up at the same time or after the first element has been practised (add this in later if the horse is very spooky so that you can be jumping the first fence confidently before adding another set of wings to ride between!). This should be a second small fence directly after the first on a straight-line distance of 7yd (6.4m), or reduce it by up to 1yd (0.9m) for ponies. Initially put the wings at the correct distance and remove all the cups and poles from the second element to the side to add in later.

How to Ride It

- Start with the familiar exercise (Exercise 32) of a place pole to a fence. Make a trot approach, and aim to land in canter, and canter quietly away from the fence (through the second set of wings if these are in place).
- Once the horse is comfortable with this, add the second element. Keep both fences small but make the second fractionally bigger so that it can be clearly seen. Continue to approach in trot, and close the leg as needed to maintain the energy to land in canter and take the one stride to the second element.
- By keeping the distance short, the young horse is encouraged to keep balance through the canter stride before the fence, and not become flat and unbalanced.
- As this exercise becomes easier you can increase the number of strides between the fences, for example, so that the second element is two strides away – 11yd (10.06m) for horses – to see if the canter and balance can be maintained as the number of canter strides taken between the elements increases.
- Keep the first element as a small step-over to set up the placement to the second element. If you do significantly increase the height, you may need to lengthen the distance between the fences slightly.

EXERCISE 35

Establishing Canter to Fences

Aim

As canter is usually the hardest pace to establish with a young horse once they are working under saddle, this exercise uses canter poles to aid the approach to a fence in canter to help the horse stay in balance and rhythm off the forehand.

Set-Up

Equipment:

- A minimum of one set of wings
- A minimum of five poles, or two poles and three half-rounds
- Six pole pods if available and using round poles
- Three cavaletti if available or similar raised pole design

Start by setting up a one-stride pole distance on 7yd (6.4m), or reduce this by up to a yard (0.9m) for ponies. Initially put the wings at the second part of the distance and remove all cups and spare poles to the side to add in later.

Later in the session, two canter bounce poles can be added before the first place pole to balance and engage the canter preceding the one-stride distance. These should be set up 9 to 10ft (2.74 to 3.05m) apart, and 7 to 8ft (2.13–2.44m) for shorter-striding ponies.

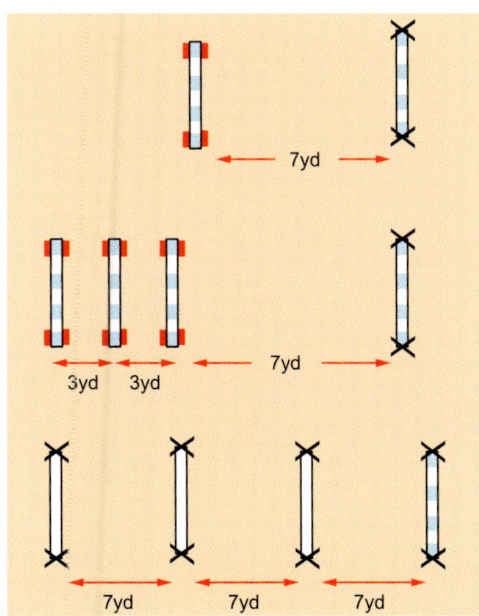

These are some basic set-ups for a canter approach to a fence.

If cavaletti are available these can be used on a low setting instead of the poles to create the three bounce strides, or can be set on the one-stride pole distance outlined above (this is slightly less intense for the horse). These will help to maintain the length of stride, and because they are also slightly raised it can also help the horse to maintain balance.

How to Ride It

- For the basic canter exercise, start by establishing a steady, rhythmical canter and approach the two poles on the one-stride distance. If the horse is forward-thinking and inclined to rush, you can trot the majority of the approach and ease into canter a few strides before the poles.
- Add in the small fence as the second element and repeat.
- You can now add in the canter bounces if you want to help maintain the canter rhythm better. When adding the bounces, start without the fence at the end of the line and then add it back in once the horse is confident with the exercise. Start at 3yd (9ft or 2.74m) and adjust as needed to suit the horse.
- If you lack a way to secure your poles but have cavaletti, these can be used on the lowest setting as they won't be much higher than poles on pods.
- Alternatively you can replace the first pole in the one-stride distance with a cavaletti, and add more cavaletti on a low setting on a 7yd (6.4m) distance before it, to create a line of one-stride canter steps between the cavaletti and to the fence so that the horse has to maintain the same stride length throughout the approach.

TIPS ON KEEPING BALANCE IN CANTER EXERCISES

The key to riding canter exercises with a young horse is for the rider to keep their balance. A neckstrap can be useful, but also think of keeping your chest up so you don't drop on to the forehand with the horse (they often do that well enough on their own!), and keep your chin out – this will help you to keep looking ahead and allow you to follow the jump more easily, whether the horse stands off or gets close to the fence, without being out of balance.

LOOSE JUMPING AND GRIDWORK EXERCISES

Loose jumping can be a good way of introducing a young horse to fences, and allows you to observe his technique (although this is no guarantee of his technique under saddle). If you are selling a young showjumper, it is also often a method by which horses are demonstrated for auction purposes when they are not yet backed, so if you intend to use this method of sale, it is well worth making sure the horse is familiar with it.

Gridwork under saddle is useful for training horse technique, rider technique, or both. Different configurations can help achieve different things in terms of the horse's technique. For the rider, the grid format allows them to focus on themselves more, as once they have entered the grid everything is, to some extent, set up for them.

EXERCISE 36

Starting Loose Jumping

Aim

There are specific formulae for loose jumping in an auction format, which will be covered in the next exercise. This exercise is designed to help you introduce the horse to loose jumping safely, and can be adapted depending on your set-up.

Set-Up

It is important that this exercise is carried out safely in a sufficiently secure environment, so that the horse does not jump out of the arena. Ensure that the surface and equipment are good and not likely to cause the horse to sustain any injuries. Ideally, set up this exercise in an indoor arena with doors that can be shut, so there is no opportunity for the horse to jump out. Another option might be if you have an outdoor arena but with very high boards round the sides.

Equipment:

- A minimum of eight poles plus wings

Using one long side of the arena, locate two wings near the mid-point: one should be against the wall, and the other should be a pole distance apart, but do not introduce poles or cups until later.

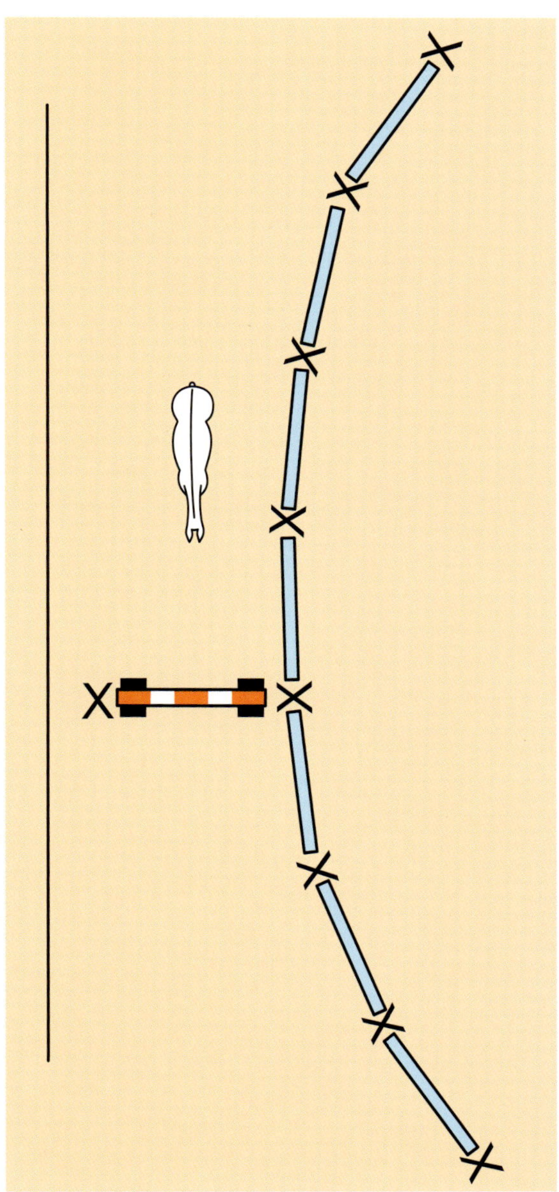

This is a basic set-up for loose jumping. The blue poles denote the angled rails used to create the jumping lane.

Parallel to the wall and in line with the inside jump wing, create a slightly curving line of poles, which can be straight a little before and after the jump wings but can then curve out away from the wall to each side after that. Now raise the poles up on to cups with wings. I tend to angle the poles slightly from about 5ft 9in (1.50m) on one side down to 4ft 7in/5ft (1.20/1.30m) on the other, unless you are loose jumping something small, in which case reduce the height so they can't wiggle under!

How to Do It

- Ideally you want a minimum of two people to do this safely, and how you do it depends on the size of your arena. If the arena is relatively small, it is easy to manage it with a couple of people to direct the horse and allow him to work loose.
- If the arena is quite large it can be difficult to direct the horse down the loose-jumping lane, so in this instance I use bribery! Have one person lead the horse to the start of the lane: make sure they are capable handlers and are wearing a hard hat, so they don't get hurt releasing the horse. Have someone else with treats at the other end of the arena in a safe place (so they don't get flattened!) and the food-orientated horse will happily travel down the lane to the food, and be recaptured to start again.
- Once the horse is travelling down the empty jumping lane safely, secure a pole on the floor between the wings and allow him to repeat the exercise a couple more times. You can also do the same thing on the other rein. The pole could then be slightly raised and given a groundline to complete the first session.
- When you repeat the loose-jumping session, still build it up in the same way, but you can build the fence slightly bigger with a groundline on each side (so that it can be jumped either way), and allow your horse to learn how to judge his own take-off point.

TIPS: HOW TO KEEP CALM AND IN CONTROL

Having a lunge whip to hand can be useful to help point and direct the horse, but try not to chase him down the lane with it, as this can cause him to rush and flatten.

Loose jumping can be quite exciting for the horse, so try to keep the atmosphere calm, and have experienced people in the arena with you. It can be sensible to have the horse in a simple snaffle bridle to help with control if you need to lead him, and looping a rope through the bit rather than clipping it on can be better for ensuring a safe release.

EXERCISE 37

Loose-Jumping Grid

Aim

This exercise presents one of the specific formulae for loose jumping in an auction format (this one is from the Dublin Horse Show), to give an idea of what might be expected. It is much more prescriptive in terms of the set-up so that the horse is put into a good place to jump, and it then demands more physically with the sequence of fences. It is therefore a set-up that I would not use too often with a young horse, but is useful to practise for sales purposes, and can be used to introduce the idea of combinations.

Set-Up

Ideally this grid should be set up in an indoor arena, with doors that can be shut, so there is no option for the horse to jump out.

Equipment:

- A minimum of sixteen poles plus wings
- One half-round pole or a pole on pole pods

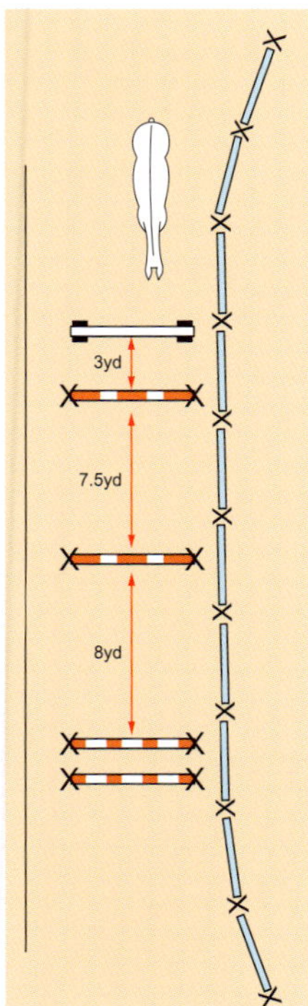

This is a grid for a loose jumping auction, to give an idea of the set-up a horse being sold by this method will encounter.

Create a similar set-up to exercise 1, but add in two more sets of wings for additional verticals plus a set of back wings at the third set of wings to make an oxer later (if desired).

In front of the first set of wings, which should be near the beginning of the jumping lane, set up a place pole using a half-round pole or a pole fixed in place securely.

Once the horse has worked down the line confidently, start to add in the elements progressively at the following distances:

Pole to a small vertical (max height 2ft 6in/75cm): 3.28yd (3m)
Vertical to vertical (max height 2ft 6in/75cm): 7.44yd (6.8m)
Distance to a final (third) vertical (max height 2ft 6in/75cm): 7.98yd (7.3m)

To complete the grid, the final element would become an oxer once it has been jumped successfully as a vertical.

How to Do It

- As with the initial loose-jumping exercise, have an assistant to help manage the horse, and start with an empty jumping lane or just the place pole, before adding further elements.
- Then add the first small vertical at the distance outlined above. Keeping it small allows the horse to make adjustments more easily if needed.
- Once he has completed the single fence sequence a couple of times, add the second fence, also keeping it small.
- Introduce the horse gradually to the sequence of jumps: it might be better to leave the third fence until a subsequent session, and again, rebuild from the place pole but add in the final element, which can be a little taller once the horse is confident down the grid (90cm to 1.10m for a three-year-old).

TIP: KEEP THE SESSIONS SHORT

Remember that this new experience will be mentally and physically fatiguing for the horse, so keep the sessions short, even if his enthusiasm says he could keep going all day!

EXERCISE 38

A Basic Trot Approach Grid

Aim

The easiest way to approach a grid is in trot, as it is easier to control pace and stride. This exercise is a basic grid using this type of approach.

A basic grid such as this allows you to work on rhythm and to focus on your own balance and position over the jump, as well as building your horse's confidence working over a consecutive line of fences.

Set-Up

Equipment:

- One place pole using a half-round or a pole secured with pole pods or similar
- A minimum of seven poles
- Three sets of wings and cups

Gradually add in the elements (*see* below), but set up the wings as follows:

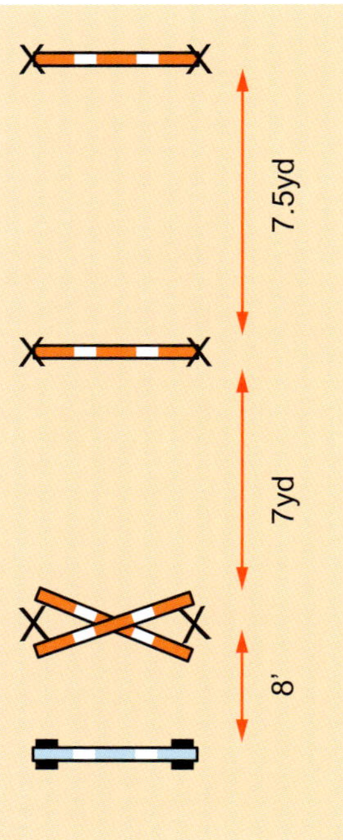

This is a basic grid with a trot approach. The distances can be adjusted to accommodate your horse as needed, especially if he is less experienced, in order to make the set-up comfortable for him to execute.

Place pole to cross-pole – 8ft (2.44m)
Cross-pole to vertical – 7yd (6.4m)
Vertical to vertical – 7.5yd (6.85m)

Be prepared to adjust the distances slightly if needed, lengthen the distance for bigger fences and shorten the place pole distance by about a foot, and the distances up to a yard for small and/or shorter-striding ponies.

How to Ride It

- Begin by riding over the place pole in trot and through the line of wings to familiarise the horse if this is a new exercise to him. Keep your eyes up, and focus on riding a straight line between the wings.
- Add in your first element, which is a cross-pole. Keep the two poles apart from each other by about 4in (10cm) so they can fall independently of each other if knocked. The cross-pole should help to keep the horse straight, but have your focus on your line after the jump to the end of the grid to maintain straightness throughout. Approach in trot, but aim to land from the cross-pole in canter, and canter to the end of the line.
- If the horse hesitates or lacks impulsion, think of closing your leg as you cross the place pole, and ride positively forwards and away afterwards.
- Once this is riding well, add in the next element, which is a small vertical placed about 7yd (6.4m) away. Keep all the elements small while you build the horse's confidence through the grid, and be aware of your straightness down the line, but also of your own position.
- Add the final element once the first parts are jumping well, and keep focusing on straightness and maintaining the same energy down the line – be ready to close your leg to keep the forward momentum if needed.

> **COACHES' TIP: HAVE THE WINGS IN PLACE**
>
> Having the wings in place throughout the grid progression helps rider and horse straightness, but is also useful to gauge whether the distance is likely to be comfortable for the combination you are working with before you add each element, as you can observe the horse's landing strides in relation to the wing location.

EXERCISE 39

Trot Approach Bounce Grid

Aim

This bounce grid will be helpful for horses that get quick or flat to their fences; it requires some athleticism and engagement from the hind legs.

Set-Up

Equipment:

- One place pole using a half-round or a pole secured with pole pods or similar
- A minimum of eight poles (if you are short of poles or wings but have cavaletti, the earlier parts of this grid could be replaced with cavaletti on their highest setting)
- Four sets of wings and cups

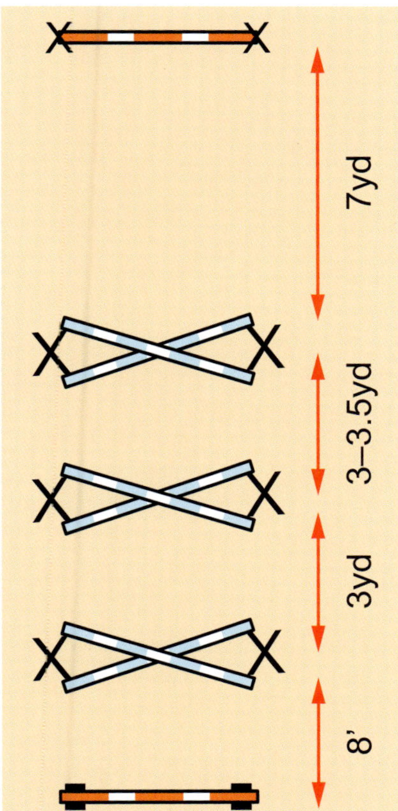

This grid demands engagement and suppleness of the hind leg through the bounces, which should help the quality of the canter through the one stride distance to the vertical afterwards.

Gradually add in the elements (*see* below), but set up the wings as follows:

Place pole to first cross-pole: 8ft (2.44m)
First cross-pole to second cross-pole: 3yd (2.74m) to 3.5yd (3.2m)
Second cross-pole to third cross-pole: 3yd (2.74m) to 3.5yd (3.2m)
Third cross-pole to vertical: 7yd (6.4m)

Be prepared to adjust the distances slightly if needed, particularly if the horse is finding them a little long, and keep the sides of the cross-poles relatively low to start with; also place the poles so they have a 4in (10cm) gap between them so they can fall easily if knocked (the cross-poles can be replaced with small verticals if preferred, the cross-poles just help to keep the horse's shoulders lifted and moving well, in addition to aiding straightness).

How to Ride It

- Begin by riding in an energetic trot over the place pole to the first cross-pole, aiming to ride away in canter, maintaining straightness through the other sets of wings.
- When you and the horse feel confident in this, add the first bounce by forming the second cross-pole. The key is to have plenty of energy in the trot, and to keep the leg closed through the bounce to help maintain the power if needed, as this effectively becomes the first canter stride. Keep your shoulders up and just flex at the hip, allowing your hips, knees and ankles to absorb the bounce. Make sure you keep looking up and ahead to help maintain your balance, as riding a bounce is more demanding of your balance as a rider than other related distances.
- Now add the third fence, and focus on your position and balance as you continue the line of bounces.
- To complete the grid, add a vertical 7yd (6.4m) after the last cross-pole for a one-stride distance to finish. Keep holding your position through the final stride, and ride a straight line away afterwards. Depending on your horse – whether he is forward thinking or not, and how long his natural stride is – you might find the distances need to be adjusted to keep the shape of the jump; however, be aware that if you increase the height of the last fence significantly this will have the effect of shortening the distance a little, so bear this in mind when making any adjustments.

EXERCISE 40

Trot Approach Oxer Grid

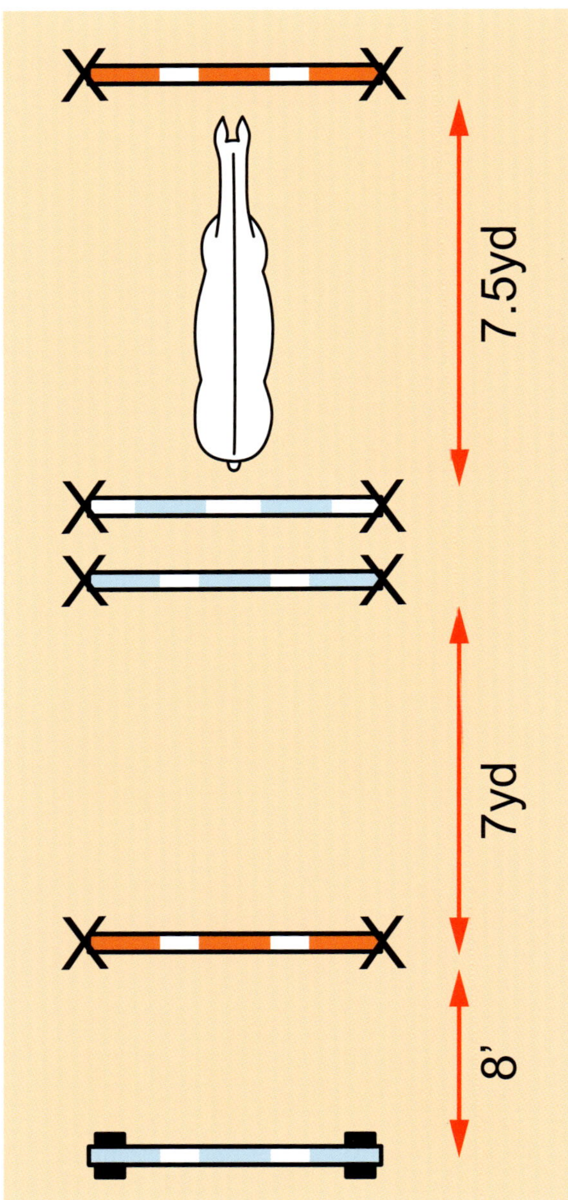

This grid demands power for the oxer element in the middle, and control and balance to complete the line over the final vertical.

Aim

Adding an oxer into a grid demands power and athletic ability on the part of the horse to extend his frame across the spread, and challenges his balance to then readjust his body for the vertical afterwards.

Set-Up

Equipment:

- One place pole using a half-round or a pole secured with pole pods or similar
- A minimum of seven poles
- Four sets of wings and cups, including two safety cups

Gradually add in the elements (*see* below), but set up the wings as follows:

Place pole to vertical: 8ft (2.44m)
Vertical to oxer: 6.5yd (5.94m) to 7yd (6.4m)
Oxer to vertical: 7yd (6.4m) to 7.5yd (6.86m)

Be prepared to adjust the distances slightly if necessary to suit the horse.

How to Ride It

- Make sure that you have an energetic trot to start over the place pole to the vertical, and ensure you ride away in canter.
- Once this feels comfortable, add the oxer element, keeping an easy width to begin with. On landing from the vertical, ensure that the horse is travelling forwards with energy and in balance to jump the oxer, and focus on sitting up and riding a balanced canter afterwards.
- Build the oxer a little wider and ride the exercise again before adding the final element.
- When riding the full grid, be aware of the horse's balance on landing from the oxer, particularly with a bigger spread, so that you can be ready to help him rebalance for the final element through your upper body and leg if necessary.

EXERCISE 41

Canter Control Grid

Aim

This exercise is designed to be ridden in canter right through the grid. More bounces could be added in front of the suggested set-up to regulate the canter for longer.

Set-Up

Equipment:

- A minimum of three cavaletti
- Three jumps

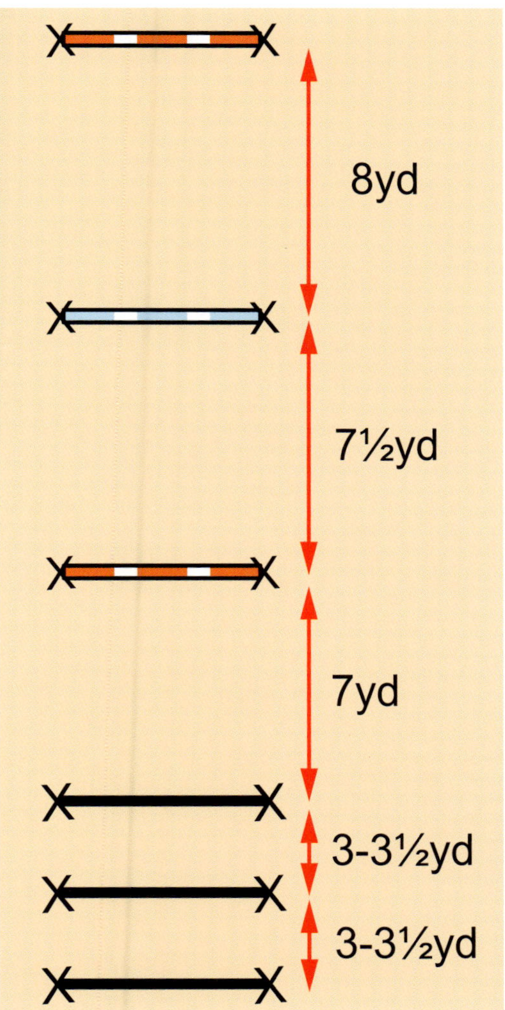

This grid controls the canter into it through the cavaletti bounces and can help work to regulate stride.

Set up the full grid as follows, then remove the poles and cups from the later elements for the warm-up section:

Cavaletti set at 3 yards (2.74m) apart (lowest setting) to 3.5 yards (3.2m) (high setting)
Final cavaletti to the first vertical: 7yd (6.4m)
First vertical to the second vertical: 7.5yd (6.86m)
Second vertical to the third vertical: 8yd (7.32m)

Be prepared to adjust the distances slightly if necessary to suit the horse, and shorten them slightly if the fences are very small.

How to Ride It

- Once you have warmed up on the flat, start by riding over a single cavaletti or small fence, elsewhere in the arena ideally, so as to warm up the horse's jumping muscles before tackling the bounces.
- Then approach the grid in a balanced, rhythmical canter, being careful not to get too quick on the approach.
- Once you have ridden the cavaletti bounces a couple of times and are happy with the approach and your ride through the line, add your first vertical.
- As you continue with the grid, progressively add the other elements, and increase the height of the last two elements as required.
- Keep focusing on straightness and rhythm, and keep your shoulders up throughout so that the horse does not increase his pace or run on to his shoulders too much.

TIP: HOW TO PREVENT RUSHING

If the horse is still rushing to the cavaletti, add a place pole 8ft (2.44m) to 9ft (2.74m) before the first cavaletti to help him hold his stride on the approach. Also ground poles can be used, so long as they are well secured, between the jumping elements to help him hold a level stride.

01282 834970
EQUESTRIAN
SURFACES LTD
equestriansurfaces.co.uk

POLE AND FENCE COMBINATIONS

This chapter combines polework exercises with jumps as an alternative to straight-line gridwork. It is designed to provide more comprehensive training sessions that can be used by coaches as ideas for clinic settings or group sessions, as well as giving varied training set-ups that you can use to work with your horse on a broader range of exercises.

Some of the pole and jump combinations I have designed over the years are particularly suited to (and have been used in) small arenas, so you will find a few more ideas in the next chapter as well!

EXERCISE 42

Straightness and Control Exercise

Aim

This exercise is designed to aid straightness when riding to and from a fence. Including the angled fences and trot or canter poles at the end of the grid increases the challenge of riding with control and accuracy.

Set-Up

Equipment:

- Eight poles or half-round poles for trot poles
- 22 pole pods (if possible) if using round poles for trot and canter poles
- Eight poles for canter poles and jumps (nine poles if you prefer a ground pole on each side)

Set up the exercise as in the diagram, starting with trot or canter poles for the central fence location (depending on the experience of the horse and rider combination), and building it to a fence later in the session.

Set the distance between each trot pole at the top and bottom to measure 3ft 6in (0.9m) for a small pony, and 4ft 6in (1.22m) for a horse. Ensure that there is room outside the poles to ride a turn between them, and that the middle two poles are positioned so the horse can go between them and ride a straight line between the wings of the central fence.

The canter poles should be set about 7ft (2.13m) apart for a small pony, and up to 10ft (3.05m) apart for a horse – generally start at 9ft (2.74m) for horses when introducing the exercise, and adapt as needed.

How to Ride It

- Start by riding the trot poles on both short sides of the arena, focusing on the quality of the turn

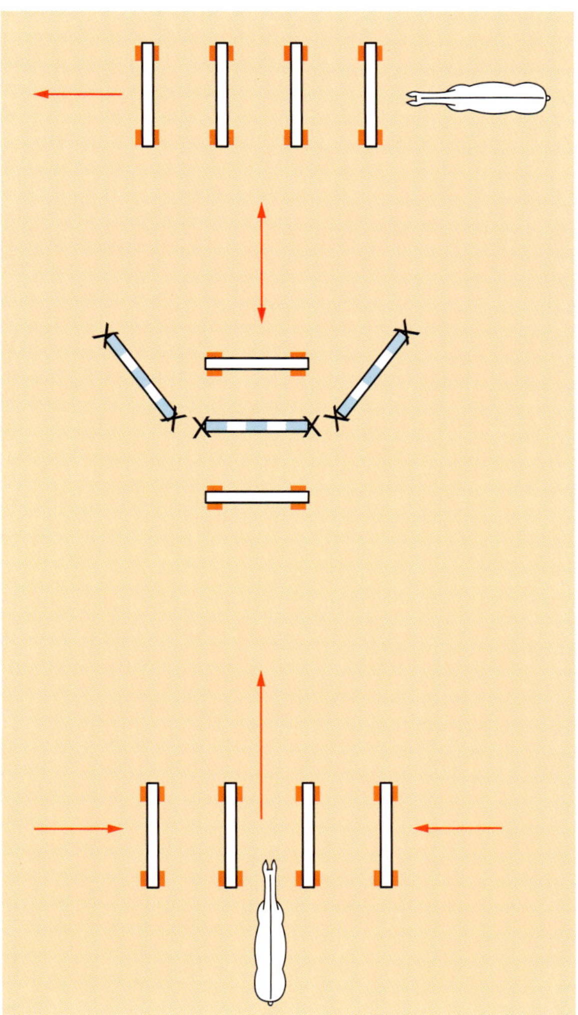

This exercise uses the centre line to address straightness and can also work on supple turns, control and straightness by adding in the angled fence elements and linking these to the trot poles at each end.

before and after the poles. Notice whether the speed and rhythm of the horse stays the same, or changes on the turns and the long sides between the poles – work to have the same speed and rhythm throughout. Do this exercise on both reins.

- Then ride the turn between the trot poles at each end, and over the central poles whether these are set in trot or canter. In canter the turns at the top and the bottom become more challenging, so make sure you are looking and planning ahead and that there is room to turn!
- The exercise can then be progressed to a single fence on the centre line (using the additional poles as groundlines on each side); be sure to ride between the middle of the trot poles at each end to ensure a straight approach and departure from the fence, and a controlled turn before and after.
- To progress the exercise further, introduce the additional fences that are ridden out of a turn. For control purposes these can then be followed by the trot poles at either end with transitions between, or the trot poles can be adjusted to a canter-pole distance to regulate the canter before and after the jumps.

TIPS: RIDING IN CONTROL

If on the initial trot-pole exercise the horse increases speed on the long side, include a trot-walk-trot transition in the middle of the long side to improve control of pace.

Coaches' tip: This can be a useful group exercise as the initial exercises can be ridden together, provided all riders are kept on the same rein and with clear rules! With novice combinations, begin the centre-line exercise in trot, and ensure that they understand the aids to make a clear turn at the end so that both horse and rider know where they are going before trying the canter turns!

EXERCISE 43

The Egg Timer

Aim

This exercise is about maintaining rhythm and needs a longer arena to create enough space to complete it fully; although it can be adapted for less space, it might not be possible to ride the full shape.

Set-Up

Equipment:

- Six poles or half-round poles or cavaletti
- Twelve pole pods (if possible) if using round poles
- Four jumps, which can be placed together so it is possible to share multidirectional jump stands

Create an 'X' of jumps in the centre of the arena, as shown in the diagram. On the short sides of the arena, set up two curving lines of canter poles or cavaletti. These are likely to fit best on a one-stride distance of 7yd (6.4m), but in a larger arena they could have two or three strides between them. Leave enough room to ride around the outside of the poles.

How to Ride It

- Warm up over the canter-pole curves before starting to jump.
- The exercise also allows you to jump the single fences in the centre in any order you want.
- To increase the challenge, ride through the canter-pole curve and then ride the curving line to one of the fences on the X. You can also ride this in reverse, jumping first, then riding to the canter poles afterwards.
- The canter poles should help you to keep rhythm and balance through the turns, and will test control after the fence to get back on to the same length of stride.
- To ride the full exercise, ride one set of canter poles to a fence, then ride the curving line to the other set of canter poles, then to the next fence, and continue until you have jumped all four fences.

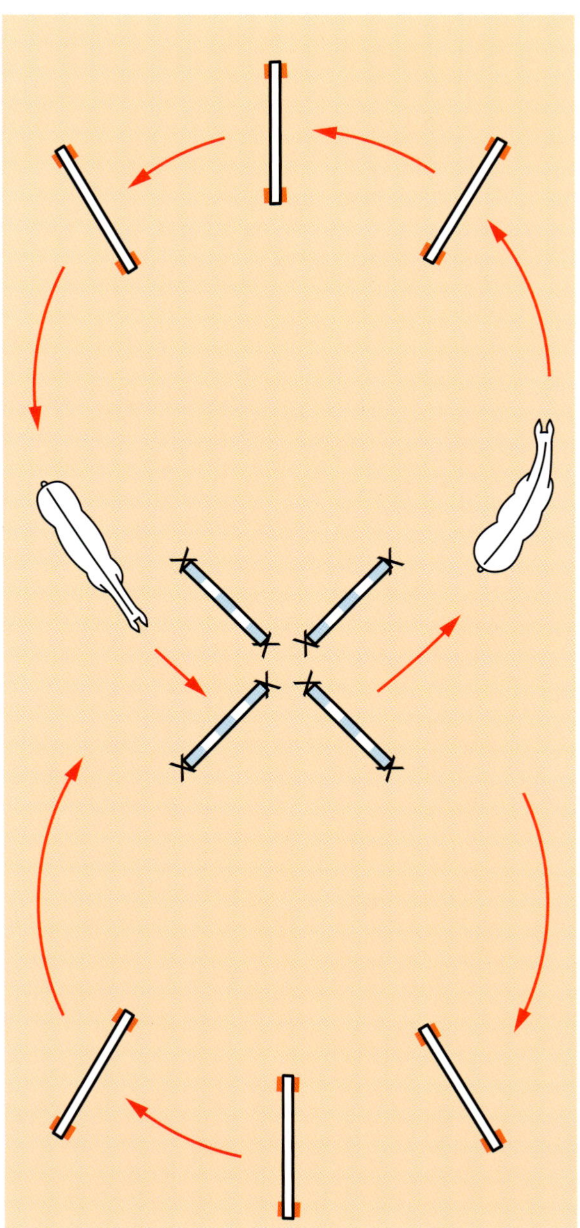

By using the canter curve at each end to establish a quality canter, this can help the ride to the central fences. To increase the challenge, add the second set of canter poles afterwards.

EXERCISE 44

Double Double

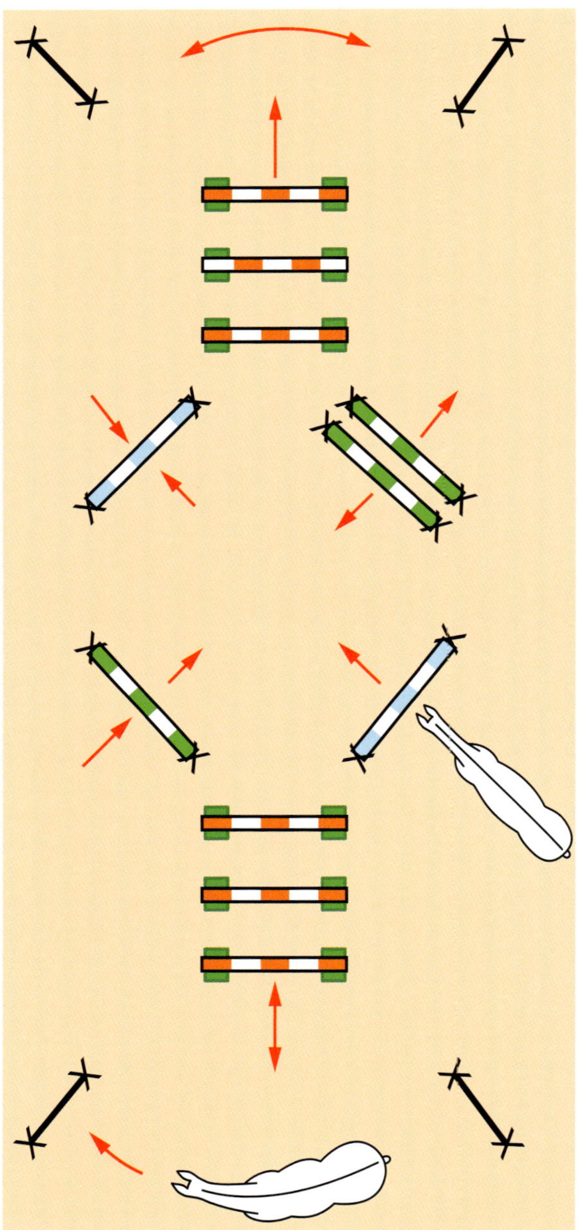

This exercise gives options to work straightness and suppleness before training through doubles or related distances (depending on your arena size and what you need to work on).

Aim

How this exercise is set up will depend on the size of the arena you are working in, but at its more challenging setting it has two doubles set up across the central area, and canter poles and cavaletti to help develop the canter before riding the doubles. It is a useful exercise to work on straightness and an appropriate length of stride.

Set-Up

Equipment:

- Four jumps for the doubles
- Six poles or half-round poles
- Twelve pole pods (if possible) if using round poles
- Four cavaletti (these can also be jumps)

Down the centre line of the arena, build two sets of three canter poles with a distance between each pole of between 9 and 10ft (2.74 to 3.05m) with a gap in the middle of at least 14yd (12.8m), or longer if needed to accommodate the two doubles (depending on the shape of the arena).

In the centre, as in the diagram, build two doubles or related distances, one on each diagonal line. Depending on the size and shape of the arena, these could be on 8yd (7.3m) for one stride, 12yd (11m) for two strides, or it can be a related distance on three strides or more at 16yd (14.6m) plus if it is a large space.

At each end of the exercise, build a curving line of two cavaletti on a distance that again can vary, but for example on three strides would be about 14yd (13m) and four strides would be 18yd (16.5m) if the cavaletti are on a relatively low setting; this would be extended to up to 20yd (18.3m) if you replace the cavaletti with jumps on a four-stride curving line depending upon height. The degree of the curve can be made quite gentle for an easier warm-up exercise.

The exercise can be set up so that the central fences are not directly in line and so each fence can be worked individually; alternatively the second element can be removed completely if space is tight.

How to Ride It

- Use the central canter poles to warm up, focusing on straightness and rhythm over the poles and through the gap between the two sets of poles.
- Now ride the cavaletti curves, focusing on steering with your legs and looking and planning ahead. You can also then link the canter poles and the cavaletti by riding the cavaletti at one end of the arena, cantering down the long side and then turning up the centre line to the canter poles and vice versa.
- To make the exercise progressive in terms of the doubles, start by removing one element and ride them as single fences. You can precede them or follow them with any of the other sections already ridden.
- To complete the exercise, ride up the centre line over the canter poles, then ride one double, which can be followed by cavaletti before riding the second double, or ride straight to the second double. There are lots of options depending on space and whether you want to keep focusing on stride length, in which case the central canter poles can keep being revisited, or if you want to maintain the quality of the canter, in which case the cavaletti curve might be most beneficial.
- Depending on the distances, if you have set up related distances rather than doubles, there is also an option to ride one set of canter poles and then a dog leg to one of the fences if the distance has been set up to do so (this would need to be 1yd (0.91m) shorter than a standard related distance, to factor in that one element is only a pole).

EXERCISE 45

Mercedes Options

Aim

This is another exercise that can be adapted depending on the size of your arena: for smaller arenas it can be set up as for Exercise 52, the Mercedes exercise, in Chapter 6, with added canter poles to help establish rhythm and stride; while for larger spaces the exercise can be extended as outlined here.

Set-Up

Equipment:

- Three to five jumps, depending on arena size
- Six poles or half-round poles
- Twelve pole pods (if possible) if using round poles

First set up the straight-line exercise down the centre of the arena. If you are using the Mercedes shape due to limited space, it can be set up off-centre to create more space to turn if needed.

Set up the central fence for the exercise, and then, if you are using only three fences, set out a 7yd (6.4m) distance to three canter poles set at 9ft (2.74m) to 10ft (3.05m) apart for horses. If you are using five fences, then it will make fence location and angle easier if the distance from the central fence to the canter poles is on a two-stride distance, which is about 11yd (10.06m).

As in the diagram, adjacent to the central fence place two to four additional fences, making sure that they are angled so that you can ride to them by going round the canter poles, and that there is sufficient room on landing to ride away.

As an extension of the exercise, you can adapt the canter poles to make a small grid using cavaletti or additional jumps. For example, for a canter approach on a two-stride distance, you could change the poles for a single cavaletti to the central fence on 11yd (10m), then the central fence to a second fence on 12yd (11m).

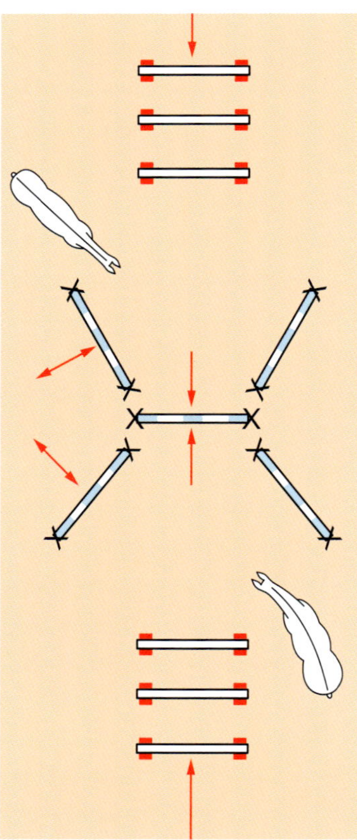

This set-up allows you to establish a quality canter up the central line and then add in the other fences, which can build up to a small course.

How to Ride It

- Warm up in trot over the canter poles without the central fence, or use one or two of the angled fences to begin your warm-up.
- Progress to riding the straight-line exercise, focusing on maintaining a good rhythm over the poles to the fence, and the same on the ride away.
- Now ride the angled fences and link these together, or add them to the centre-line exercise by completing the straight line and then rolling back out of that line to one of the angled fences. Use the space well to keep the horse's rhythm and flow through the turns, and see if you can maintain the same quality in the canter that you have achieved through the centre-line exercise.

COACHES' TIP: KEEP STRAIGHT, KEEP A GOOD CANTER

If a rider is struggling to make the distances in the central straight-line exercise, make sure that you observe them from the end of the straight line to see if they are straight, as this outcome is often caused by the horse and/or rider not being straight. Alternatively it might be caused by a loss of quality in the canter through the turn.

EXERCISE 46

Centipede

Aim

This is a useful exercise to introduce dog-leg lines and clarity of the aids, as well as providing options to work on straightness and turns.

Set-Up

Equipment:

- Four jumps, depending on arena size (these can be oxers and verticals)
- Six poles or half-round poles
- Twelve pole pods (if possible) if using round poles

Down the centre of the arena create a straight line with two ground poles, ideally at least six strides apart, which for horses will be 26yd (23.77m). On either side of the central pole, put two poles on an angle to create an open 'U'-type shape, as in the diagram. This works quite well on a 7yd (6.4m) distance, but keep the angle quite gentle, or widen the location of the poles to add more strides.

From the centre-line pole at the bottom of the arena, measure a dog-leg distance to a fence, taking 1yd (0.9m) less than if the distance were fence to fence. (Five strides will therefore be about 23yd (21m) – although if the lines are tight due to the space available, or the fences are very small, you might need to shorten the distance slightly, at least at first.)

Repeat this in a dog-leg line in the other direction. If there is space to do so, you can then add in the other set of 'legs' for the centipede by creating a shorter dog-leg distance in the remaining space.

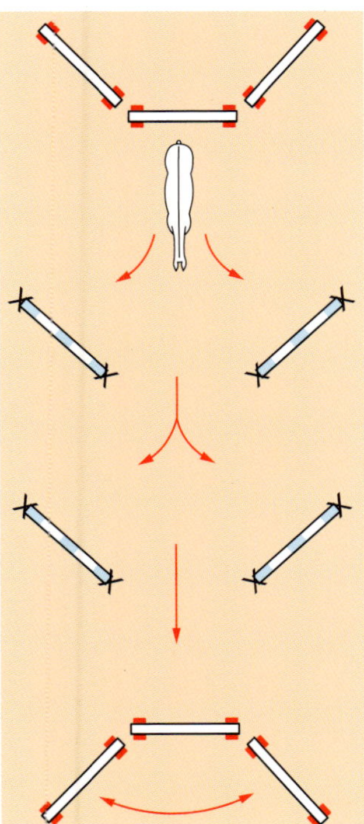

This can be adapted as poles or fences to work on steering through dog leg lines, and has the option of a curving one stride distance at each end as well as a central line to work on straightness.

How to Ride It

- Start by trotting and cantering over the two poles down the centre line, focusing on straightness; notice the number of strides taken in canter, which you can adjust up and down to practise rideability.
- If you have set up the angled poles to ride between, you can also then practise riding an accurate, balanced line through the curve at either end of the arena.
- Once you have warmed up and are happy with the length of stride and rhythm in the horse's canter, start to ride the dog-leg lines, steering with your legs and directing the horse by looking ahead and moving your weight slightly into the seatbone in the direction of travel, keeping the rein aids as subtle as possible.
- You can also ride the curved line of the two poles in canter, and then ride down to a fence on the outside of the exercise to practise a more open line, with the option to roll back afterwards.

> **TIP: KEEP THINGS SMALL**
>
> When introducing the dog-leg line for less experienced horses and riders, keep the fences small, or even replace them with poles at first (in which case reduce the distance by 1yd (0.9m).
>
> **Coaches' tip:** Tramlines or cones on the centre line can help guide accuracy, as it can be tempting for rider and horse to drift in towards the fence for the dog-leg lines.

EXERCISE 47

Kidney Bean

Aim

This exercise is good for practising controlling the horse's body through curves and turns, backed up by a straight-line exercise that uses tramlines to correct any drift that might be creeping in elsewhere.

Set-Up

Equipment:

- Two oxers and two verticals
- Four cavaletti or similar (alternatively can be poles or half-rounds)
- Two poles or half-round poles for tramlines
- Pole pods if using round poles, or block these in with the arena surface

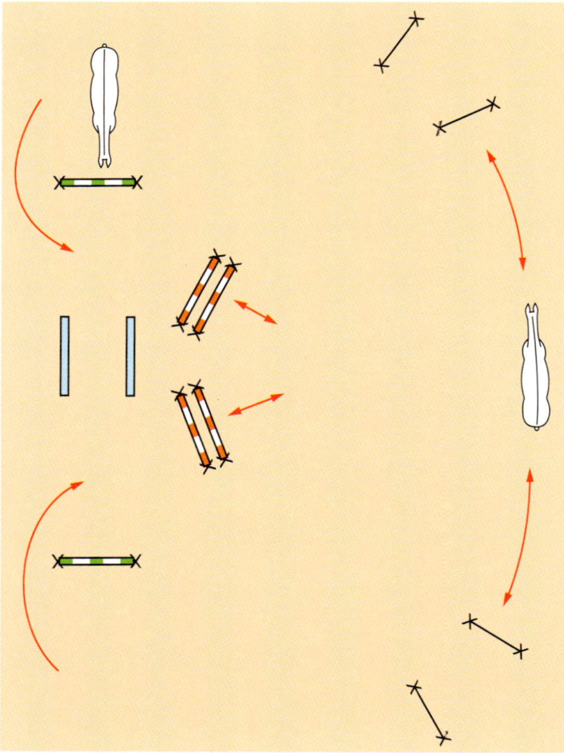

This set-up uses tramlines on a straight line distance to correct any loss of straightness encountered when using the curving line exercises elsewhere.

On one side of the arena, near the edge but allowing enough room to ride round the outside comfortably, build a straight-line related distance on five or six strides – about 24 or 28yd (21.95 or 25.6m) respectively.

In the middle of the related distance, place two tramlines about 2yd (1.8m) apart. These need enough space between them to ride comfortably through, so they can be wider at first and made narrower later if needed.

Next, place two oxers on a diagonal line that allows you to approach from round the vertical and through the gap between the tramline and the vertical, as shown in the diagram. If you want to be able to jump the oxers in both directions be sure to have safety cups on both sides, and appropriate ground lines.

Making sure that you are not impinging on the lines to or from the oxers, on the other long side of the arena place two cavaletti on a 7yd (6.4m) distance in each corner, but away from the track so you can ride round the outside of them. If you want to ride the distance between the cavaletti, then ensure that the curving distance will work on an even stride pattern – therefore the cavaletti could be 30yd (27.4m) apart for example, which would be about seven strides, depending on how wide the curve is then ridden.

How to Ride It

- This exercise could be started by using the two cavaletti on a 7yd (6.4m) distance on a curve to establish a quality canter, and work on accuracy riding the correct line through the middle of the curve. This can then be progressed to relate one set of cavaletti to the other, maintaining the same number of strides between the two sets of cavaletti in each direction, each time.
- When riding the straight-line related distance of verticals through the tramlines, keep the fences smaller to start with while the horse becomes accustomed to riding through the tramlines, and then build them up. This exercise can be jumped in both directions provided it has a groundline on each side.

- A good way to introduce the oxers is to ride to one pair of cavaletti on the curve, then ride round the outside of the vertical to approach the oxer. This will help establish the quality of the canter round the turn before riding to the jump. Depending how much space is available, the challenge can be increased on landing from the oxer by riding to the other set of cavaletti afterwards instead of riding round them.
- Again, dependent on space, it may also be possible to ride from the cavaletti to the straight-line distance and so begin to link all the segments together.

COACHES' TIPS ON KEEPING AN ACCURATE LINE

This exercise is quite good for working on accuracy of lines when approaching and riding away from a fence or grid as there are other fences or poles to help guide the less experienced rider on to the correct line, if the exercise is set up well. For very inexperienced riders, the whole exercise can be set up as trot and canter poles and worked over in the same way as is described for the exercise when jumping.

01282 834970
EQUESTRIAN
SURFACES LTD

SMALL ARENA EXERCISES

One of the biggest challenges that can be faced as a coach and as a rider is creating varied and interesting training exercises in small arenas, by which I mean arenas that are variations on 40 x 20m or smaller. These require careful placement of fences to provide enough room to ride safely to and from a jump, which, as a rule of thumb, should be 15yd (13.7m) from the edge of the arena, if at all possible.

In this chapter I have outlined some exercises that can be relied on to work well in smaller spaces, and have included some of the more complex pole and showjump combinations that I have used in clinic settings in small arenas.

Key to creating a successful set-up is to lay out the poles first and walk the lines to check that they all work! Once you know that nothing will lead to you crashing into something, and that the fences are a safe distance from the edges of the arena, you can build your showjumps and complete the set-up – although I always follow that up with a final check before starting the training session.

EXERCISE 48

Straightness and Turning Exercise

Aim

There are plenty of options with this exercise:

- Assess and work to improve straightness using the central vertical.

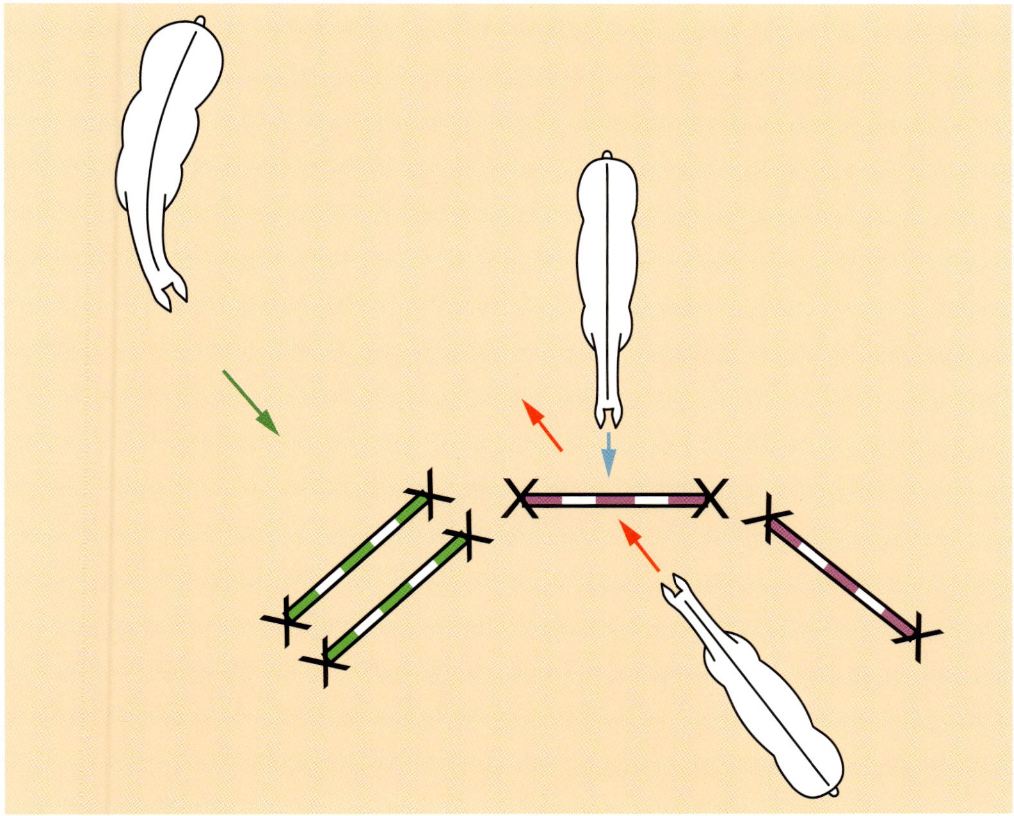

Some options for this set-up include working on straightness (blue arrow), working through rollback turns (green arrow), and jumping fences on an angle for jump-off practice (red arrow).

- Work on maintaining energy and rhythm through the turn by riding between the two angled fences.
- Work to improve energy and straightness out of a rollback turn, including looping between the two angled fences.
- Practise jumping on an angle using the central fence.
- Link the three fences together as a course.

Set-Up

Equipment:

- Three jumps will be needed. These can be oxers or verticals – for oxers use safety cups on both sides if they are to be jumped both ways (if there are limited safety cups try to have at least one on each pole). If wings are limited but these are multi-sided wings, then they can be useful for this exercise as verticals.

Set up the exercise as in the diagram: place the central jump in the middle of the arena; the two angled fences can be touching the central fence wings. Try to ensure that the line of approach is easy to achieve. Ideally there should be 15yd (13.7m) before and after the fences to give enough room to approach and ride away.

How to Ride It

- To work on straightness, use the central fence and try to find a focal point beyond it to line up with – be particularly aware of any drift just before the fence, and whether you are able to ride straight afterwards.
- To work on rollbacks, ride round the top turn to the first angled fence and then ensure that the horse stays straight on landing. Focus on maintaining the energy, rhythm and length of stride through the turn, and then, as you complete the rollback, focus on getting the horse straight in the middle of the other angled fence. Make sure you ride away accurately after the jump, using as much available space as possible.
- To jump on an angle (*see* Exercise 73 in Chapter 8), use the more enclosed approach to the central jump (which also gives you the angled fences to help with straightness), and gradually increase the degree of angle at which you approach. Focus on a point to ride to afterwards, and make sure you plan where you will be going (usually this would be a change of rein) by looking towards and giving the aids for the new direction of travel.
- If these three fences are built so they can be jumped safely in either direction, it is possible to keep riding between them and jumping any number of times to get nearer to replicating riding a course.

EXERCISE 49

Zigzag

Aim

This exercise helps you to work on riding round a turn and getting straight to a fence. As all the fences can be linked together, it is also a good exercise for practising maintaining rhythm riding over a number of fences, and can be used to practise tighter turns to fences for jump-offs.

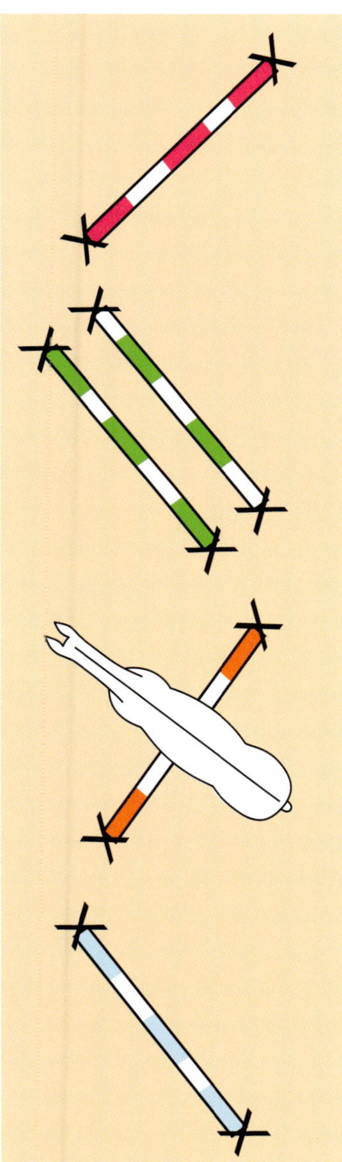

This very simple set-up fits most arena sizes in some form, and allows for changes of rein and riding linked fences together as a small course.

Set-Up

Equipment:

- Any number of jumps from two upwards will be needed – for smaller arenas four is usually optimal. They can be oxers or verticals – for oxers use safety cups on both sides (ideally on all poles, but on at least one side of every pole on the wings).

Set up the exercise on the centre line of the arena, as in the diagram. Make sure there is still room to turn and approach the fences safely at each end of the zigzag.

How to Ride It

- Each fence will be approached out of a curve, so focus on maintaining rhythm through the turn (as horses tend to decelerate when turning), then riding straight to the fence before riding a smooth, balanced line afterwards.
- Start with the central fences and then ride the lines to the outer fences individually before starting to link them together.
- For jump-off practice, tighten up the curving lines so you have a shorter approach to each fence, and try jumping some on the angle.

COACHES' TIP FOR TRAINING WITH ADDITIONAL PRESSURE

This exercise can be useful for training riders to cope with additional pressure (which is obviously something they will experience in the ring). Instead of the rider knowing the course, try calling out the next fence for them to jump at a timing to suit the challenge you want to present – for example on landing from the previous fence, or when you see that the canter has improved so that they are ready to approach another fence. (It helps if the fences are different colours!). Giving the rider less notice to prepare for a fence increases the requirement to react quickly and organise themselves, so although the pressure is not the same as that in the competition arena, it is pressure nonetheless.

EXERCISE 50

The Circumflex

Aim

This exercise is a very simple way of addressing both straightness and suppleness as the fences to each side need to be approached straight and ridden away from straight so the rider can then complete a turn and work suppleness to the fence on the diagonal.

Set-Up

Equipment:

- Four jumps will be needed. These can be oxers as well as verticals, but if oxers you should use safety cups on all poles on both sides if you want to jump them in both directions. For a more advanced exercise, and if there is space, a second element can be added to the fences on the angle to create a double.

Set up these fences across the central area of the arena to suit the arena dimensions. The angle of the middle fences needs to be adapted so the approach and rideaway are comfortable within the confines of the arena space – a wider arena will allow an easier approach from a wider turn at the top. If the arena is wide enough, the warm-up will be easier if you can allow a little space on the outside of the jumps so that you can work round the outside track without a jump in the way.

How to Ride It

- Focus on riding to the fences on the outside edges first, making the horse as straight as possible both before the fence and afterwards.

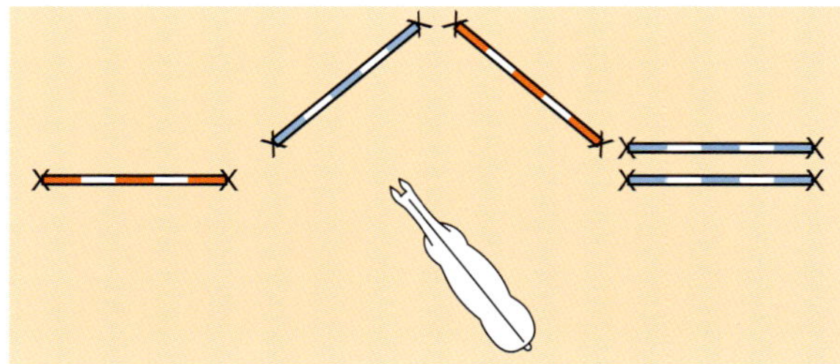

Another easy exercise to create that works straight line approaches and fences out of a turn allowing a change of rein. If you can create enough space either side to ride past the fences, it will give you more scope to keep riding between the different jumps.

- If there is space, or if someone can take down the poles for the other straight fence for you, start by working over just one jump in both directions before progressing to riding a rectangle shape to include both straight fences.
- Be aware of whether the horse's head is in the middle of their shoulders, and the shoulders and hindquarters on the same line. See if you can maintain the same speed and rhythm both on the straight line and round the turns at the end of the arena.
- Next ride the two fences on the diagonal, riding a curve at each end of the arena to approach the next fence.
- If the horse is less experienced and lands on the incorrect lead, keep him supple and continue through the first turn, then correct the lead through trot if necessary before completing the second half of the turn. For more experienced horses, or those learning flying changes, this part of the exercise is a good opportunity to practise these.
- Apply the outside leg on the approach to the fence to indicate to the horse that you will need him to be supple in the other direction on landing, which can help create the change. If there is space to go a little wider and leg yield back into the centre of the fence this can also help to set up the change of leg. Be careful not to throw your upper body to one side to try to get the change of leg, as this can cause the horse to become unbalanced; try to keep the aids to your leg, and look and plan ahead, putting just a little more weight into the seatbone and stirrup on the side you are turning to.
- Complete the exercise by riding from a straight-line fence to a fence on the diagonal, and then to either another diagonal fence or straight-line fence – and continue as much as is required. Keep the speed, rhythm and lines as smooth and consistent as possible.
- If you want to add a double, you must check that there is enough room to ride two to three straight strides before and after the fence. The distance between the two fences should be 24ft to 25ft (7.3 to 7.6m) for horses for a one-stride double, and from 19ft (5.8m) for 12.2hh ponies to 23ft (7m) for 14.2hh ponies, although the distances can be adjusted to a little shorter for smaller fences or short approaches.

EXERCISE 51

Serpentine

Aim

This is a great exercise for working on suppleness and rhythm through the turns and straightness to the fence. The central fence can help you work on changes of direction and accuracy of lines.

Set-Up

Equipment:

- Start with three fences, but more can be added if the arena is long enough. These can be verticals or oxers – for oxers use safety cups on both sides (ideally on all poles but on at least one side of every pole on the wings).

If the arena is rectangular, build the three fences on the centre line facing the long sides of the arena.

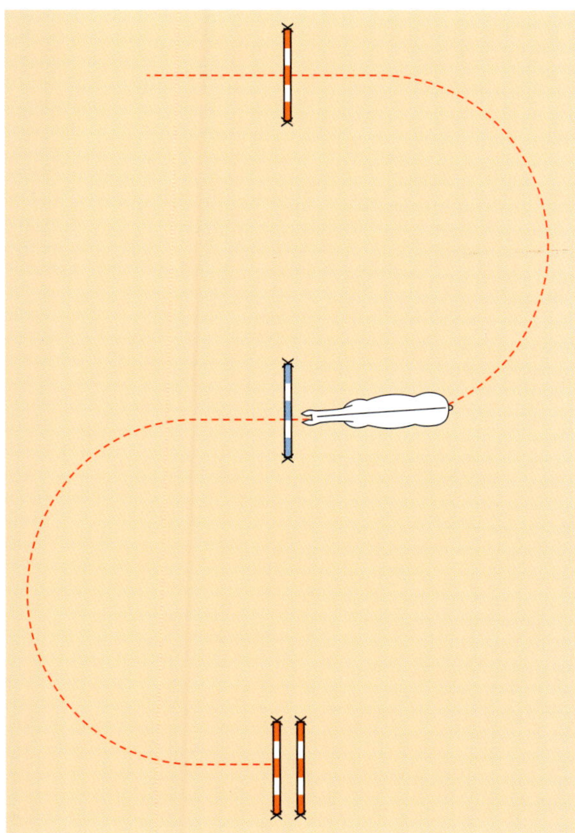

This fence location can be ridden around the outside track between the fences at either end of the arena, or include the central fence to practice changes of direction.

If the arena is very narrow then it would still be beneficial to set up the exercise with just trot poles or single canter poles in place of fences to achieve the aims of the exercise.

How to Ride It

- Start by riding a single fence at one end of the arena. Focus on riding a good turn and getting straight on the approach, and keep looking and planning ahead so that you ride a good line after the fence as well.
- Progress the exercise by adding in the second fence at the other end of the arena.
- Focus on keeping the same rhythm throughout. As both fences are central, if the arena is an even shape you should be on the same distance down each side of the arena to the fence, so a good add-on to this exercise is to count how many strides you get between the two fences on each side and see if it can stay the same when you repeat it, and whether it is the same on both sides of the arena and on both reins!
- To complete the exercise, add in the central fence, so that you are changing direction each time you jump it and progressing to a fence at the end of the arena.
- Be aware of riding straight at the central fence and getting as straight an approach and rideaway as possible. By applying your outside aids on the ride in towards the centre fence, you can help to prepare your horse for the change of direction. Make sure you are very clear in looking where you are going next at this central fence so that there is no misunderstanding!

COACHES' TIPS ON HOW TO RIDE THE CORRECT LINE

Often riders will try to jump the central fence on an angle to make the next turn, or will cut across immediately after the fence, rather than riding the curve. Using cones or similar safe markers to encourage them to ride the correct line can be very helpful, but be careful to leave sufficient room for them to turn, and ensure they have somewhere to focus on as they approach the turn so they don't just ride straight at the wall!

EXERCISE 52

Mercedes

Aim

This exercise can be used to address straightness with the single fence, and to work through curves and rollbacks to the other two elements; it also gives the option to practise tighter turns between elements for jump-off practice if needed.

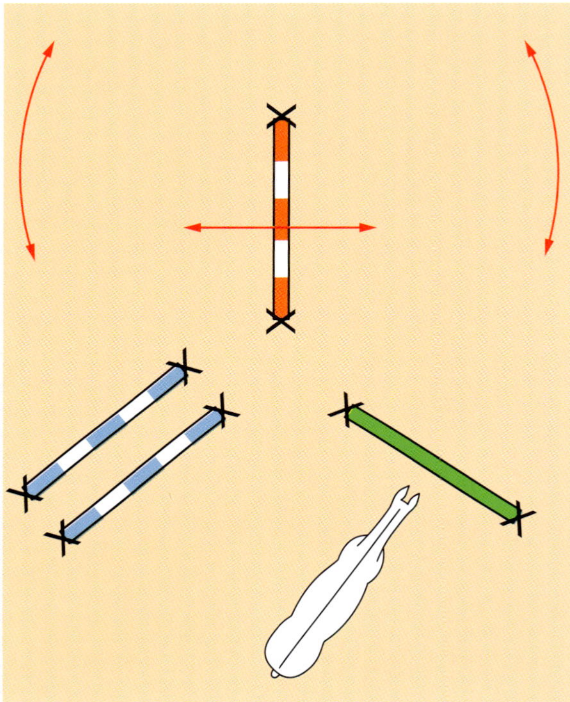

This exercise is a very easy arrangement, including with limited wings (multi-directional wings can be used if needed), and it will fit most small arenas.

Set-Up

Equipment:

- Three jumps will be needed, which can share wings if you are using block-type wings with several sides.

This exercise is incredibly flexible and will suit most arena sizes. It can be set up in the middle of the arena, or with the straight fence nearer the three-quarter line if more space to approach the other fences is needed. The fences can all be touching each other, or there can be a gap between, depending how much space you have.

How to Ride It

- This exercise can be worked through in any sequence, depending on what you and your horse would find easiest first.
- The straight-line approach needs you to focus on keeping the horse's body straight, and to be aware that if he is inexperienced the other two fences might encourage him to drift to the outside away from them.
- The angled fences can be approached along a standard curving line, or you can make the turn tighter and ride a rollback , always ensuring that you are straight at the fence and not facing the other one on landing!

EXERCISE 53

Related Distances

Aim

Working on riding related distances well in a small arena can be difficult as it's challenging to come to a fence off a tight turn on a good enough canter, especially for bigger fences. This exercise allows you to still work down a distance, but it is easier to establish a good canter to a pole out of a tight turn than doing the same to a fence, and it allows you to focus on riding the distance well instead.

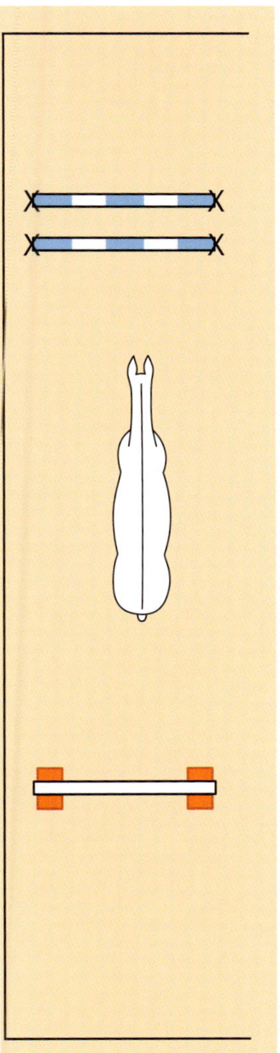

Using a pole as the first element of a related distance is a useful way of practising these when space is limited.

It is also a useful exercise to train the rider's eye to judge distance, and to become aware of the likely take-off spot.

Set-Up

Equipment:

- One fence with two sets of wings built so that it can be a vertical first, and then an oxer later
- One additional ground pole (use pole pods if using a round pole to prevent it moving)
- If you want to be able to reverse the exercise to ride it on the other rein, put wings at the ground pole as well, and then switch over the poles to change direction

Set up the fence on the long side of your arena, ideally leaving enough room to ride past the fence during your warm-up and cool-down.

For a 40m long arena, a three-stride distance is the most manageable, to give enough room to ride away safely afterwards, given that there should be at least 15yd (13.7m) on landing before the end of the arena.

The distance between the pole on the ground and the fence needs to be 1yd (0.9m) less than it would be if it were two fences. So for example, a three-stride horse distance would normally be 16yd (14.6m), so the pole-to-fence distance becomes 15yd (13.7m).

How to Ride It

- Focus on riding a strong, quality canter round the corner to the pole, but keeping your eyes ahead and lining up for the fence beyond as you would do for any straight-line related distance.
- Start with a smaller fence and focus on keeping the canter strides even down the distance if the horse is inclined to rush, or maintain power if the horse is behind the leg.
- It can help to count the strides out loud, or have someone do that for you – but be careful not to include the stride over the pole!
- Once you can be consistent, increase the size of the fence, or vary it by adding a back bar to create an oxer.
- Ideally work this exercise on both reins as the stride length can be different if the horse is less balanced or supple in one direction.

EXERCISE 54

The Diamond

Aim

This exercise focuses on straightness and maintaining rhythm. It allows for short or long approaches to the fences, depending on what you would like to focus on.

Set-Up

Equipment:

- Four fences will be needed. These can be oxers or verticals, but ensure that safety cups are on all poles if you intend to jump the oxers in both directions.

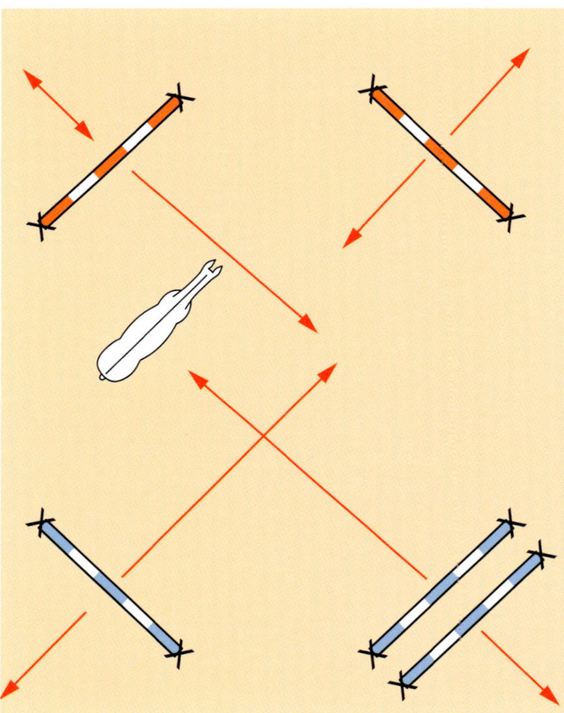

By moving the fences slightly out of alignment to make the diamond effect, four fences can be fitted into a relatively small area to create a mini course to jump.

Set up the fences in the centre of the arena, as in the diagram. The fences can be moved to be short related distances if there is space, but as a starting point keep at least two as individual fences.

How to Ride It

- For your warm-up, ride up the centre line between the fences, focusing on keeping your horse straight through his neck and body. You can do the same through the middle of the exercise riding across the midpoint of the arena.
- Once you start jumping you can choose whether you want to approach from the longer direction, or use a shorter approach.
- The challenge of the short approach is to get straight quickly, whereas on the longer approach it is easy to become flat or increase pace towards the fence.
- If the fences are built to be ridden in any direction, they can form a wide variety of 'courses' to link together.

TIPS ON HOW TO RIDE LONGER APPROACHES

If you find it challenging to ride longer approaches, try counting out loud in time with your horse's stride – not to find the take-off spot, but just to focus on the tempo your horse is on, and to notice whether it changes – it can help *you* not to rush, and to breathe too! Counting to four strides and starting again, as in 1-2-3-4, 1-2-3-4, works quite well for this purpose. However, be careful you don't end up counting your own rhythm and not the horse's....

EXERCISE 55

Canter Curve

Aim

This exercise helps to improve engagement and maintain stride length in the canter through the turn and to establish rhythm and a consistent stride length to continue to a fence.

Set-Up

Equipment:

- Two showjumps, which can be oxers or verticals
- Three canter poles or cavaletti – if using round poles use pods, or block them in to prevent them rolling. You can add more of these if you have them and if there is space to do so

Position the canter poles on a gentle curve at the end of the arena, leaving space round the outside to warm up. The poles need to be 7yd (6.4m) apart for horses, and 6 to 6.5yd (5.5 to 5.9m) for ponies, measuring the distance on the middle of the curve.

From the last canter pole set out a continuation of the line on each side to a fence, which then allows a change of rein. The distance from the last canter pole to the middle of the fence on the curve needs to be about 1yd (0.9m) less than the distance would be between two fences. Aim for a minimum of three strides between the canter poles and the fence, which would be about 15yd (13.7m).

The fences can also be built in a straight line after leaving the canter pole curve, which is easier to ride to, as the outside of the arena can help with the line to the fence; however, it is a little more committed in terms of the distance, as the shape of the curved approach can be altered to accommodate more or fewer strides if needed. You may also find that a straight approach to a fence gives you less space on landing than is desirable, depending on the size and shape of the arena.

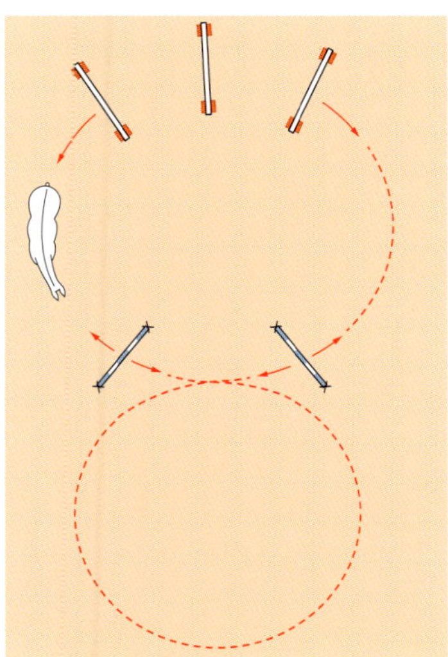

This exercise uses canter poles on the curve to ensure the quality of the canter is maintained through the turn, which will help with the ride to the fence afterwards. Depending on space, you can then loop back to the second fence or ride back to the poles on the other rein.

How to Ride It

- Start by working the canter over the curved line of poles. Focus on riding the curve in the middle of each pole, and on keeping the same canter quality round the arena as you achieve over the poles.
- Once you have established a consistent ride over the poles on both reins, ride the poles on one rein and add in the curve to the fence, making sure that you are looking and planning ahead, and using your outside leg to help bring the horse's body round the turn.
- Focus on riding an accurate and balanced line away from the fence to change the rein.
- Once that direction has been practised a few times, try changing the rein and repeating the exercise but to the other fence.
- To complete the exercise, ride the curved poles to the fence one way, change the rein over the fence, and return immediately to the poles on the other rein and to the other fence. The challenge here is to keep the same pace over the poles the second time as the horse is likely to have increased either stride, speed or both after jumping a fence.

COACHES' TIP ON BUILDING THE CURVED LINE

For group lessons with varying heights of horse and pony, building the curve so that the inside line suits a pony and the middle to outside line suits a horse will allow you to work the initial exercise over poles, at least, for all without changing the distance – although it will demand accuracy from the riders!

EXERCISE 56

Straightness and Suppleness

Aim

This set-up can be used in relatively small spaces and addresses straightness through the use of pivot turns (*see* Exercise 63) and tramlines, as well as suppleness using fences that can be ridden off a gentle curved approach or via a tighter rollback line.

Set-Up

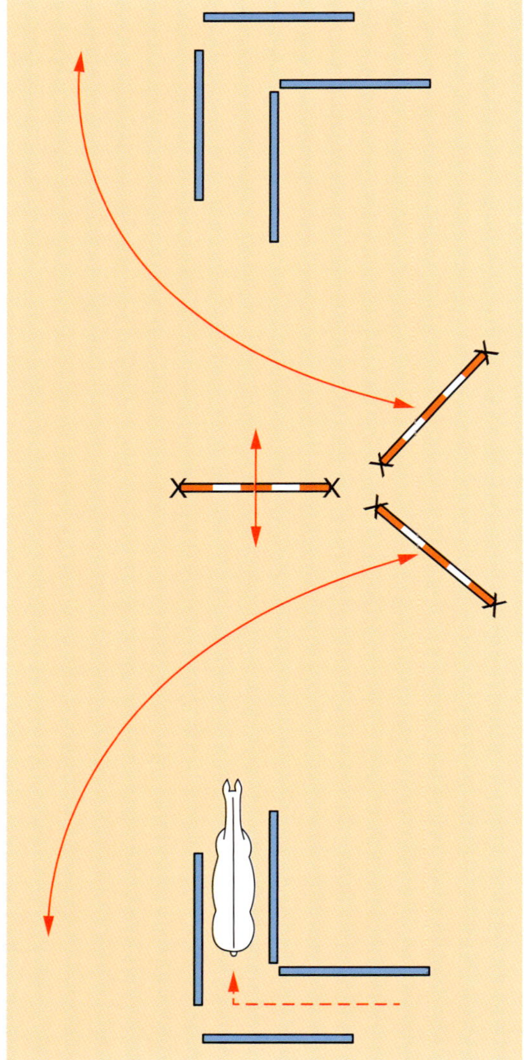

Tramlines create corners to practice pivot turns and straightness to a fence, whilst there is the option to ride around the outside of the tramlines to the other two fences.

Equipment:

- Three fences (these can be oxers or verticals, provided they are built to jump either way, with safety cups all round on the oxers)
- Eight poles or half-rounds for tramlines plus pole pods (x 16) to secure them if using round poles (or block the poles in with arena surface if not).

Set out the pivot turn exercise first using poles or half-rounds to make square corners (corner to corner should measure a minimum of 4yd (3.7m) so you can canter through the turn). Ensure there is room to canter round the outside of these tram lines to the other two fences (*see* diagram). For the fence that is approached through the tramlines, try to ensure that ideally there are at least three strides (15yd/13.7m) before and after it.

How to Ride It

- Start by riding round the outside of the tramlines to the fences across the diagonal of the arena. Focus on maintaining engagement and rhythm through the turn and getting straight to the fence. Try to make the rideaway from the fence through the next turn as balanced and supple as the approach.
- Next ride the pivot-turn exercise. Start with a pole between the wings on pole pods or a small vertical, and build from there. If you haven't practised pivot turns before, start with a pole and ride the pivots in walk before increasing the speed.
- Ride through the pivot by keeping the horse's neck straight using your outside rein, put your weight into the inside seatbone, and open (but don't pull!) the inside rein at the same time as using your outside leg near the girth to push the horse round the turn.
- Once you are jumping a fence on this line and riding successful pivots through the tramlines before and after, you can progress the exercise by, for example, riding from one of the fences on the diagonal of the arena to the tramlines for the straightness exercise, then ride out of the second set of tramlines and roll back to the other fence on the diagonal. This last fence will require more accuracy on landing to work round the outside of the tramlines and negotiate the corner successfully.

EXERCISE 57

Multiple Exercises 1

Aim

This more complex set-up combines polework and fences, which is great for clinics, including group sessions in small arenas, as it can help to meet the training requirements for a broader range of horse and rider combinations. The initial exercises here focus on straightness, and there are jumping exercises working curving lines plus obedience to the outside aids, which also helps horses that tend to rush fences and get flat.

Set-Up

Equipment:

- Six showjumps – the fences on the curving approaches can be oxers, but use verticals for the leg-yield exercise.
- Eight poles for trot and canter work – ideally half-round poles or similar. If using round poles ideally you will need sixteen pole pods to secure them, or block in the poles with some arena surface so they can't roll.

Set up the exercise as in the diagram, keeping all the fences, where possible, a minimum of 15yd (13.7m) from the wall or fence. This set-up has been used in an arena smaller than 20 × 40m, but lay out the poles first and get the angles to work well before building it fully.

The trot poles should be set 3ft 6in (0.9m) apart for a small pony, and 4ft 6in (1.22m) for a horse. The canter poles should be 7yd (6.4m) apart for horses, and 6 to 6.5yd (5.5 to 5.9m) for ponies.

The two verticals on the straight line can be built on a two-stride distance (or a bit longer if space allows, for example three strides), which would be 35 to 36ft (10.7 to 11m) for horses, and from 29 to 33ft (8.8 to 10m) for ponies, depending on their height.

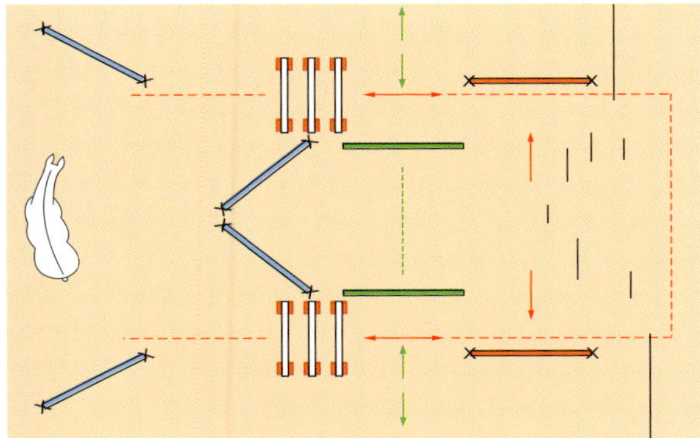

This is a multiple exercise set up for a small arena. The red dotted line denotes the trot-pole exercise, and the green poles and line are a straight-line canter exercise. The blue fences can be ridden individually, or the two on the left can be ridden as a curving line related distance if there is space to do so. The orange fences and black broken line indicate the leg-yield exercise, working outside one fence and leg yielding into the second fence, which can be done on either rein.

How to Ride It

- Start with the trot poles, which can be ridden on the same rein as a rectangle, or as a serpentine if there is enough room at either end. The canter-pole placement helps stop the horse moving in, and the location of the verticals on the long side stops the horse falling out on that side of the arena, so then you can focus on your straightness on the other side.
- To work straightness and length of stride in canter, ride down the two poles that are located inside the verticals on the straight line (green on the diagram), trying to ensure that the canter stride length and energy remains the same through the turn so that you don't need to ride forwards to achieve the distance.
- The two verticals built on a straight-line distance (orange poles) can be used to work on acceptance of the outside aids and engagement of the hind leg without rushing by riding just past the outside wing of fence one and leg yielding in to jump fence two. Keep the fences small while you and your horse become accustomed to the exercise, and try to keep the horse's neck and body straight as you move across.
- The two fences on the other side of the arena can be set up as a curving line related distance, or can be ridden separately from either direction if built to do so.
- The two fences in the middle (blue poles) allow you to ride a change of rein across the diagonal over the fence. By riding round the outside of the other exercises they can help with a correct approach and control of the line before and after the jump.
- All six fences can be linked together in a variety of patterns so you can ride a small course at the end of the session.

EXERCISE 58

Multiple Exercises 2

Aim

This is an arrangement of exercises for a small arena with several different options to work with to increase variety and provide different challenges.

Set-Up

Equipment:

- Four fences, which can be oxers as well as verticals depending on available equipment
- Two small fences, which can be cavaletti, or use larger pole pods or small jump blocks
- Nine poles for trot and canter work, which can be half-rounds or poles; the latter should be blocked in by the arena surface or pole pods

Set up the exercise as in the diagram, keeping all fences, where possible, a minimum of 15yd (13.7m) from the wall or fence. This set-up has been used in an arena smaller than 20 × 40m.

The trot poles should be set 3ft 6in (0.9m) apart for a small pony, and 4ft 6in (1.22m) apart for a horse, and are positioned in straight lines parallel with the long side of the arena. The canter poles should be about 9ft (2.74m) apart at the centre, but this distance can be lengthened to 10ft (3.05m) or shortened to 7ft to 8ft (2.13m to 2.44m) for ponies, depending on how tight the approach is, and the horse you are building for – go for a shorter distance where there is less room, with the inside of the curve narrower and the outside wider (this allows for horses with different stride lengths to be accommodated in a group session).

The two fences on the centre line can be cavaletti or just raised poles, as the approach to these is likely to be tight in a small arena.

The two fences located towards the outside of the arena can be ridden as a curving line related distance, so measure this to ensure it is on a level stride in case you decide to use it.

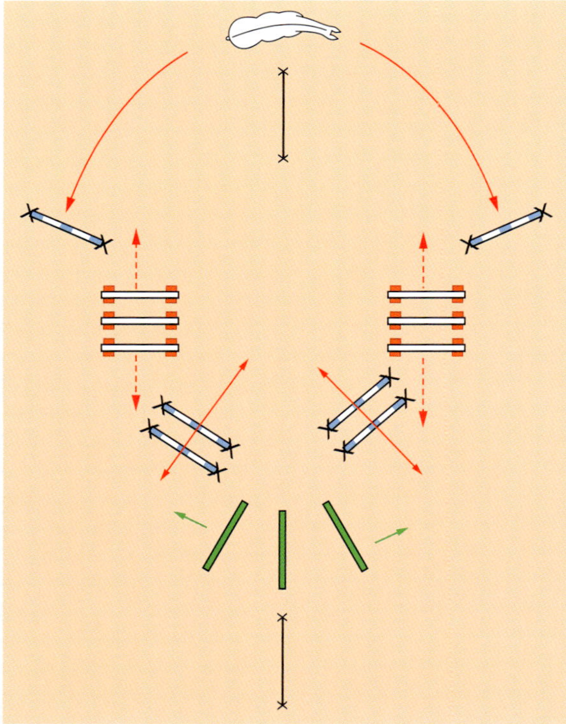

For this multiple exercise the cavaletti are located at each end of the arena and can be ridden as a rectangle in all three paces. The red line denotes the trot-pole exercise, and the green poles and arrows denote the canter bounce curve. The blue and white poles are jumps that can be built to jump in either direction.

How to Ride It

- Start with the trot poles, focusing on straightness and accurate turns. Depending on the width of the arena you may be able to ride from one set to the next, or you may need to switch between the two sets if the turn is too tight.
- The small step-overs or cavaletti can also be set up initially as trot poles, as single poles or with more poles added to create a set of three at each end.
- The canter poles on the curve (green on diagram) are set on a bounce stride to encourage engagement and suppleness in the canter through

the turn. They also test rider accuracy and their ability to keep riding the curve on the middle line and not drift in or out.

- Canter straightness can be worked on using the two cavaletti-height fences as these can be ridden on a rectangle with the focus being on straightness before and afterwards. You can also practise maintaining canter stride length between the two as the distance between them should be equal, and should require the same number of strides between them.
- The top cavaletti can then be linked to the canter poles on the curve to mix up straightness to the cavaletti and suppleness through the curve.
- The two fences towards the outer perimeter of the arena can be ridden on either rein. Try to keep a smooth canter through the turn round the outside of the cavaletti to link the fences.
- The two fences towards the centre of the arena can be ridden across the diagonal and then linked to the other two fences for a small course.

COACHES' TIP: RIDING A RELATED DISTANCE

The two fences on the outer area can be on a related distance on a curving line riding round the outside of the step-over, but the line is flexible enough that the number of strides can vary. Alternatively you can increase the accuracy challenge and, for example, ask the rider to consistently ride the same line on the same number of strides and see if the stride pattern remains the same on repetition and on both reins.

EXERCISE 59

Multiple Exercises 3

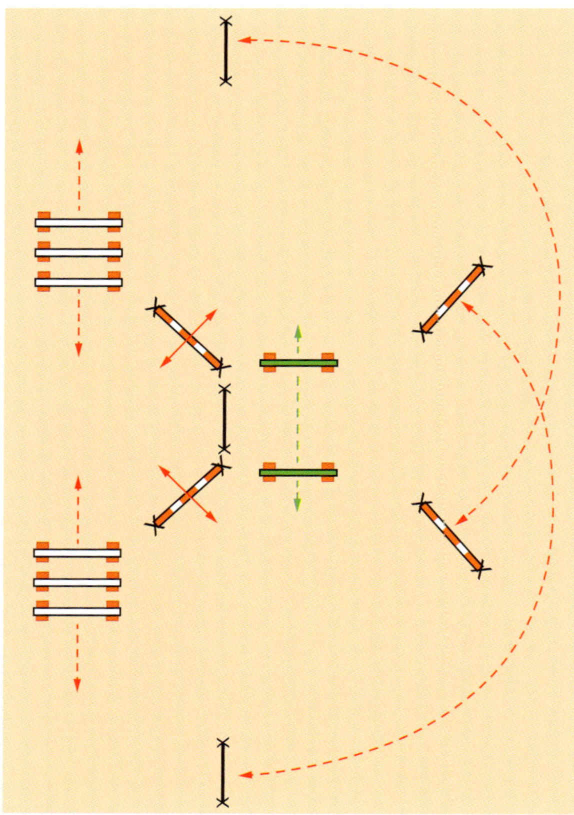

The cavaletti for this exercise are all on the centre line and can be ridden as rectangles or as a figure-of-eight. The red arrows denote the straight-line trot-pole exercise, and the green ones denote the canter-pole exercise. The dotted black line shows how you can include a related-distance curve from the cavaletti to a fence. To make the exercise easier, ride round the outside of the cavaletti instead to jump the fence on its own.

Aim

This is another set-up for a small arena that encompasses trot- and canter-pole options plus various showjump arrangements for a diverse training session.

Set-Up

Equipment:

- Four showjumps, which can be oxers as well as verticals depending on available equipment
- Three small fences, which can be cavaletti, or use larger pole pods or small jump blocks
- Eight poles for trot and canter work, which can be half-rounds or poles; the latter should be blocked in by arena surface or pole pods

Set up the exercise as in the diagram, keeping all fences, where possible, a minimum of 15yd (13.7m) from the wall or fence. With the angled fences, the key is to make the angle work to create enough space and still maintain the flow through the turns.

The trot poles should be set out near the three-quarter line, and be placed 3ft 6in (0.9m) apart for a small pony, and 4ft 6in (1.22m) apart for a horse. Leave the gap between the two sets wide enough to ride through to the central fences. The canter poles should be about 7yd (6.4m) apart, and positioned so that the central cavaletti and other fences are not affected by them.

The three fences on the centre line can be cavaletti or poles raised on small blocks. Leave enough space outside the end ones to ride comfortably round them.

Place the two fences towards the long side of the arena so that you can ride round the end cavaletti to them, and ride away without being impeded by the other fence – the angle is key to this! If you want to add an extra challenge to the set-up, try to place them on a related distance to the cavaletti at the other end of the arena, so that you can ride the cavaletti and then round the turn to the fence, or vice versa. (If you are doing this, then make the distance about 1yd (0.9m) shorter than it would be if it were two jumps.)

The other two jumps should be placed adjacent to the central cavaletti and set on an angle to allow a fluent rideaway afterwards to change the rein round the end of the arena.

How to Ride It

- Begin by using the trot poles as a warm-up exercise to focus on straightness, including through the gap between the poles. You can also work control here by adding a transition in between if there is space.
- You can then move on to the canter poles, or use the cavaletti to work straightness out of the turn and a change of rein over the central cavaletti. This can be done in trot or canter or both.
- Ride round the outside of a cavaletti towards the end of the arena and jump one of the fences that leads out to the edge of the arena, repeating to the other fence on the other rein.
- Then jump the fences near the centre of the arena, taking care to ride a balanced turn afterwards as this line might be quite tight depending on the size of the arena. Keep these fences small if space is limited.
- A further option is then to ride the related distance either from one of the fences angling out to the wall to the cavaletti afterwards, or from cavaletti to fence.

INDOOR SEASON EXERCISES

The indoor season for showjumping in the UK starts in October and concludes in March. There is a noticeable difference between what is required to compete indoors and competing outdoors, and this chapter seeks to provide some exercises to help you prepare for that transition.

One of the most noticeable factors in moving indoors is the inevitable constriction of space. Most show centres have larger outdoor arenas than indoor, and this means that competing indoors you will find that related distances become shorter, there is less time to prepare for each fence, and you are more likely to find that fences come up quickly out of a turn or you are having to ride tighter movements to get between the fences.

EXERCISE 60

Rollback Exercise

Aim

In the indoor showjumping season you are likely to encounter 'rollback' turns frequently, where you have to turn back on yourself to a fence, and these are likely to be on a tighter line than those you might see outdoors. This is more challenging than fences in a straight line as it is much easier to lose the power and quality of the canter through a turn. It also requires the rider to get the horse straight when he comes out of the turn to perform the jump as well as possible.

Set-Up

Equipment:

- Two jumps, which can be oxers or verticals – for oxers use safety cups and a groundline on each side of the fence so that it can be jumped in either direction.

Set up the exercise as in the diagram towards the centre line of the arena, with at least 15yd (13.7m) to the end of the arena from the fence to allow room for the approach/landing.

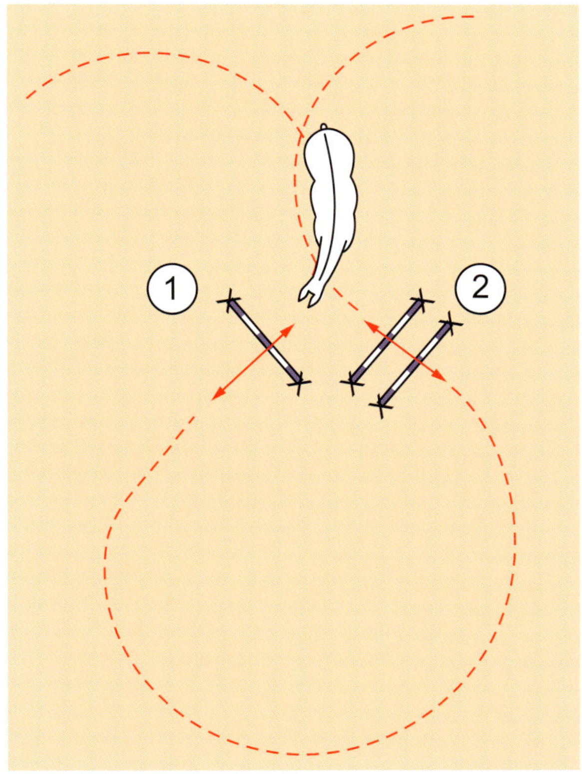

Depending on where the fences are located in the arena, one approach will be smoother and less tight and the other will be more of a rollback out of a tight turn, which may be encountered in competition.

How to Ride It

- Keep the fences small to start with and focus on a good, energetic canter with an even rhythm.
- Begin by warming up over both fences on the more open approach, coming out of the corner and riding the jump so that you land heading towards the middle of the arena before making a change of rein at the top.
- Once this is established, canter down the long side of the arena on the right rein and ride to the end of the arena to then perform a right turn back to the vertical.

- From the top corner of the arena, be looking over your right shoulder for the fence. Use your inside leg to maintain the energy and balance into the turn, supporting the horse to use all the space through the outside rein and using a slightly opening rein to direct him. (If the horse is looking to the outside and falling in, then an indirect inside rein to create poll flexion can help to correct this and allow you to use your inside leg more effectively.) To complete the turn, use your outside leg and outside rein to straighten up the horse for the jump.
- On landing, ride a straight line away.
- Repeat the exercise on the left rein to the second fence.
- You can then link the two fences together as in the diagram, maintaining the same rhythm and energy all the way round and focusing on straightness to each fence out of each turn.

TIPS ON HOW TO GET STRAIGHT

If you are struggling to get straight because you are turning too early to the fence, try looking at the outside wing of the fence you are approaching as you travel through the first part of the turn (for example, look at the left-hand wing of jump one for the right turn), and then move your focus to the middle of the fence as you come out of the turn – this will encourage you to ride a wider line and not to rush to get to the jump by turning early.

EXERCISE 61

Curving Related Distance Exercise

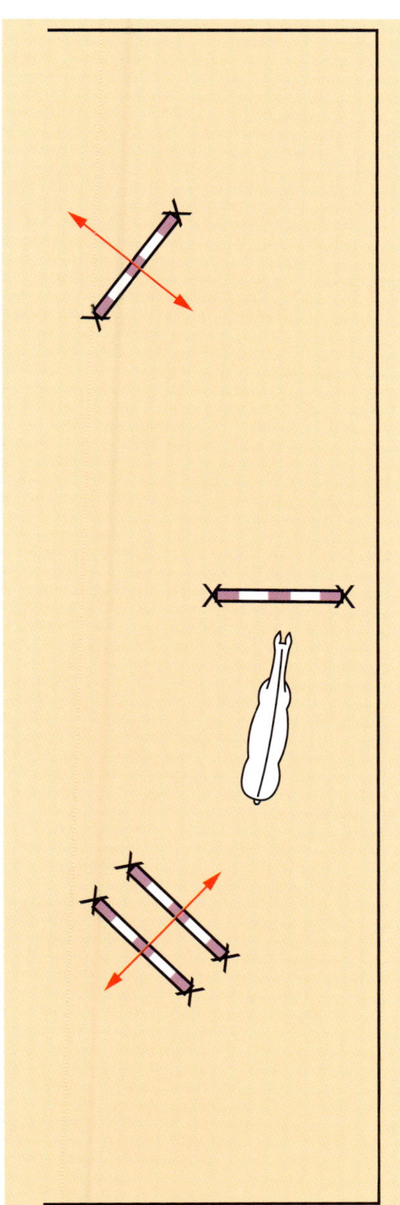

A curving line-related distance with one element against the wall is a common occurrence in indoor competition.

Aim

A regular feature in showjumping tracks is a curving line on a related distance. This has additional factors to consider when indoors. The presence of the wall being near the line you need to ride can have a magnetic effect, pulling the horse out on to a wider line, whereas if there is a lot to look at along the side of the arena it can sometimes have the opposite effect.

Once there are three fences on a curving line like this, accuracy is key, and addressing any drift and reacting quickly to the influences of the fence location is important to complete the distances successfully.

Set-Up

Equipment:

- Two or three jumps. These can be oxers or verticals – for oxers use safety cups on both sides. When beginning the exercise start with verticals, and include oxers once you are riding it confidently.

Set up the exercise as in the diagram – if using three fences put the middle fence near the edge of the arena on the long side. The other two fences should be a minimum of 15yd (13.7m) from the end of the arena to allow room for the approach/landing.

If using two fences, set out a minimum of five strides in between if possible. For horses, that equates to between $23\frac{1}{2}$ and 24yd (21.49 and 21.95m) – choose the slightly shorter distance if the turns before and after the fences are near the wall, as this usually shortens the stride. The apex of the curve should be near the wall for the full effect in training. (For ponies the distance would be from $19\frac{1}{2}$yd (17.83m) for a 12.2hh pony, and a maximum of 22yd (20.12m) for a 14.2hh.)

Only add the third fence once you are successfully riding the two fences on a curve, ideally on a similar distance – for example, both distances on five strides.

How to Ride It

- Start with two verticals and establish an energetic, balanced canter, keeping your eye up to ride the curving line – as you jump the first fence, you should already have your eye on fence two.
- If the horse drifts out, use your outside leg to correct him. If he moves in, correct the line with your inside leg. In both instances, support the horse with the outside rein to control the outside shoulder and help him to balance through the turn. The inside rein is only a guide – too much pressure here and the stride length will be impacted, and you will risk losing control of the outside shoulder.
- Focus on the horse's rhythm and your line.
- When you are successfully completing the exercise on both reins you can add the third fence, and play with the location of oxers – for a novice horse, the oxer as fence three could potentially be the most challenging if he makes mistakes at fences one and/or two, whereas jumping an oxer followed by two verticals is more forgiving but can make the distance feel shorter.

TIPS: VIDEO REVIEW CAN BE USEFUL

Video review can be useful so that you can see where your horse moves in or out on a line, and it can help you make corrections to improve it, whether that is in your body position or your horse's.

Usually the line from the middle fence by the wall to the fence away from the wall is more difficult to ride as your horse may assume he is continuing straight on, whereas riding from a fence to the fence nearer the wall is a more natural line. When riding the line away from the wall, look and plan early for your next fence and use your outside leg to indicate clearly the direction of travel. Some of the flatwork exercises covered in Chapter 1 can be useful here as you will have trained the correct response to the outside aids.

EXERCISE 62

Related Distance Exercise Against a Wall

Aim

When competing indoors there is a greater likelihood of finding some fences placed against the wall of the arena. This tends to cause the inexperienced horse to draw back and lose impulsion, or to move away from the wall towards the inside of the arena, especially if there are banners or spectators there. When a related distance is added into the question this can make for a greater challenge as the horse may not maintain his stride length throughout the distance, or he may move off the central line, making the distance ride longer.

By building two fences against the wall, we can train the horse to be more confident in this scenario; so we start by riding in canter over two poles, and progress to confidently working down a related distance of two fences.

Set-Up

Equipment:

- Two jumps: these can be oxers or verticals; for oxers use safety cups on both sides – when beginning the exercise start with poles on the ground and progress to fences.

The distance between the two fences can be anything from one stride upwards, and this may depend on the length of the arena you are using. Try to have a minimum of 15yd (13.7m) from the wall to the fence in either direction to allow room for the approach and landing. Both fences should be positioned against the wall of the arena *provided it is safe to do so* – for example, be sure there is nothing projecting from the wall of the arena, and that the eaves of the building have enough clearance!

As an example, set up the two fences on a four-stride distance of about 20yd (18.3m) for a horse, or 16½yd (15m) for a 12.2hh pony to 18yd (16.5m) for a 14.2hh pony. If you are starting with poles, bring the poles in 1yd (0.9m) from the fence at each end so that the distance is 2yd (1.8m) shorter overall.

Related distances, whether doubles or longer distances, can be more challenging located against the edge of the arena.

How to Ride It

- When first introducing this exercise, start with two poles on the ground and aim to ride the line at the centre of both poles with a straight line before and after. If the arena is quite small, a pivot turn will help with this (*see* Exercise 63).

- Once you and your horse are confidently riding straight between the poles on the correct number of strides, move one pole out to its set of wings and build it into a jump. Repeat the exercise, but now you are riding from a pole to a fence. Check that you are still able to stay straight before and after both the pole and the fence.
- You can also ride the distance from the jump to the pole to check control on the landing strides.
- When you are confident with this, build the second fence and repeat the exercise. Check that you can have the same straightness and number of strides on both reins, as it is generally easier to attain straightness on one rein than the other.

TIPS ON ACHIEVING STRAIGHTNESS

If you are struggling to achieve straightness, it may help to ride between some poles or similar placed between the two fences as tramlines. These can be quite wide at first (for example the width of the fence poles), then narrowed if necessary – the horse may be surprised by these, so it can be helpful to start using them while cantering over poles, then build the fence afterwards. Similar tramlines can be built before and after the fence if needed. Try to have any guide poles like these at least 3yd (2.7m) from the fence so they are influencing the ride between the fences, and not the take-off and landing.

EXERCISE 63

Square Turns

Aim

Often fences come up quite quickly indoors, and where space is tight it can be hard to get straight after a turn. Square or 'pivot' turns can be very useful for getting the horse straight quickly, and can also be an advantage in a jump-off to help the horse turn quickly. This exercise trains the horse to understand the aids for a pivot turn with the help of poles to guide him.

Set-Up

Equipment:

- Eight poles or half-rounds or square poles
- One jump (not essential!)

Make a corner in your arena as shown in the diagram, with 4yd (3.7m) from corner to corner between the poles. If you have space you can do the same at the other end of the long side and build a fence between the two corners – make sure there are at least 15yd (13.7m) from the corner to the fence at each end.

How to Ride It

- Start in walk, riding between just the poles that form the corner (or corners if you have built more than one).
- To perform the pivot turn, first think about keeping the horse straight through his neck by holding the outside rein. If he looks a little to the outside that is not a problem for this exercise.
- Look where you want to go and start to apply your outside leg just before the turning point, but keep the horse straight with the outside rein until you are ready to turn.
- At the point where you want to turn, open the inside rein away from the neck (but do *not* pull it!) and push the horse round from your outside leg.
- The horse should load his inside hind leg and pivot round it, resulting in a relatively square, tight turn (I sometimes describe it as a 'cheating' pirouette, as we take the correct bend away to remove the need for collection).

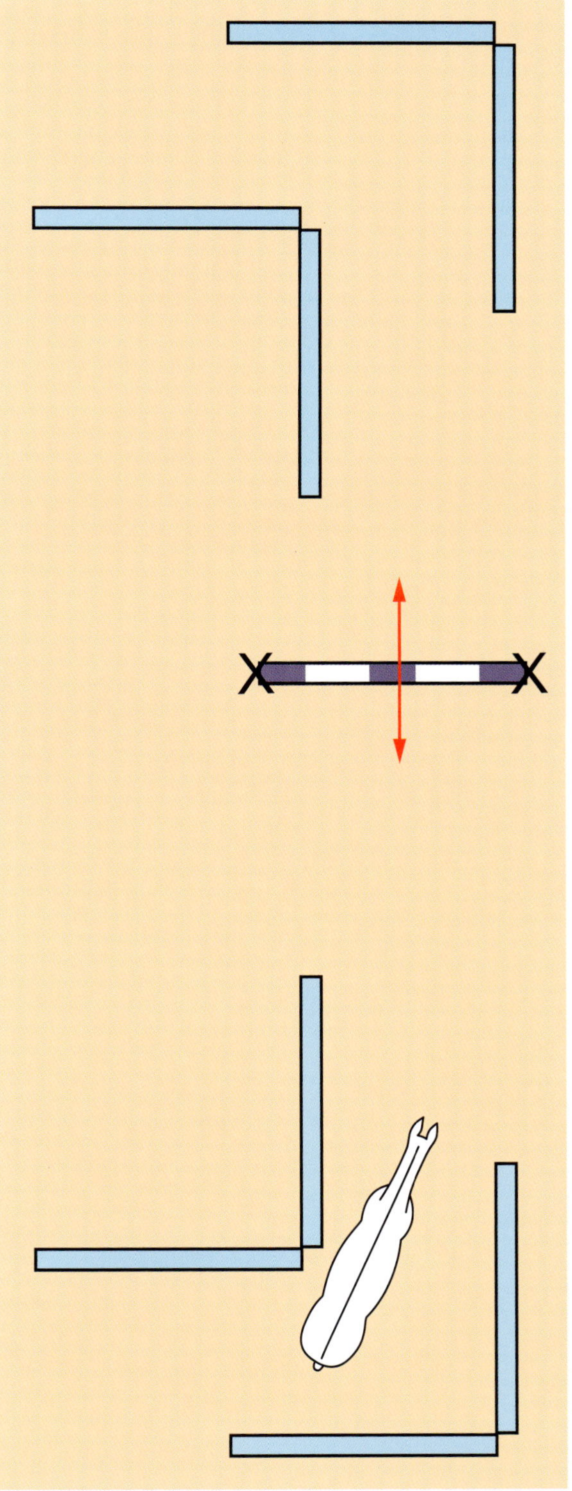

Pivot turns are very useful to create straightness quickly out of a tight turn. These tramlines help create the effect in training.

- Once you are both confident riding it in walk, progress to trot and then canter.
- To progress the exercise, a small jump can be added after the corner, and a corner after the fence tests control and rideability.
- Once you have mastered the pivot technique, try removing the tramlines and riding it without.
- If you have a course to practise over, find places where you can ride a pivot – for example, where the fence is at 90 degrees to the end of the arena, as a right-angled turn lends itself to a pivot; or you can use it to slow down a speedy horse at any fence! These turns are also useful where you need to get straight quickly out of a short approach, particularly with a related distance or double afterwards.

TIPS ON MAKING PIVOT TURNS MORE EFFECTIVE

Think of your outside leg like an indicator: using it on and off is more effective than just closing it on the horse's side, and can indicate movement in time with a specific leg when you get more practised at it. By using it near the girth you are asking the outside foreleg to move across, hence creating the pivot effect round the inside hind leg.

Coaches' tip: Pivot turns can be very useful for horses that are a little narrow behind, as it encourages them to stabilise with the inside hind, widening the hind feet and creating better power out of the turn as a result.

EXERCISE 64

'Which Fence' Exercise

Aim

In smaller indoor competition arenas particularly – although it can be a factor in any – there can be more than one option in front of you in terms of fences as you come out of a turn. In this situation it is obviously important to be clear to the horse which fence you intend to jump, and this exercise is good for practising the skills required, including giving the correct aids and looking and planning ahead.

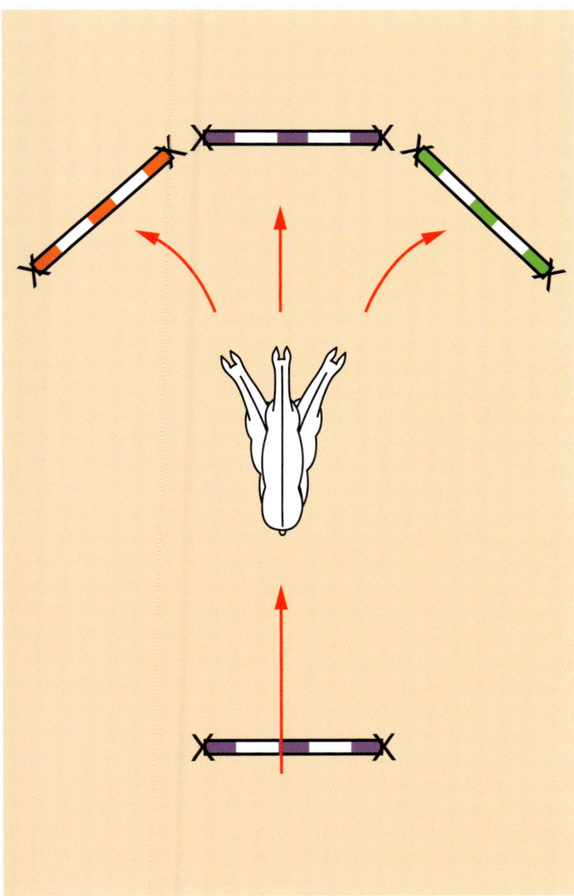

With this set-up you can practise giving clear signals to your horse as to which jump you want to approach each time, whilst also being careful not to allow him to fall in or out on the intended line.

Set-Up

Equipment:

- Four jumps – three of the fences can be oxers or verticals, although when introducing the exercise it would generally be better to start with verticals. The initial jump can be a pole to start with (*see* below for distances).

Set up the exercise as in the diagram – usually it is best built centrally in the arena so there is room to ride away on either side.

First build the two fences on the centre line. Ideally the distance between them would be five strides, or a little more if space allows. A five-stride distance would be $23\frac{1}{2}$ to 24yd (21.3 to 21.9m): build on the shorter distance initially, as it can always be increased for bigger fences or if including an oxer as the first element later. If you decide to use a pole first on the approach but will use a fence afterwards, leave the wings in the correct place for a jump and move the pole 1yd (0.9m) closer to the second element. Make sure the pole is secured on blocks or similar so that it doesn't roll if knocked.

The other two fences should be positioned on either side of the central fence (as shown in the diagram), and should be angled to create a curving line from the central initial fence to each. The easiest way to build these so as to keep all the fences adjacent to each other is to build on the same distance – for example five strides: walk the distance from the middle of the poles on the curving line you want to ride.

How to Ride It

- Once you have warmed up, a good initial exercise is to ride a pole to the fences first. Ride the straight-line distance first, focusing on a good approach and looking ahead, planning the straight line to the fence and keeping straight on landing before planning and riding the turn. Make sure you are riding the correct number of strides between pole and fence.

- Next ride one of the curving lines. First approach the pole straight, and as you are going over it, look to the fence you want to jump. Think of steering to it with your legs – as you rode straight the previous time you are more likely to need more outside leg, but some horses are quick learners and you may soon find that your curve is more of a diagonal line. In this case start with the inside leg to hold the line straighter on landing before turning using the outside aids.
- Once you are happy that you can ride each line, replace the pole with another fence and repeat the exercise.
- To increase the challenge you can ride the exercise in reverse, so jump one of the outside fences and ride the curve to the straight-line fence afterwards. This demands more accuracy to achieve a good line to the first fence and to maintain a good canter on the curved approach.
- You can make a small course from the exercise by riding some of the fences without the related distance in order to change the rein.

TIPS ON RIDING A CURVING LINE

Think of using an opening rein to indicate the direction you want to go, rather than a direct (pulling) rein, as an opening rein encourages the horse to step into the space, whereas a direct rein can cause him to overbend the neck and fall on to the outside shoulder.

Coaches' tip: Cones can be a useful addition to this exercise to ensure that the curved line doesn't become a diagonal line, which would make the distance shorter.

EXERCISE 65

Short Approach or Departure

Aim

The limitations of indoor space can mean that you have very few strides away from the edge of the arena to the fence, and very few strides afterwards. For less experienced horses (or riders) it can be a challenge to get the horse focused on the fence when there is a short approach, and if there is not much room on landing the horse can back off on the approach if they are uncertain of how much room there is afterwards, or if there are banners or other distractions round the edges. Practising this scenario at home and at arena hires, for example, can help to prepare the horse for this. It can also help more experienced horses after they have been jumping outdoors all summer to pay attention coming out of turns as they can be taken a little by surprise when they return indoors and the fences come up more quickly!

Set-Up

Equipment:

- A minimum of two jumps: these can be oxers or verticals – for oxers use safety cups on both sides.

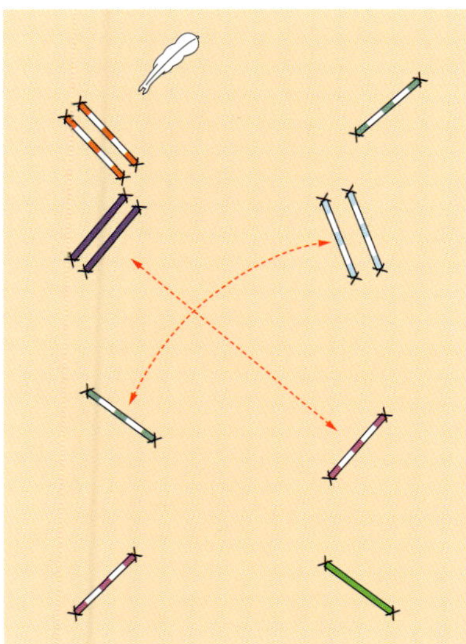

This is a suggested set-up to help practice riding to fences with a shorter approach or with limited room on landing, as will be encountered in indoor competition, so helping the transition between outdoor and indoor competition.

Set up the exercise as in the diagram, or use another set-up to suit, ensuring that the fences are a minimum of 15yd (13.7m) from the edge of the arena, but keeping the approach and landing relatively close to the edge for the purposes of the exercise.

How to Ride It

- This exercise can be ridden in any pattern, and can be jumped in any direction as long as safety cups are used all round on the oxers and appropriate groundlines used. It is usually best to start with a vertical for your initial warm-up, selecting the fence that has the easiest approach (which will depend on the layout of the arena).
- The most important thing to remember when riding fences with a short approach or short departure is to look and plan ahead so there are no miscommunications between you and the horse in terms of direction.
- To ride a shorter approach to a fence, make sure that the canter stays powerful and energetic before riding the turn, and prepare the horse with a half halt before maintaining a balanced canter through the turn, straightening as soon as you can out of the turn to the fence.
- When riding to a fence with limited space on landing, ensure that the canter stays the same on the approach. If the horse is new to this, keep the fence small to start with and approach from a slightly steadier pace, then build up to competition pace as his confidence increases. Try to ensure that you are looking ahead to the route afterwards, and on landing, control the line so that the horse doesn't cut the corner and make the turn even tighter – but be clear as to where you are going!

TIP ON RIDING A GOOD TURN

If you struggle more on one rein than the other to ride a good turn because the horse bends his neck too much and falls out through the shoulder, then try using a pivot turn (Exercise 63) as this will make him straighter more quickly by removing inside bend.

OUTDOOR SEASON EXERCISES

The outdoor season for showjumping in the UK starts in early April and concludes at the end of September, although there are outdoor shows all year round at some venues. Generally these feature larger arenas, and in the summer this can include grass arenas as well as larger events, such as county shows and horse trials; here, showjumping is an additional event alongside other equestrian and non-equestrian activities, which present their own challenges.

The outdoor show season also sees the introduction of open water in courses. These are a feature of Newcomer and Foxhunter second round competitions, and otherwise are mostly seen in Grand Prix classes and other high-level competitions, such as Area Trials.

This chapter covers some of the areas that you may want to practise in preparation for the outdoor season, depending on the level you want to compete at, and includes jumping on grass, jumping open water, and riding the longer distances that are encountered outdoors.

EXERCISE 66

Riding on Grass

Aim

It is now more common for horses to be predominantly trained and jumped on all-weather arena surfaces. As a result, to ride and compete on grass can present a very different feeling. These initial exercises use poles to help you understand how your horse is affected by performing on grass, and to build confidence in riding and training in this environment.

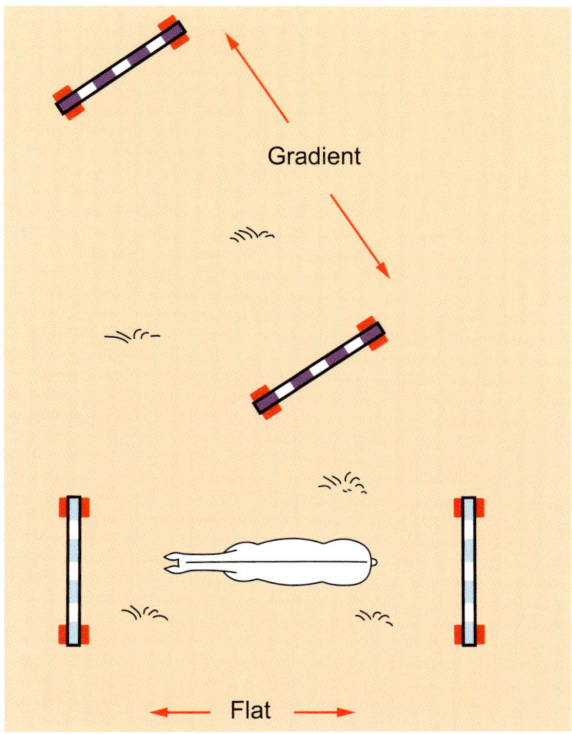

This pole exercise starts on the flat so that you can assess your horse on grass without a gradient. Then relocate the poles onto the gradient and see how it affects your horse's stride length and balance.

Set-Up

Studs: Horses can be ridden on grass without shoes or without studs in their shoes, but fitting studs can help them maintain their balance and have better grip when ground conditions are damp or muddy and can therefore be slippery. Choosing the most appropriate studs for the going is something that is worth experimenting with at home, and it is not the intention here to discuss the finer art of studs – but as a basic guide, pointed studs are helpful for firmer ground, and rounded studs are designed to help if the ground is soft. If you are using studs, it is also advisable to use a stud guard on your girth.

Equipment:

- Two poles or cavaletti
- Four pole pods if using round poles

Set up the poles or cavaletti on a four-stride distance of about 18yd (16.5m) on a relatively flat piece of ground to begin with. Ideally, once you have trained over these on the flat, this exercise should then be relocated to the same distance on a gentle gradient in the same area.

How to Ride It

- Start by working the horse on the grass surface in all three paces, including riding circles, turns and transitions. Be aware of his rhythm and balance, and ride half halts as necessary to help them. This helps the horse to become familiar with being ridden on the grass, and gives you a chance to feel if his movement or stride length alters.
- If there is a gradient to work on, include working up and down the hill and along the gradient as well – this is also very good for strengthening the horse's core. Whether you are working uphill or downhill, keep your seatbones slightly lighter to help the horse use his back more effectively, and with the lighter seat, keep your lower leg underneath your body and your chest up.
- Once you and the horse feel happy with this work, add canter work over the two poles and notice how easily the horse can fit in the four strides. Normally the horse will travel more forwards in the open spaces on grass if the ground is good, so the four strides on 18yd (16.5m) might feel a little short.
- Progress to experimenting with the poles on a slight gradient. Riding the four-stride distance uphill will require more power as the stride will naturally shorten going uphill. The reverse is true of riding downhill, where the same distance will feel shorter as the stride naturally lengthens. The horse is more likely to end up on the forehand going downhill, so you will need to hold your own balance well and keep a light contact to help support him.

TIP: RIDING ON A SOFT OR UNLEVEL GRASS SURFACE

Riding on a good grass surface gives natural spring, which artificial surfaces try to imitate, and many horses love it. When the ground is less perfect due to softening with rain or because it is unlevel, the key is to increase the power in the canter without increasing the length of stride or speed. This will give the horse the impulsion to cope with these other factors that can cause the power to diminish.

EXERCISE 67

Jumping on Grass

Aim

This set-up is designed to allow you to train your horse over a few key jumping exercises on grass to make sure that you have practised the things that are likely to be different when jumping on grass as opposed to on all-weather surfaces.

Set-Up

Equipment:

- Seven fences

This set-up uses a slight gradient to aid the training of the horse and to help understand how different gradients affect a horse's stride pattern and balance.

It is suggested that the double be ridden slightly uphill, in which case the distance between the two elements should be about 8yd (7.3m). The curving-line related distance could be built on seven strides, which is 32yd (29.3m). Place all the fences so there is plenty of room to turn and establish a good canter.

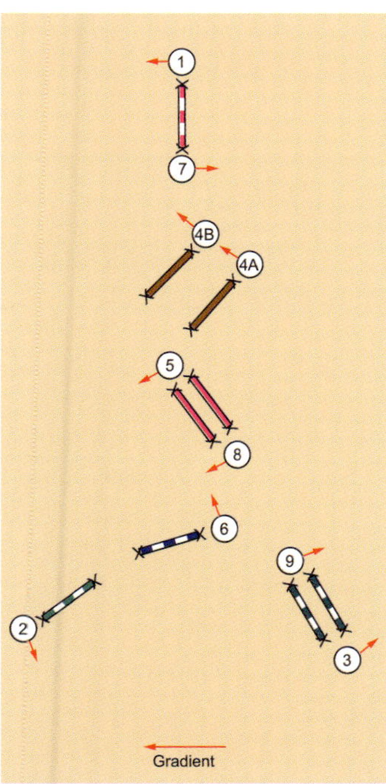

This is a basic suggested set up of a small course to allow you to practice riding individual fences and related distances on grass, with some slight gradient added in if possible.

How to Ride It

- Warm up on the grass surface, being aware of how the horse is travelling on the ground (which might change depending on the ground conditions), and how he is in his balance.
- Start your jumping warm-up over a vertical on the flat or an uphill gradient. Ensure that the canter is balanced, forward and engaged.
- Using the same sort of approach, continue your warm-up over an oxer.
- You can then start to link some of the fences together. When riding the curving-line related distance travel uphill first. Focus on landing from the first element and adding power if needed as you land to ensure you keep the momentum and energy travelling up the gradient to make the correct number of strides. The curving line allows you to ride wider if you need to add a stride if, for any reason, the horse's jump does not result in him landing in a good, forward canter. (A straight-line related distance is less forgiving so might be introduced when you and your horse are more familiar with jumping on grass.)
- To ride the fences downhill, including the curving-line related distance, keep the same engaged and balanced canter but be aware of keeping your shoulders up slightly to help the horse stay balanced and off his shoulders, and think of the same feeling through the second half of the parabola of the jump. On landing, be ready to help the horse rebalance if needed with a half halt, using the leg to push his hind leg under and help elevate the shoulders if he has fallen on his forehand due to the effect of the gradient.

TIPS ON WHICH STUDS TO USE

If the horse slips on the grass (which is more likely if it is damp or the ground is muddy or very soft), it is worth putting studs in his shoes – and if you have studs in already, review which studs you are using and how many, so that you achieve the right balance between grip and still having freedom to move. For example, massive studs in the wrong ground can provide too much resistance and the horse can become a little 'stuck', so use the smallest studs you can that are still effective.

EXERCISE 68

Open Distances

Aim

One of the key differences between the outdoor and indoor seasons might sound fairly obvious, but it is space! When you have been competing indoors all winter it can feel as if there is almost too much space between the fences when riding outdoors. The set-up in this exercise creates a more 'open' feel so you can practise being back in an outdoor competition arena, and can regulate pace across longer related distances.

Set-Up

- Six fences

In this diagram is a suggested basic set-up for practising more open distances. The curving-line distance is on seven strides, which is 32yd (29.3m) for horses, and the straight-line distance is on eight strides, which is 36yd (32.9m).

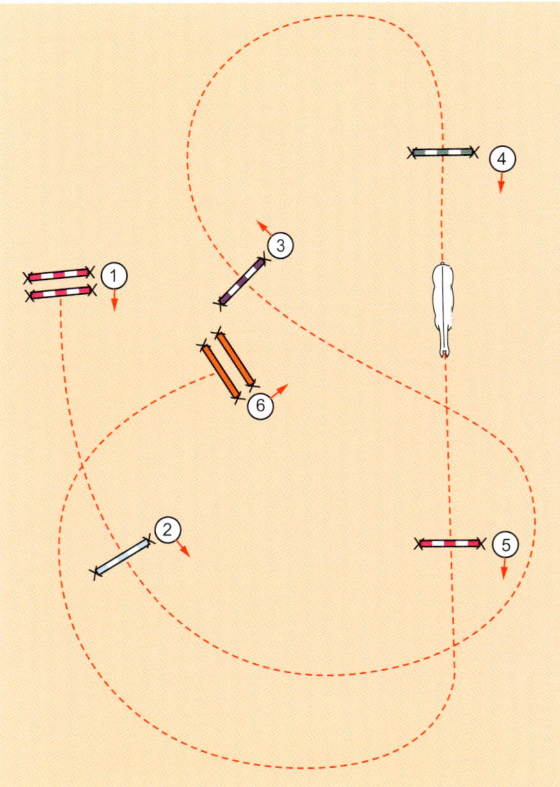

Outdoor competition tends to have longer distances between fences, so this set-up is one suggestion for creating this in training.

How to Ride It

- Start your warm-up over the fences in the middle of the arena, focusing on maintaining a good rhythm to and from the fence.
- Once you are happy with the warm-up fences, start adding the distances. It is generally easier to ride a related distance after a single fence as this helps to establish the quality of the canter.
- As you link the fences together, think of keeping the horse travelling forwards through the outer spaces before rebalancing him through a half halt to ride to the next fence. Even if your horse is forward thinking, you will often find that he slows down through the turns and then speeds up to the fence, so keeping the canter more forwards through the turns can help to maintain a more consistent pace.
- In a large arena you will usually find that the course-builder has not measured a line going out to the edges, so practise riding a natural line between the fences that does not use all the available space, as using too much arena space is an easy way to incur time penalties!

COACHES' TIPS ON MAINTAINING RHYTHM ON A LONGER APPROACH

With a longer approach to a fence it can be harder to maintain rhythm as riders start to adjust and change their minds on the way in. Staying on the same rhythm makes it much easier for riders to 'see' the stride, so getting them to count their horse's rhythm round the course can be helpful. Counting up to four is often sufficient, as in '1-2-3-4-1-2-3-4', but encourage them to count out loud, as they can end up counting the rhythm they *think* they should be on, and not the rhythm of their horse's canter! It also tells you if they're breathing and when their focus switches to the fence, as the counting often then becomes erratic, much quieter, or stops completely.

EXERCISE 69

Open Water

Open water is a showjumping feature of the outdoor season. Although you will encounter water trays indoors, the open water element is not a feature of the winter season. It is compulsory for International Stairway, International and Area Trial classes as well as Newcomer and Foxhunter second round competitions for horses, and is optional for Senior BS classes from 1.30m upwards as well as classes for six- and seven-year-old horses and Young Rider competitions. For Juniors it is compulsory for the Pony Showjumper of the Year qualifiers and the Pony Foxhunter second rounds, as well as being optional in some other classes, including JA, JC and Pony Opens.

The open water can have a maximum spread of 3.7m (12ft) for some pony classes, whilst for Senior Newcomer second rounds the maximum is 3m (10ft); however, this can increase to up to 4.25m (14ft) for classes such as the International Stairway.

Aim

The structure in this exercise aims to help you introduce a horse to open water and teach him to jump it confidently.

Set-Up

Buying an open water tray is quite expensive and only really worth the investment if you have several horses or ponies needing to jump one regularly. These can be found at many competition venues that offer arena hire, and at coaches' training facilities. However, a great, inexpensive alternative that is more helpful for introducing a horse to open water was once suggested to me by my coach mentor, Susie Gibson, and has proved invaluable ever since:

create an extendable water jump by attaching a blue tarpaulin-style sheet to a wooden slat at each end, which can then be rolled in or out to suit.

An open water tray should be built up to full width gradually. It helps to have a second set of wings located alongside the fillers at the front to create an oxer effect. The poles over the water should all be on safety cups.

Equipment:

- Adjustable open water
- Two to four wings
- Two poles with four safety cups (ideally the poles should be at least 3.7m (12ft) long)
- A small take-off element such as a small sloping gate filler about 60–70cm (2ft–2ft 4in) high
- Set up the water jump with the filler at the front (if you have enough wings, place some beside the fillers to create an oxer effect) and the water tray rolled up to the equivalent of a standard water tray – for example 90cm (3ft). Beside the back edge of the rolled-up water tray put the wings, with two sets of safety cups and two poles set to a relatively low height – for example 80cm (2ft 8in).

How to Ride It

- It will help to have other fences to jump preceding the open water, so have at least one other vertical and an oxer to warm up over and use before you approach the open water.
- Work round the open water, in its extended form, in your warm-up so the horse becomes familiar with it being in the arena.
- The key to jumping open water is to have a powerful, strong canter that is connected into the bridle, so you are not galloping flat out at it all the way in, but have good impulsion and a little length to the stride without the horse going fast and flat. Close the leg a little more strongly in the last couple of strides to encourage the horse to open his frame over the spread of the water.
- Once you are both jumping the narrow version of the water confidently, extend the water so that it gradually gets nearer to 3m (10ft) – although you don't need to do this all in one training session.
- To progress towards the requirements for competition, you will need to practise over a full open water about 3 to 3.5m (10 to 11.5ft) wide. You might need to do this away from home if you don't have one. Once the water tray is being jumped confidently, add some water into it if there is none in already and repeat the jump, as there is usually water in the open water element, not just the tray.
- The other aspect that often comes into competition is a vertical or set of planks after the open water to test rideability and control on landing. This can be positioned at perhaps a seven- or eight-stride distance – 32ft (9.75m) or 36ft (10.97m) – after the open water to allow time to rebalance the horse after he has opened the canter, and to replicate that experience for him.

EXERCISE 70

Establishing Pace

While there is a 'time allowed' for all affiliated showjumping tracks, it is often easier to make the time at the lower levels indoors as it is usually measured quite generously by the course builder within the confines of the indoor space. Once you get outdoors it can be easy to use too much space in the larger arenas, and if you are also not riding at the stipulated speed it is easy to get time penalties: at one penalty per second over the time allowed these are quite costly.

Aim

This exercise gives you the basics of how to gauge the pace that is required for each level of showjumping track. It is also useful for eventers to assess their cross-country pace.

Set-Up

A measuring wheel is useful for this exercise to measure a distance accurately, but a measuring tape, or any other system for measuring, can be used, including various apps.

Ideally you need about 55yd (50m) of straight-line distance with space before and after to establish the pace and bring the horse back down out of the pace.

As a follow-on you can use the measuring wheel to measure a natural line round a track of showjumps, and then ask someone to time you while you ride the track following as similar a line as possible.

How to Ride It

- Using the straight-line measured distance, ask someone to time you from the moment you pass the first marker to the end of the 50m stretch where you pass the second marker.
- Establish a good quality canter and then approach and proceed down the straight-line distance.
- The speeds you are trying to attain depend on the level you are jumping at – for example:
  - Horses competing at 1.10m and below: 325m per minute (mpm)
  - Horses competing above 1.10m: 350mpm
  - Grade A & B horses competing outdoors: 375mpm (350mpm indoors)
  - International Trials: 400mpm
  - Pony classes range from 325 to 350mpm
- As an example to calculate how long it should take to cover 50m at 325mpm this is the sum:
  - 60sec divided by 325m = 0.1846sec for 1m × 50m = 9.23sec
- Bear in mind that jumping efforts also need to be included within this time, so although this gives you a general idea of pace, it is then useful to measure and ride a short course with fences to find out whether you are riding at the correct pace once jumps are included. Some horses take more time in the air than others, so this can be an added factor.

Start

TRAINING FOR A JUMP-OFF

Historically, British Showjumping ran most classes as Table A7, which meant that you only tackled a jump-off if you had completed your first round clear and left the arena, following which those who had also jumped clear would also return at the end of the first round to jump a bigger, shorter track against the clock.

Currently, most classes are run as single phase or two phase, and incorporate the jump-off in the second section. In two-phase competition it is just one round, but you can only continue to ride the jump-off section if you have gone clear in the first phase; while for single-phase classes you complete the entire course including the jump-off element even if you have had faults in the first part of the track.

Regardless of the format of the class you are competing in, there are several techniques that you can train to achieve with your horse so that you can be more competitive in a jump-off; in this chapter there are some exercises to help learn these techniques.

EXERCISE 71

Turning Quickly on Landing

Aim

This exercise explains how to practise turning quickly on landing, which is probably the easiest way to save time in a jump-off.

Set-Up

Equipment:

- A minimum of one fence, starting as a vertical

The single fence can be placed towards the middle of the arena if it is to be used on its own – just ensure that there is room to turn easily each way on landing.

How to Ride It

- Every horse will be slightly different in terms of what they can do best in a jump-off. Some are naturally quick, some are very careful and can turn tight to a fence, and some are very good with their hind legs and can turn tightly on landing. Finding out what your horse does best helps you form a strategy for future jump-offs, and can improve their performance in doing so. Most horses will find turning quickly after a fence easier than turning tightly to it on the approach.
- Start by riding to and from the fence straight. Keep the fence at a comfortable height and make a point of looking straight ahead and keeping your body position central. There would be no point in allowing the horse to dive left or right on landing at the outset to then encourage that with the turns. The turn should be on your aids, not when your horse feels like it!
- When you look to introduce a turn on landing, be aware of preparing for the turn but not asking too soon, particularly once you are trying it over an oxer, as your horse is more likely to drop his hip in the direction of travel if you ask too early and

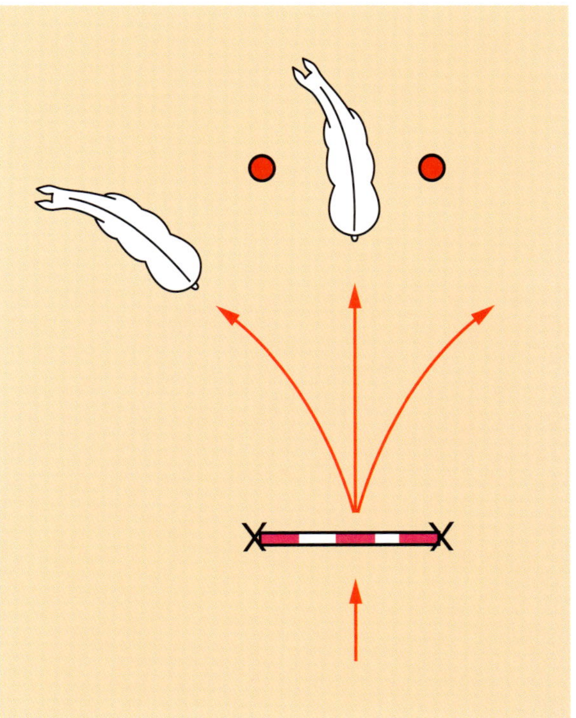

Cones can be used on landing after a fence to help provide a 'target' to turn inside and to see how easy it is to turn in either direction. One way is usually easier than the other, and it is worth factoring this into your jump-off plans.

knock down the back rail as a result. The timing of the aids is key, which is where this exercise plays its part as, again, every horse is slightly different.

- Key to a successful turn is looking ahead. As you are about to take off, turn your head in the direction you want to go after the fence. Through the jump, start to think of moving your weight slightly more towards the direction of travel on landing (but be careful not to lean over and unbalance the horse), and you can start to close the outside leg to help indicate the direction to the horse as well as slightly opening the inside rein.
- Be careful not to pull on the rein over the fence as this will unbalance the horse's jump. Keep your shoulders level, just think of your weight being slightly more in the inside stirrup and hip rather than dropping your shoulder.
- As you land, keep looking round the turn, opening the inside rein and closing the outside leg more to push the horse's body round the turn; then ride forwards away from the fence.
- Try first approaching and riding away from the fence in the same direction, then approach from one direction and change the rein over the fence. Mix up the turns with riding straight away from the fence so that a turn is not anticipated every time you jump.
- If you want to increase the accuracy challenge in one of these training sessions, use cones or another fence in the arena on the landing side of the main jump, positioned so that you can ride round the outside of it but can also turn inside it. Start off with it located at least four strides – 20yd (18.3m) – away from the main fence to turn inside it, then if you find that easy, start to shorten the distance a little at a time to see how easy it is to turn inside the obstacle, and how much space you need at this stage of your horse's training to turn on landing. This means that in competition you will know whether a particular turn is achievable for you and your horse or not.

EXERCISE 72

Turning Tightly to a Fence

Aim

Turning tightly to a fence gives you competitive options in the ring, and if the horse is careful and brave, you can dare him with a very short approach once he is experienced enough to do so. As with everything, practice and confidence is key, and knowing your horse and his level of training allows you to judge how tightly you can turn to a fence. This exercise helps you to educate the horse, and to learn how much space before the fence you will need to allow for his level of training and his capabilities.

Set-Up

Equipment:

- A minimum of one fence, starting as a vertical

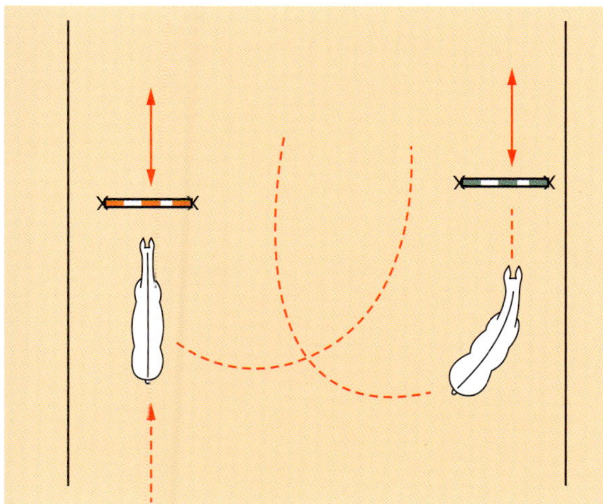

By locating the fences near the edge of the arena, you can warm up riding to the fences in a straight line and then try coming through the middle area of the arena, turning back up to one of the fences. Give yourself a few strides straight before the fence at first and then make the turn tighter if you feel you can increase the challenge a little. Be careful that you get straight to the fence and aren't angling it so much that you might be aiming as if to jump out of the arena!

This exercise can be practised with more fences, and is perhaps slightly easier when the fence is located near the edge of the arena (or on the three-quarter line) as it provides more of a visual guide for the turn (though you will need to be straight on landing to stay in the arena!). So for example, have a fence near each long side of the arena that can be jumped straight, or turned back to.

How to Ride It

- Start by riding the fences in a straight line to warm up. Notice the quality of the canter and check that the power stays the same through the turn.
- When you start to try the turn up to the fence, keep the fence small to begin with.
- Ride a curving line to roll back to the fence, initially making sure that at least the last three strides are straight before take-off.
- Look over your shoulder back at the fence you want to turn up to, and think of using your legs to create the turn and maintain the energy – so use your inside leg to keep the curve and stop the horse falling in, then the outside leg to complete the turn and straighten him up. It can help to open the inside rein to 'invite' the horse round the turn, but take care not to pull the rein if possible as this tends to cause neck bend and the horse will fall out through the outside shoulder.
- Ensure the horse is straight for take-off, and ride straight away after the fence.
- As the horse becomes familiar with the approach, you can try riding the turn a little tighter so there are fewer straight strides before the fence – however, this is not something to aim for in the first session.
- The main challenge with this sort of turn, other than the horse learning to be ready for a jump when he doesn't have much time to see it, is being able to maintain the power and the balance in the canter while turning, so make this a focal point and ensure you are achieving this before increasing the height of the jump too much.

EXERCISE 73

Jumping Fences on the Angle

Aim

Being able to jump fences on an angle confidently can save quite a lot of time by reducing the number of strides taken to approach and ride away from a fence. The set-up in this exercise is one way to practise doing this.

Set-Up

Equipment:

- Up to four fences will be needed to create this set-up, but you can train over a single fence or practise using fences set within a course, depending on what is available to you.
- Half-round poles as needed to help guide straightness.

Set up the fences as in the diagram for one basic exercise to practise this, making sure there is enough room to the outside of the fences to approach and ride away safely on landing.

How to Ride It

- Warm up by riding the fences with a normal approach and keep everything to a height that is comfortable and straightforward for the horse to jump. Whilst doing this, focus on the horse's straightness through his body and neck, as this will be key to the subsequent exercise.
- It can be helpful to use some half-round poles as tramlines for the initial attempts to ride fences on the angle, as it helps to keep the horse straight in his body. To do this, put two half-round poles on the ground approximately two strides from the fence – about 11yd (10.1m) – on a slight angle as in the diagram, and approximately 2yd (1.8m) apart.
- Canter round the arena and then, looking and planning ahead, leave the track using the outside leg aids to help keep straightness and ride between the poles to the fence, aiming to keep the same line on landing.
- To begin with make sure the angle is not too acute; you can increase the challenge of a greater angle later in the horse's training.
- From a rider perspective, think of helping the horse to stay on the line by sitting evenly in the saddle, with an even contact on the reins and channelling the horse's body to be straight and remain engaged in the canter by using your legs as needed. It helps to have a focal point to ride to that is on the line you intend to ride, so try to find something in the eyeline on the landing side of the fence that you can line up with on the approach.
- Once you are riding to the fence on the angle confidently, remove the tramlines and repeat the exercise, then add the other fences in the diagram and try each one with a slight angle.

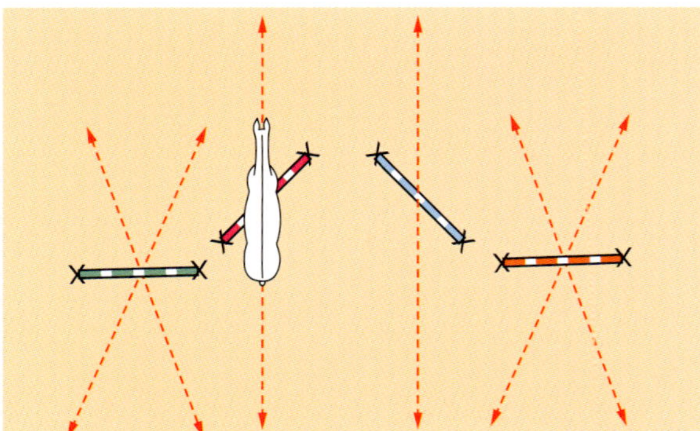

This set-up can be jumped on the standard lines, but then progressed to include jumping on the angle. The outside fences can only be jumped like this if there is enough space to the outside of the arena to create an angled line safely.

> **COACHES' TIP ON ADDRESSING LOSS OF STRAIGHTNESS**
>
> Notice whether one direction is riding more easily than the other on the angle. If one direction is proving harder, try and observe from a position where you can see the horse from in front (so long as you are not in the horse's direct line of sight and therefore a distraction) to check whether he is losing straightness through the neck and shoulders or through the quarters. Revisiting the tramlines might then be helpful, or return to riding a small fence in a straight line and get the rider to notice and address the straightness before attempting the angle again. If the loss of straightness is happening at take-off, you can place the half-rounds on the floor nearer the wings to help guide the jump, then narrow them a little if necessary once the horse is familiar with them being there.

EXERCISE 74

Riding Between Fences

Aim

Sometimes the best jump-off line, especially when competing indoors, is to go between fences through a relatively narrow gap. If the horse is not familiar with doing this, he can 'cramp' or draw back in the canter and lose the power you will need after the turn to jump the next fence. This exercise can be ridden in any space with a course of showjumps, but if your equipment is limited, the basics of this concept can be practised using just one or two fences, although larger wings rather than blocks are better to give the effect that you would encounter in the ring.

Set-Up

Equipment:

- A minimum of two fences, ideally with full wings

These can be located almost anywhere in the arena, provided there is room to ride between them on either rein if there are two fences – or for a higher level of challenge, build one fence as an oxer so you can ride through the middle of it.

If using two separate jumps the gap between the wings needs to be at least 2yd (1.8m) to start with, and if building an oxer to ride through, the width between the front and back rail needs to be around 1.7yd (1.6m).

How to Ride It

- This exercise is not necessarily about riding to a fence, although depending on what is available to you, jumps can be incorporated.
- Begin by working in walk and start to ride between the fences – if you are using a course already set up there will be various options in terms of the space between the fences, in which case it would make sense to ride through the bigger gaps first before attempting the smaller spaces. Otherwise incorporate riding between the gap in your set-up as part of your warm-up.
- If you are using the gap between the front and back rail of an oxer, warm up a little and then ride through it in walk first. If the horse is likely to be nervous about this, start with poles on the floor, then build up the oxer later: the gap you are riding through is much longer, so the constraints of the smaller space last longer, with more of a tunnel effect, and this can be more of a challenge for the horse.
- Focus on keeping your eyes on the line through the gap and riding confidently from your leg into a consistent and even contact so that the horse stays straight. If he starts to wobble, widen your hands a little so they are further apart from each other and create a 'tunnel' effect, and close your legs – this can help to channel him straighter.
- Once you and the horse are confident with this, increase the pace to trot and repeat the lines between the fences, then try the same in canter.
- If you then add fences, the challenge is to keep control of the body with the likely increase in power and pace, and to maintain the energy after riding through the narrow space to ride to another fence.

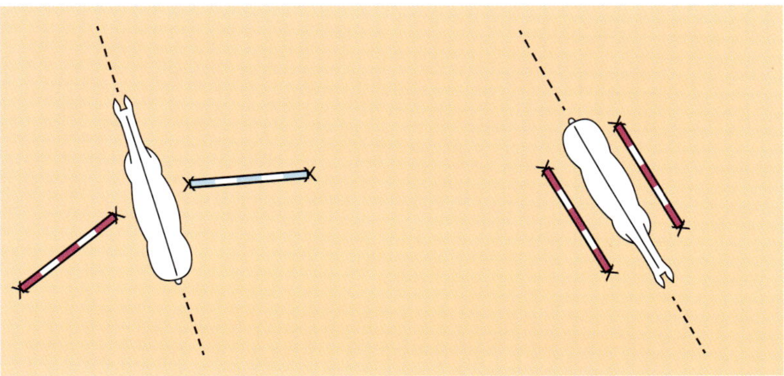

Practice riding through relatively narrow spaces between fences, which can also include riding between the front and back bar of a wide oxer for a slightly different challenge.

EXERCISE 75

Adjusting the Stride Pattern

Aim

This exercise allows you to practise adjusting the number of strides that the horse takes down a distance. In a jump-off there may be related distances where you can be a fraction quicker by taking one stride less than the other competitors – but this must be done in balance to avoid flattening the second obstacle. This exercise aims to help rider and horse train so they can achieve this.

Set-Up

Equipment:

- Two half-rounds or round poles placed on pole pods or other blocks to prevent them rolling

Set up the two poles on a straight-line distance 24yd (21.95m) apart.

How to Ride It

- This is a very simple exercise to enable you to practise adjusting the horse's stride.
- Approach the first pole in a good canter and ensure that the horse is straight. Ride down the straight line to the second pole, and notice how many strides you get without interfering too much with the canter. With most horses on this distance it is likely that you will get six strides the first time.
- The idea now is to add and remove strides from that number. From a jump-off point of view it is most relevant to be able to ride for one stride less, but from a control point of view it is also good to train to be able to add one stride more. And a great challenge to set yourself is to be able to mix it up each time you ride the line – for example six strides, seven strides, five strides, seven strides, and so on.
- To get fewer strides, ride into the first pole with a little more energy but keep the connection and balance. Landing over the pole, lighten the seat slightly and close your leg strongly to ride the first couple of strides forwards, before growing a little taller again to be in balance for the second pole. Try to achieve as much of the lengthening as you can in the first few strides, as this will allow you to have the horse back in balance for the next obstacle.
- To add an extra stride, still ride into the first pole with power (after all, you will need that power to jump the fence), but then on landing grow tall in your body, tighten your core muscles, close your leg and ride a half halt to shorten the stride, repeating on the next couple of strides if needed in order to close down the canter enough to make space for the extra stride. Be careful to soften the hand in between each half halt, so it doesn't become a wrestling match all the way between the two poles, but stay tall in your body to indicate to the horse that you still want him to wait.

TIPS ON SHORTENING AND LENGTHENING THE CANTER

It is important when you are wanting to shorten or lengthen the canter not to adjust the stride too much on the ride in, because this usually results in the horse becoming less balanced and potentially 'chipping in' a short stride to rebalance himself, which then makes the distance more difficult to ride. Keep the canter engaged and with power on the approach, riding the connection between leg and hand, then seek to adjust the stride on the landing side of the pole.

EXERCISE 76

Taking Out the Curve

Aim

Another way to save time in a jump-off is to take fewer strides between fences by reducing or straightening out the curve on a bending line. This exercise explains how to set this up to practise it in training.

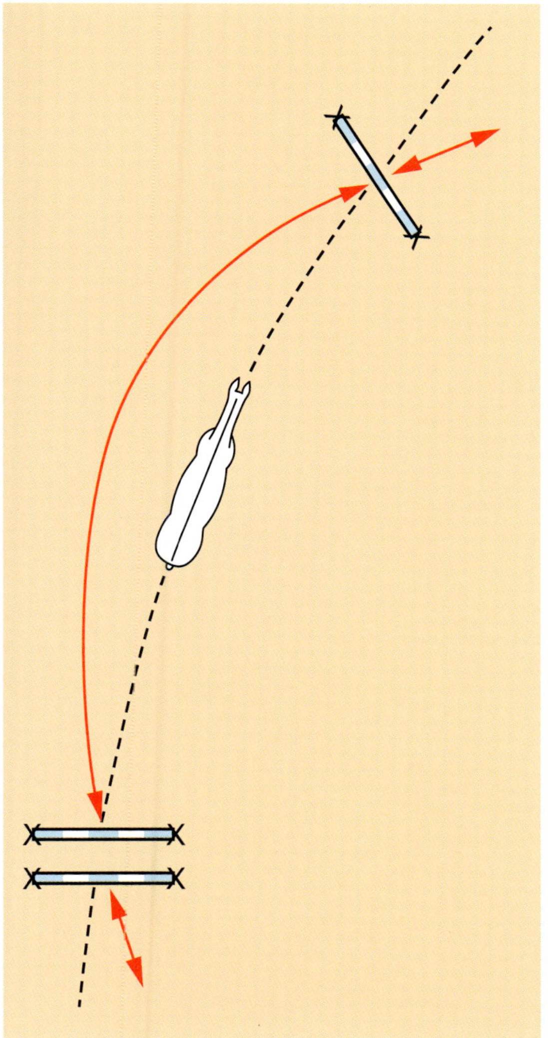

This exercise begins with a normal curving line related to distance, denoted by the red line, and can then be practiced taking the curve out to ride fewer strides between the elements, denoted by the black dotted line, but make sure you can ride an angled line away clearly on landing without the edge of the arena or other jumps in the way.

Set-Up

Equipment:

- Two fences: the first element can be an oxer, but start with a vertical as the second element.

Set up the fences as in the diagram, with a curving line on six or seven strides – that is, 28 to 32yd (25.6 to 29.3m). Make sure there is enough room on landing from the vertical to ride away afterwards on the angle without encroaching on the edge of the arena.

How to Ride It

- Warm up over the fences individually first. When you are first attempting this, as with any new exercise, keep the fences relatively small so they are an easy jumping effort for the horse.
- Begin by riding the curving line, using the full space for a natural line and working to achieve the distance comfortably on a good quality canter.
- When you are riding this comfortably, try riding the line without the curve. Ride the first fence from a slightly wider approach to jump it slightly on the angle (make sure you have practised this, *see* Exercise 73) and keep your eye on the direct line to the middle of the second fence.
- Using the techniques practised in Exercise 75, land from the first fence and ride forwards and straight on the direct line for the first couple of strides to be able to take one less stride between the fences. You will be jumping the second fence on an angle as well, so make sure you have your eye on the line after the fence, and a plan for where you are going next!
- Keep the horse channelled between leg and hand to maintain straightness on the direct line, and think of the pace being early in the distance so that you can have the horse balanced for the second element.

TIP: PRACTISE THE OTHER EXERCISES IN THIS SECTION FIRST!

This is quite a challenging exercise demanding accuracy and a straight horse, so make sure you have practised the other exercises in this section before tackling this one!

BIG BEAR FENCES

INTRODUCING DIFFERENT TYPES OF FENCE

This chapter explains how to tackle some of the less common fences you might encounter in a showjumping competition, as well as how to introduce fillers and water trays to a young or inexperienced horse.

EXERCISE 77

Introducing Fillers

Aim

Although trends for using fillers vary, there are usually some in a showjumping course, and the following exercises are designed to help build your horse's confidence with them. However, some horses seem to be bold from the outset, in which case most fillers don't phase them! Training with them at home allows you to learn how your horse is likely to react in the ring.

Set-Up

Equipment:

- A minimum of two standing fillers (one pair)
- A minimum of one showjump

How to Ride It

- It can be useful to start by doing flatwork with fillers in the arena, and to make a habit of riding through a gap between them as part of your schooling. Place them far enough apart to get comfortably between them and build up from walk, through trot and into canter as your horse's confidence grows. Key to this is to make sure that, even if your horse is uncertain, you never allow him to run past the obstacle. If necessary, get someone to make the gap wider for you, but keep the horse in front of the question quiet until he decides to walk through the space.
- To introduce fillers in a fence, use the same fillers initially that you've worked with on the flat, and place them to the edge of the fence, overlapping the wings, to begin with.
- Gradually as the horse gains confidence, bring the fillers in from the side until eventually you are jumping the fence with the fillers fully underneath it.
- Keep focusing on remaining in the centre of the fence and riding straight with the horse connected between leg and hand.
- Fillers with a bigger contrast – such as black and white – tend to cause more reaction as they stand out more to the horse's vision, which makes less distinction between different colours.

These standing fillers are placed slightly to the outside of the fence to create a gap to ride between whilst introducing your horse to them for the first time.

TIPS ON COPING WITH RUNNING OUT

If your horse goes to run out, try to hold him to the middle of the fence, and if someone is there to help you, if the horse has stopped, keep him in front of the fence and have your assistant make the fence into poles on the floor or on a very low setting, pulling the fillers out a little if needed. Then ride the horse over the poles to 'complete' the jump, before rebuilding the fence and re-presenting to it. This means that the horse has always crossed the fence despite any difficulties presented, and he will usually jump it the second time with fewer issues.

There are now apps that allow you to see jumps as the horse sees them, but the basic principle is that most colours become a more green-grey, blue-grey or yellow-grey, and therefore blend more into the background so that the contrast between different colours is slight; however, white stands out.

EXERCISE 78

Jumping Planks and Walls

Aim

Planks are often used as fillers in fences, however a full set of planks presents a slightly different question for the horse and can be quite an imposing fence depending on the design and how many planks are used. A wall used alone has a similar profile, and there is an increasing trend for the wall to have a relatively square top rather than the traditional curve that is seen on a Puissance wall. In these instances, the same challenge is presented. Most riders don't have easy access to a full wall, but the same principle can be applied with the practice over planks.

Set-Up

Equipment:

- A minimum of two planks plus wings (remember to use the flat side of the jump cup for the planks)
- One pole or half-round pole

How to Ride It

- The main challenge with a set of planks is that it can draw the horse closer to the fence as it has a very upright profile, and with the planks having, by their nature, a larger, flat front, they don't have the slightly more forgiving curve of a pole if a limb touches one. This means that ideally the horse doesn't want to take off too close to the fence, as it might be more likely that he will then hit the plank on the parabola of the natural jump.
- To help you to jump planks well, you can use an open groundline in front of the fence, around 0.5yd (0.46m) from the planks (although it can be pulled out further). Keep the planks fairly small to begin with and think of riding the canter in an uphill but powerful way so that the energy is carried on to the hocks. The open groundline will encourage you and the horse to give the planks a little more room at take-off.
- Once you are jumping this successfully, remove the groundline and try to replicate the same feeling in the canter and the same rhythm so that you can keep the take-off in a good place in good balance.
- A variation on straight planks are wavy planks. The decision to be made here is whether you aim for the lower part of the wave and stay accurate to jump the smaller part, or aim for the higher section so you are not caught out on height if the horse moves across. Generally I would suggest aiming for the higher part, as the wave is a more difficult line for the horse to judge, and aiming for the lower part also depends on how much room in that lower section there is. Hopefully the horse will give them enough clearance so you don't need to worry about it, but if you have at least put the higher section in his line of sight you can hope that you've done enough to help him judge it.

Wavy planks can be harder for your horse to judge and these are one version of planks you may encounter in competition.

EXERCISE 79

The Liverpool Oxer

Aim

This type of fence has become common with a water tray under it in Senior Foxhunter classes in Great Britain; however, it can also be found in courses without the water element, and this is how it is considered here.

A Liverpool oxer can have several poles on the back set of wings, which should all be on safety cups, with the front rail kept very low so that it is usually not particularly influential to the jump.

Set-Up

Equipment:

- A minimum of four poles
- Two pairs of wings plus four safety cups

The Liverpool oxer usually comprises of about two poles set low in front (these can be just 60 to 70cm high), then on the second set of wings there are another two or more poles on safety cups, all located higher than the rails on the front wings.

How to Ride It

- Although this fence can look a little unusual, its profile is very forgiving for the horse to jump.
- The key to riding to it is basically to almost ignore the front rail and make your judgement based on the back element.
- This is because the front rail is so small it doesn't impact on the jump even if you take off just in front of it. The distance between the front and back elements is usually less than the take-off distance for the back bar – that is, less than 2yd (1.83m) in front of the back element. Therefore you can make a judgement on the take-off point based purely on the back bar, and can get relatively close to the front rail without worrying about it, treating the fence almost like a vertical with an open groundline, as it is very unlikely that the horse will knock the front rails.

EXERCISE 80

The Triple Bar

Aim

The triple bar is a spread fence with a slightly more forgiving profile but a bigger spread than a standard oxer. It tends to have the effect of opening out the stride, and so is often followed in competition by a combination or short related distance in higher-level classes, to test control and rideability.

Set-Up

Equipment:

- Three pairs of wings with safety cups for all the poles on the second two sets of wings
- A minimum of three poles, but generally more

Build the triple bar with the first element small, using one or two poles, then build the middle element on safety cups using one or two poles placed slightly higher than the first element. Finally, build the third element using one or two poles on safety cups placed slightly higher than the middle element.

To give an idea of size, a standard oxer in a Foxhunter (1.20m) class has a maximum spread of 1.40m, whereas a triple bar in the same class has a maximum spread of 1.80m.

How to Ride It

- As with a Liverpool oxer, you can almost ignore the first element of the triple bar, treating it like a slightly raised groundline, and ride to jump the second and third elements. However, because of the nature of the spread and the forgiving profile of the fence, you will want to approach with good power and potentially a little more pace, depending on the size of the triple bar.
- Make sure that you are straight on your approach and that the horse is balanced and travelling in a powerful way between leg and hand.
- Keep your focus up and ahead, and close the leg at take-off to encourage the horse to open out his frame over the full spread. Complete the jump by riding a straight line away from the fence afterwards. This is not a fence to tackle on the angle if you can avoid doing so.

A triple bar is over a wider spread than standard oxers with three sets of rails. The front rail is kept very small, with the next two sets of wings needing to have safety cups on all poles used.

EXERCISE 81

Water Trays

Aim

The inclusion of a water tray in British Showjumping classes is mandatory in Newcomer (1.10m) and Foxhunter (1.20m) classes, and optional in most other competitions. It is generally not encountered in classes below this level, but can still be included in all except four-year-old age classes.

Set-Up

Equipment:

- Two pairs of wings plus safety cups
- Four poles
- One water tray, or preferably, an adjustable water tray (*see* below)

For open water training (*see* Exercise 69) I reference the equipment that I prefer to use for training the horse over water trays: this is something like a blue tarpaulin, with a small structure at each end such as a wooden slat that can be used to roll up or extend the tarpaulin to suit your needs. This allows a gentler introduction to the water tray than immediately tackling a full water tray, as it can be made into the dimensions of a blue pole and then gradually rolled out.

How to Ride It

- Having warmed up, including over standard fences, I prefer to introduce the water tray under a slightly ascending oxer.
- Keep the adjustable water tray slightly rolled up at first so it is more of a blue pole, and jump the fence once or twice, keeping your focus up and ahead.

Water trays can be a feature of most classes, but are normally seen at Newcomer level and above. The water tray in this photo is made of blue tarpaulin, and can be rolled in to begin a horse's introduction to water trays before extending it out once the horse is confident with it.

- Once you have jumped this confidently, roll out the water tray gradually until it fills the space between the front and back rails.
- Over a few training sessions, and once the horse is confident with this, the complete effect would be to add water to the water tray, as this will be encountered in the ring.
- You can also experiment with different fences with the water tray underneath. For vertical fences, if the water tray is behind the front profile of the fence, you can use standard cups. However, if the water tray extends in front of the fence as well as behind it – that is, if the jump sits over the middle of the water tray – then safety cups should be used.
- For young horses stepping up to Newcomer and Foxhunter level, you should also introduce the water tray under a Liverpool oxer (*see* Exercise 79), as this is the most likely form that they will encounter in competition.

TIPS ON DESIGNING AND RIDING WATER TRAYS

There are many different types of water tray, including hexagonal trays and rectangular ones of differing sizes that can also be found in black rather than blue. A little creative design at home can help replicate some of them with plywood or tarpaulin so that you are less likely to encounter something in the ring that you've not seen at home; alternatively a few arena hires may provide the variety needed.

Whilst the water tray can make your horse look down, make sure that you don't do so as well. It can help to stick your chin out slightly in the last stride so your head is employed in a different movement – this also helps your body to be aligned for the jump. Close the leg in the last stride to keep the forward momentum going.

EXERCISE 82

Weird and Wonderful Poles

Aim

Over the last few years, course designers and showjump manufacturers have come up with a huge range of new and innovative designs far beyond the traditional two-colour bands of old. Some of the new designs do not cause any issues at all, where others seem to, and it is not always clear why, even though our understanding of what colours horses see has improved significantly. Amongst the unusual poles that can be encountered are horizontal stripes, spirals and spots.

Set Up

A paint pot and a little creativity can help replicate unusual poles to practise over, if you don't want to buy new ones, and using tape to create spirals or stripes with a crisp edge can be a useful technique. Some companies also manufacture fabric wraps to cover poles, which can make for a quick and easy change of design or colour.

How to Ride It

- This is more about introducing the horse to an unusual pole design than applying a different technique in your riding.
- Ride the fence as normal, as most of the time the designs have no negative impact on the horse.
- Occasionally with poles that are harder to read, such as some spiral designs (but not all), the horse will approach normally, but may take a deep final stride in preference to standing off, as they sometimes seem to double check how the fence needs to be jumped.
- It is therefore important to ride to the jump on a balanced, uphill and connected canter, keeping your shoulders up and looking ahead, being careful not to drop the shoulders forwards, and not to anticipate a forward stride if that option presents itself. Usually after the pole with the unusual appearance has been jumped once, it doesn't cause any issues again, as the horse will then understand the question.

These horizontal striped poles are one of the many designs now seen in competition, and can create an optical illusion depending on the design and the colours used.

Country Frog
British Showjumping

PROBLEM SOLVING

There are many different challenges that can be presented to us as riders, and it is our responsibility to try to find a way to reduce the challenge for our horses and ourselves.

In this chapter I have tried to cover three key elements that I believe are some of the most influential factors in the problems we encounter in showjumping. These are:

- Rideability
- Straightness
- Jumping technique

Often the issues around technique can be at least partially addressed through the improvement of the horse's rideability and straightness, so these areas are covered first.

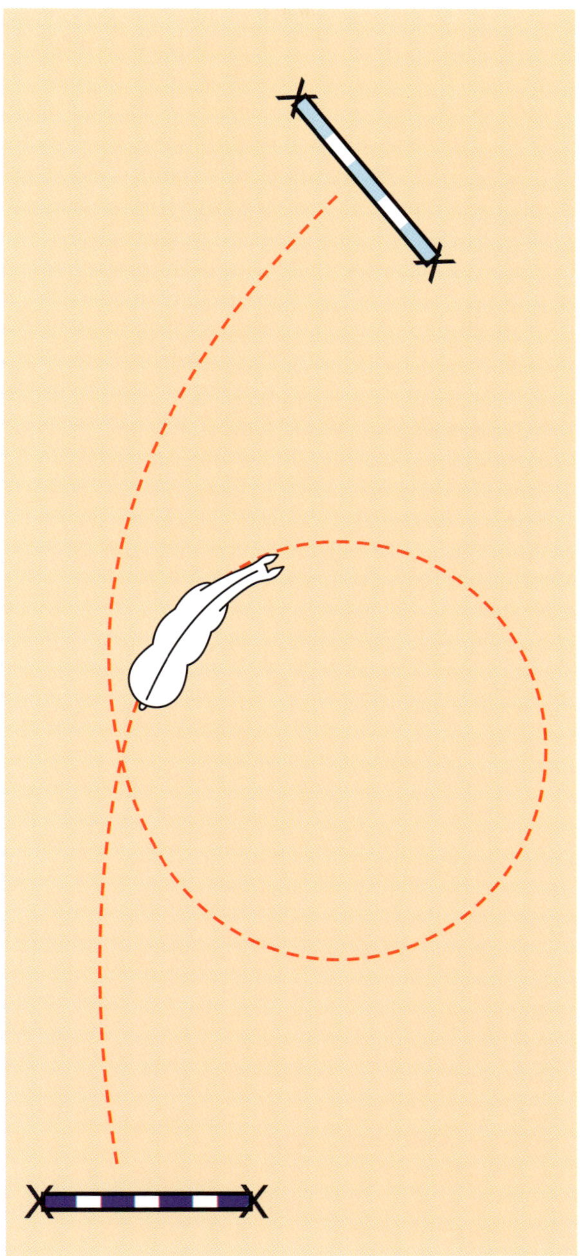

Adding circles between fences to improve relaxation and rideability can be a useful training technique.

EXERCISES FOR RIDEABILITY

EXERCISE 83

Using the Ride Away to Address the Approach

Aim

Issues with the approach to the fence can often be addressed on landing. This exercise gives a few basic options that can help train through the challenges you might encounter, and make the horse more rideable.

Set-Up

Equipment:

- A minimum of one showjump
- Optional – two tramlines using half-round poles, or poles blocked in with pole pods or the arena surface

How to Ride It

Rushing into the fence:

- If the horse has rushed into the jump, sit tall on landing, keeping him on a straight line by keeping him between leg and hand, and ride a halt transition. For this you can use some tramlines on the landing side of the fence to provide the straight line and a target to ride into for the transition – make this at least four strides – 20yd (18.3m) – after the fence to make it achievable. (It may take a lot longer to achieve the halt at first.)
- Once you have ridden the halt, praise the horse. The idea is not that you are punishing him, so make it clear that you just wanted a halt transition, and that there is no issue. With a forward-thinking horse the purpose of consistently riding a halt on landing is to get him to anticipate the halt and therefore be starting to slow after the fence, rather than rushing away. This anticipation often leads to a less speedy approach too.

Landing short from the fence/being lazy on approach:

- Sometimes more backward-thinking or laid-back horses will drop down from the fence closer to it than is ideal, so their jump loses its shape in the second half.
- The solution to this is the same as if you have a horse that doesn't travel forwards to the fence, so doesn't stay in front of your leg aids.
- As soon as you land from the fence, lighten your seat and apply your leg to send your horse forwards away from the fence as much as you can.
- If you are finding it hard to get a sufficient response, try riding with a relatively short dressage whip (this cannot be used in competitions, when a short, padded baton is required). This allows you to keep your hands on the reins, because the idea is not to hit the horse but to give him a tap on the hindquarters after the leg aid to help explain to him that your leg aid was to activate his hindquarters.
- Horses can be reactive to the tickle of a fly, so teach yourself to use the tassle of the dressage whip to replicate the same tickle – it is much more effective than using force, and you can keep tickling until you get the response you need.
- If you consistently use your leg aid first and tickle with the dressage whip afterwards, you will find that the horse will start to move off the leg aid before you need to follow up with any touch of the whip. This is easier and better for both of you than constantly using the leg aids and not getting any response.

Another option for speed demons!

- If you struggle to consistently achieve the halt on landing with the horse, or want to try something different, another technique is to use circles between the fences (*see* diagram).
- After jumping the fence, ride a few strides straight to create enough room to turn, and then ride a circle of about 15 to 20m diameter. Work the suppleness in the circle and stay tall and calm, closing your leg to ride the horse's hind leg underneath him – this is where you can put your leg on, as turns are where the horse will naturally go less forwards.
- Keep riding the same circle, working on rhythm, balance and relaxation. This might take a few circles to achieve, but be patient and wait for the horse to settle.
- Once the horse is letting you ride the circle in a rhythmical and more relaxed way, move on to jumping the next fence and repeat the same thing on landing.
- Repetition and calmness is the key. None of this is designed to punish the horse, so keep everything smooth and as relaxed as possible. The intention is simply to keep making him listen to his rider by giving him something else to think about on landing, rather than anticipating running on to the next fence.

EXERCISE 84

Leg Yield to a Fence

Aim

Leg yield to a fence is a good way to help control pace if a horse likes to come in too fast, and is particularly useful where there is a long run-in, as you can make your approach too wide and then move in to the fence by leg yielding, rather than having a long stretch for the horse to lock on to it. It is also a useful exercise to help improve the quality and straightness of the canter, because to perform the leg yield well requires suppleness and engagement. This will all help to improve rideability.

Set-Up

Equipment:

- One showjump

Set up the fence off the edge of the arena, perhaps on the three-quarter line to give room for the exercise to be performed.

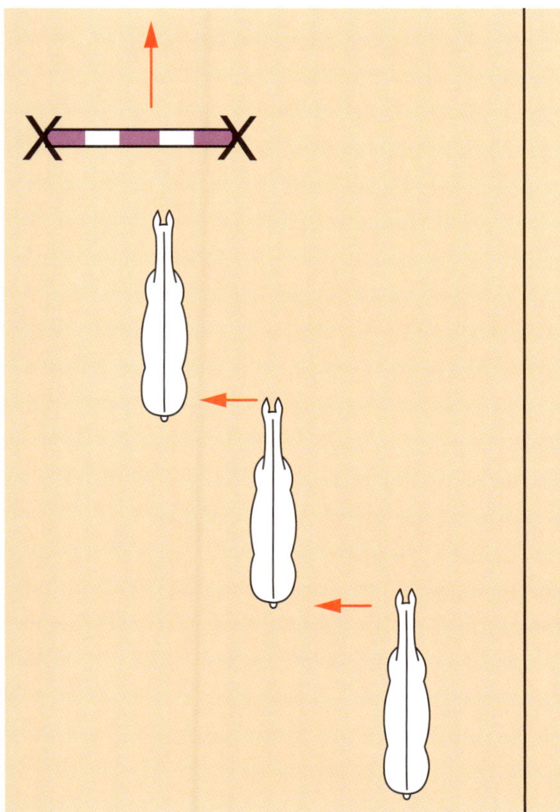

Using leg yield from the outside of a fence into the middle can help control pace whilst maintaining a quality canter.

How to Ride It

- Having practised leg yield on the flat (*see* Exercise 4 in Chapter 1), begin the exercise with a pole on the floor between the wings, on blocks or secured in place with some arena surface.
- You can start in trot if preferred when there is just a pole on the floor, then progress to canter.
- Ride out to the track and flex the horse's poll very slightly to the outside. Keeping the horse's body as straight as possible, move him over towards the jump by applying your outside leg just behind the girth. Be careful to control the inside shoulder and prevent it from falling in by keeping a connection on the inside rein, and ride a half halt as needed to ensure the outside hind leg is stepping across in line with the rest of the body.
- Aim to complete the movement across to be straight one to two strides before the fence, and ride a straight line afterwards.
- The same exercise can be used to varying heights of fences and in various places, but generally I would avoid leg yielding out to a fence as this encourages horses to drift on to the outside shoulder and doesn't help straightness. It is always better to move from the outside in, as this keeps hind-leg engagement, where often the energy falls out on to the outside shoulder moving from inside to outside.

TIPS ON ESTABLISHING THE CORRECT LEG YIELD

Try to resist the temptation to steer towards the fence if the leg yield doesn't move you far enough across. Instead reduce how much movement you are asking for by staying nearer the outside edge of the pole when you turn, so you are only moving four feet across, and then increase the movement across by riding wider once you have established the correct leg yield. It can help to think of the hind leg leading the way in from the track as this will tend to override the temptation to let the shoulder fall in – and it would be very unusual to see the quarters actually lead the way in this movement!

EXERCISE 85

Cavaletti Bounces

Aim

Cavaletti can be very useful to help control the pace with a horse that gets too hot and forwards, as they have more height than a pole so can hold the horse's frame a little more and keep the elevation in the stride, whereas bold horses can end up standing on poles. This exercise is particularly useful to hold the stride length for forward-thinking horses. It can also help engage the core and maintain their balance with power, but without allowing them to lengthen. I prefer to use cavaletti with rounded ends if possible, as these will roll out of the way if hit, rather than being fixed in the ground, which can happen with square-edged cavaletti.

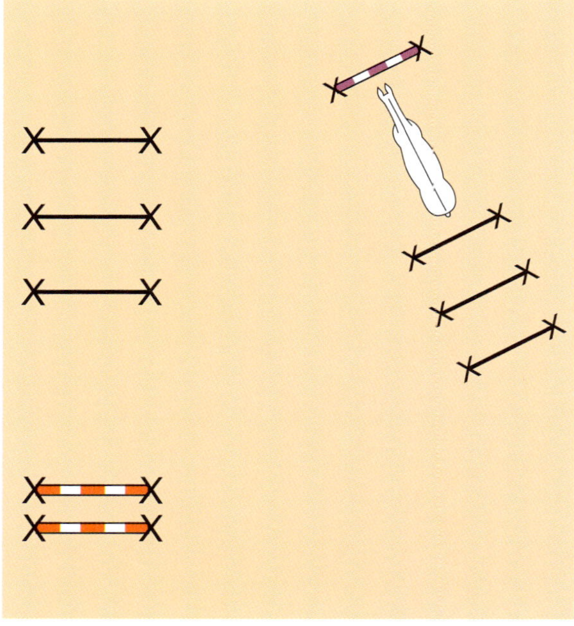

Cavaletti bounces preceding a fence can help control the pace into the jump whilst helping your horse to hold his frame and balance.

Set-Up

Equipment:

- Three cavaletti
- One showjump

Set up the exercise initially with a single cavaletti in line with the wings for the jump on a 7yd (6.4m) distance. After working over the cavaletti and adding the fence, add the preceding two cavaletti on a distance of about 3.5yd (3.2m) apart.

How to Ride It

- Start the exercise by introducing the horse to a single cavaletti, riding over it in canter, then canter the straight line through the wings afterwards.
- Add the fence on the one-stride distance and ride the rhythm over the two elements. If the horse is already getting strong, it can be helpful to ride a halt in a straight line on landing after the fence.
- Now add the other two cavaletti, so you now have a line of three cavaletti and the fence afterwards.
- Keep your shoulders up on the approach to the cavaletti, and as the distance is quite short between each of them, keep your shoulders and upper body up to help communicate to the horse that you don't want him to lengthen in between each element.
- If you are still struggling with pace in the final stride, one pole in the middle of the one-stride distance, secured with sand or pole pods, can help to keep the stride level – although generally the cavaletti will have successfully held the stride without needing to add that in.
- You can change the fence and repeat the same exercise to other fences, depending on how many cavaletti you have, or how many times you want to move them!

EXERCISE 86

Cavaletti Curves

Aim

This cavaletti exercise is useful for controlling pace with forward-thinking horses, but also encourages engagement and elevation if the horse has a tendency to run a little flat and on the shoulders or to lose power through the turns. This will help to improve the horse's rideability.

Set-Up

Equipment:

- Three or more cavaletti
- A minimum of one showjump

Set up the exercise as in the diagram, with three cavaletti on a curving line with 7yd (6.4m) in between each element on the middle line, and 7 to 7.5yd (6.4 to 6.86m) to a fence, depending on the height of the fence. Keep the curving line very slight to start with, as riding the middle line throughout can be quite challenging!

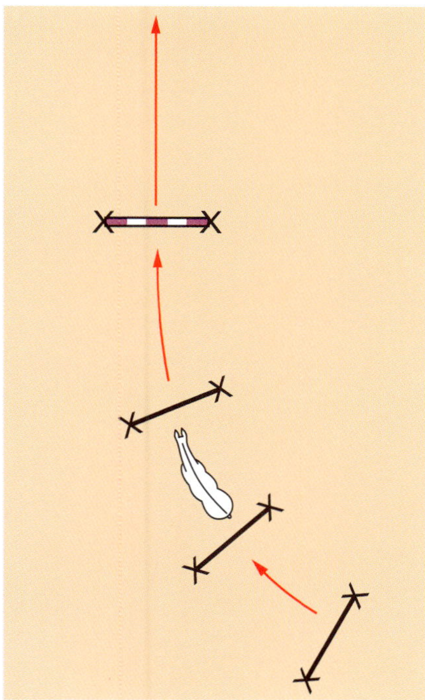

Cavaletti on a curving line helps to maintain the quality of the canter through the turn and reduces the horse's opportunity to 'lock on' to a straight line fence, whilst regulating the stride and aiding engagement.

How to Ride It

- Start the exercise by introducing the horse to a single cavaletti if needed before riding in canter over the three cavaletti on the curve and through the wings of the fence without the jump there initially.
- Think of looking and planning ahead through the curve, and be aware of controlling the line, particularly with your outside leg, as the tendency is mostly for the horse to drift out of the curve.
- Add the fence as part of the line and ride through the cavaletti curve to the fence, ensuring that afterwards you ride away straight.
- You can play with different distances to the fence depending on what you want to achieve. For example, if you have more of a challenge with the quality of the canter through the turn, rather than control of pace to the fence, it might be helpful to maintain the one-stride distance on the curve with the cavaletti and extend the distance to the fence to two strides (11yd (10m)), three strides (15yd (13.72m)) or four strides (19yd (17.4m)). You can then focus on maintaining the quality of the canter you achieved over the cavaletti through the distance afterwards.
- If you want to increase the challenge slightly and have a forward-thinking horse, you can shorten the cavaletti on the curve to about 3.5yd (3.2m) so that you ride a sequence of bounces on the curve before the one-stride distance to the fence. You can also add more cavaletti to the curve so there is a longer sequence of bounces or one-stride distances, which means that the stride is regulated to the same length throughout.
- Be aware that riding exercises of this nature is physically quite demanding on the horse (even if he says it isn't!), so include rest periods, and don't overdo the repetition of the exercise – there is always another day.

TIPS ON PREVENTING THE HORSE DRIFTING

If you find the horse is drifting out of the curve, use some flat or half-round poles on the outside of each cavaletti to help guide him round.

EXERCISES FOR STRAIGHTNESS

EXERCISE 87

Cross-Poles

Aim

Cross-poles are a very simple way to achieve straightness at a fence, but they should be built correctly, and riders should be aware that the higher sides needed to create the cross can make the horse jump the height of the sides and not the middle! They are not often seen in competition, and for this reason, alongside the potential issue mentioned above, haven't been included in the other exercises in this book. Nevertheless they have their place to help with technique and straightness at a fence.

This image shows how to set up a cross pole safely so that each element can fall independently of the other if it is hit.

Set-Up

Equipment:

- Four wings
- Four poles plus cups including a minimum of two safety cups

The important part of building a cross-pole is to make sure there is space between the two poles forming the cross-pole. This allows the front pole to fall safely if hit and does not create a fixed fence effect by being blocked in with the second pole. (*The British Showjumping Rulebook* requires a gap of at least 4in (10cm) between the poles.)

How to Ride It

- The cross-pole can be located anywhere and jumped in both directions as a vertical.
- Be aware of the potential impact of the sides being higher, so bring in any changes to height gradually. However, if you want to create more movement through the shoulders and challenge a more experienced horse, then the sides of the cross-pole can be made quite high to create a steeper 'V'.
- Another option using cross-poles is to build an oxer to train straightness and bascule over a fence. The same rules apply for the safe placement of the poles, and use safety cups all round if you want to jump the oxer in both directions.
- Keep the height of the cross-poles the same between the front and back rails, and start with a relatively narrow fence before building in width. This type of fence is not really suitable for very inexperienced horses or riders as the back element is less obvious as a cross than when it is a straight rail. You can use a cross-pole in front and a straight bar behind, but the inexperienced rider's eye can get pulled to the back bar, which can be unhelpful, so it depends on what you are seeking to achieve as to how you structure the oxer.

EXERCISE 88

Tramlines

Aim

Tramlines will have been seen in various sections of this book, because they are incredibly helpful for training the straightness that is essential for successful showjumping.

Set-Up

Equipment:
Tramlines are designed to give you and the horse a visual aid to achieve and maintain straightness.

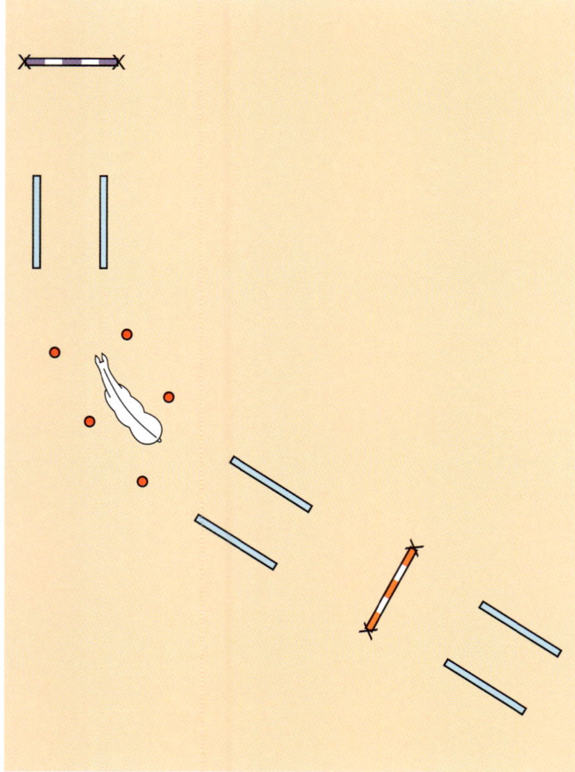

Adding cones through a curving line to guide horse and rider between them to tramlines and fences is a useful extra tool.

They can be half-round poles, flat slats, poles that are blocked in so they don't roll around if stood on or hit, and they can also be smaller guiding aids (for example round a turn) such as cones or pole pods. The latter provide less of a straightness aid as they don't have the length that poles have to help straighten the horse's body, but they are a good visual aid to help the rider be aware of the correct line.

How to Ride It

- Basic tramlines can be set up on their own, or before or after fences, to work on straightness. Ideally they should be at least a canter stride away from the fence (approximately 4yd (3.6m)) so they do not impact the jump too much.
- Set the tramlines approximately 2yd (1.8m) apart to begin with, and make them narrower if needed (as long as you can fit all four of the horse's feet between them comfortably) as the horse becomes familiar with them.
- Straightness in terms of the horse's front and hind feet following the same track is also a consideration through turns. This is where cones or pole pods can be useful to guide the line (*see* diagram), set on a similar distance apart.

COACHES' TIP: TRAMLINES AND CONES TO HELP GUIDE THE LINE

Tramlines and cones can be used throughout a course to help guide the line. This is really useful to train the eye for novice riders so they understand how a line will work and therefore learn how to ride it well.

EXERCISE 89

'A' Frames

Aim

'A' frames can be used to help guide straightness over the fence, and are also useful to help improve a horse's front leg technique by encouraging him to flex the shoulders and front limbs more.

Set-Up

Equipment:

- Two thin flat slats or half-round poles
- A minimum of one showjump

How to Ride It

- Warm up over a single fence or other plain fences before introducing the 'A' frame to the exercise.

'A' frame on the ground:

- If it is straightness at take-off that you need, rather than straightness over the fence, then the first part of this exercise, with the poles on the floor, could be sufficient.

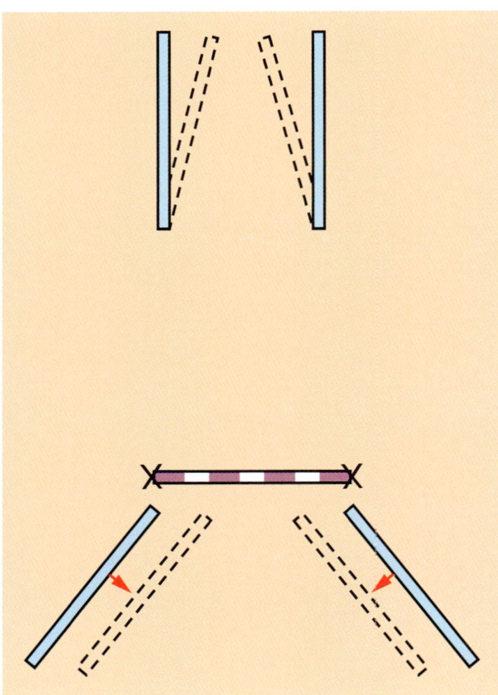

The blue poles here denote the starting point for A-frame poles at take-off and after landing. The dotted lines denote how to tighten up the 'A' once the horse is familiar with them. You may only need one set of these (for example at the fence) depending on what you are seeking to address.

- Place the two slats or half rounds on the floor near the feet of the wings. Have both slats slightly angled outwards from that point (*see* diagram) to create the beginnings of the 'A' frame. Start by approaching a small fence with the wide 'A' frame on the floor, keeping the horse in a rhythm and being ready with the leg aids if he draws back on seeing the extra poles.
- As the horse becomes familiar with the extra poles, you can bring them in slightly to make the gap in the 'A' smaller.

'A' frame on the fence:

- Once the horse has worked with the 'A' frame on the ground, you can introduce it on the fence.
- Place the slats or half-round poles on the top rail of a relatively small fence, keeping them to the outside edge to start with.
- Once you have jumped this a couple of times, you can try drawing the slats in towards the middle of the fence. Do this gradually, and be careful to ensure that they could drop down if knocked.

'A' frame after the fence:

- This does not mean putting an 'A' frame directly on the landing side of the fence! However, for horses that consistently move off the straight line on landing, drawing in the tramlines on the landing line to create a wide 'A' frame on the ground two or three strides after the fence can help to channel them straighter – keep a gap between the ends of the poles to ride through (*see* diagram).
- The narrow gap, if placed on a good point in the horse's stride (for example 11 to 11.5yd (10.1 to 10.5m) for two strides), can also encourage the horse to change to lead with the correct leg if he consistently lands on the wrong lead.
- Once you are happy that the distance suits, pull the slats close together at that point, and they will create a point to ride over that will create elevation in that step, as well as straightness, so helping the horse to change on to the correct lead. Try to time your aids for the change as the horse begins to take the stride over the point of the A.

EXERCISE 90

St Andrew's Cross

Aim

The St Andrew's Cross is not suitable for a novice horse or a novice rider, but it can be a very useful fence to encourage the horse to stay straight over the fence and improve his bascule over the jump.

Set-Up

Equipment:

- Two pairs of wings
- A minimum of four poles plus safety cups

This fence is normally built with a minimum of two poles on the front and two on the back. The poles on the back will need safety cups, and they should be used on every pole if jumping the fence in both directions. Make the jump so that the front poles are angled in one direction and the back poles are set to the same height but angled in the other direction (*see* photo).

How to Ride It

- When first introducing this fence, after having warmed up over more conventional fences, keep the height and width well within the comfort zone of both you and the horse to start with.
- Make sure that the horse is straight and has an energetic, engaged canter, then ride to the fence aiming for the middle of the cross created by the angled front and back rails. Afterwards aim to ride away straight.
- Once the horse feels confident with the question being asked of him, the height and width can be increased as needed.

A St Andrew's Cross can help improve straightness and technique over the fence. Make sure there are safety cups on all the back bars used.

EXERCISES FOR JUMPING TECHNIQUE

Exercise 91

Open Groundlines

Aim

A simple way to help your horse's technique can be to use groundlines either before or after the fence, or both. This is something that can be set up easily and doesn't require a lot of equipment to do so.

Open ground lines can be used on verticals and oxers and are designed to help open out the base of the fence to encourage the horse to take off far enough away from the fence to develop his front-leg technique, and to land far enough out from the fence to create a good shape.

Open groundlines in front of the fence can help if the horse has a tendency to run too deep, and this will give the horse more room to lift the shoulders if he is a little slow in his front-leg technique.

Open groundlines after the fence can encourage a horse to complete the bascule of the jump, and not to have too steep a trajectory on the landing side of the fence, or to land too short after the fence (which most frequently happens with a horse that is less forward going).

Set-Up

Equipment:

- A minimum of one showjump
- Two half-round poles or similar

Any groundlines need to be secure so that they don't roll and trip up the horse. Thin flat slats or half-round poles with a flat base are ideal. Soft poles made with sponge can flip up when stood on so are not ideal for this type of training, and if you need to use round poles, make sure they are well secured with pole pods or arena surface.

For horses, the take-off spot is 2yd (1.83m) from the fence and the same on landing, so an opened out groundline can comfortably come up to 1yd (0.91m) away from the fence for horses (reduce this for ponies) if necessary, but start with a less open ground line and only pull it out if needed.

An open groundline can help the horse to take off further away from the fence if he gets drawn too close. These can be useful when introducing planks, for example.

How to Ride It

- Which groundlines you open up depends on the horse and what you want to achieve. Mostly the groundline on the approach will be pulled out to improve the take-off by keeping the horse away from a very deep stride, which as a result will assist the shoulder and front-leg technique.
- If you need to use a groundline after the fence because the horse is landing too close to the fence, start with the groundline as near to being in line with the back bar as possible while the horse becomes accustomed to it, as it is less usual to see a pole here.
- Once the horse is comfortable with the pole being on the landing side, you can start to pull it out a little – but do this gradually and carefully, as it is more likely that the horse will stand on it on this side of the fence. Keep working on riding forwards away from the jump in this scenario, as doing so also helps with improving the horse's travel over the fence.

EXERCISE 92

Using Fillers

Aim

Assuming that the horse has already been introduced to fillers, their placement can also be used to help with his jumping technique.

Set-Up

Equipment:

- A minimum of one showjump
- Two standing fillers
- One plank or small hanging filler

There are various set-ups that can be used to influence the jump, which are outlined below.

To open the take-off: Small standing fillers are good for this, but they can also have a pole in front of them, secured on the ground, to help protect them from being stood on if necessary. Place the fillers slightly open to the side and in front of the fence to help open the profile of the jump and encourage the horse to jump with a better bascule.

To channel straightness: Set the standing fillers slightly apart and place them so they are angling in towards the fence, which helps create a channel to the jump to assist with straightness. Alternatively the fillers can be used independently of a fence: you can work through them as part of your straightness training on the flat, using them a few strides before or after a fence to help keep the straight line on approach and landing.

To improve the bascule: This exercise is not for less experienced combinations. Place the fillers in the middle of an oxer (*see* photo) – they can be located to either side, rather than being put close together to start with – the idea being to create more elevation in the middle of the jump to help with the shape the horse makes over it.

Using a plank to draw the eye: Often in a course, a plank will be used as a filler in the bottom of the fence to draw the horse's eye down to it and so potentially cause a rail to fall. If you need the horse to lower his head at take-off, you can experiment with the placement of a plank or small filler to see if it helps. Placing the plank as the top rail draws the eye up, but this can be an unforgiving profile and pull the horse closer to the fence; so if using it like this, to begin with it can help to put an open groundline in front of the fence to help the horse to judge the take-off point better.

Using fillers in the middle of an oxer is designed for more experienced combinations to help improve the bascule over the jump.

01282 834970
EQUESTRIAN
SURFACES LTD
.equestriansurfaces.co.uk

THE COLLECTING RING AND COMPETITIONS

The show jumping collecting ring can be a challenging environment to work in, as it can be busy and a quite high-octane environment, with many horses cantering and jumping alongside you in what is often a relatively small space. The amount of time allowed in the collecting ring can also be limited, which can make the warm-up feel more pressured, and sometimes it is not possible to work on both reins.

In this chapter are some tips and techniques to help manage this unique environment, and to help you prepare for different competition scenarios that you may encounter as well.

EXERCISE 93

How to Prepare for the Collecting Ring

Aim

For young, inexperienced horses, the showjumping collecting ring can be a daunting experience and good preparation is key to them gaining confidence to enable them to cope well with this environment. This page outlines some ideas to help with this preparation.

Set-Up

Equipment:

- One vertical and one oxer
- Ideally a separate course of jumps in another arena

How to Ride It

- In order to help your horse become familiar with the competition format, using an arena hire with a set up as outlined above can be helpful. In this situation, walk the course of jumps first so that you know the lines and the distances between the fences (see Exercise 98) before getting on your horse.
- With someone on the ground to help you, use the vertical and then the oxer to warm up having worked through your paces on the flat. This is a good opportunity to help establish a system with someone that might also come to competitions with you so that you both know what height of fences you want to warm up over and how many times you want to jump each fence before going in the ring. For less experienced assistants, it also gives them the opportunity to decipher how the cups work on the wings (especially safety cups!) and how to handle the poles to build the fences quickly and efficiently.
- Everyone will have slightly different preferences and it also depends on the horse you are riding, but as a general rule I aim for 3 to 4 verticals at increasing heights followed by the same number of oxers in the warmup with increasing height and width. If there is then a pause before my time in the ring, I might jump another fence (usually the same one as the first fence on the track) before I go in, especially if I am riding a horse that has a tendency to switch off.
- Once you are warmed up, go into the main arena and establish a good canter before riding your round. With a very novice horse, don't worry if you need to approach each fence in trot to give them time and confidence and to maintain the line to the fence, just ensure your jumps are small enough to do so and then build up from there once their confidence increases.

TIPS ON HABITUATING THE HORSE TO THE COLLECTING RING ENVIRONMENT

As well as doing some arena hires in this format where possible, there are some venues that stage training shows: in these you can have the collecting ring environment at a less intense level, and can ride round a course without worrying about penalties or elimination for errors. Other ways to help familiarise your horse with a collecting-ring environment include the following:

- Attending group lessons, where the horse has to work alongside others, but also, in a jumping lesson scenario, can watch other horses jump and canter past him as would happen in a collecting ring environment, as well as leave the other horses to jump exercises on his own.
- Ride in an arena with friends to familiarise the horse to other horses working in the same space if you mostly school alone – big-moving horses can make quite a lot of noise as they canter and jump and so can be quite intimidating for a young horse if he has not encountered these before.
- Dressage competitions are one of my favourite ways of educating a young showjumper to the competition environment, as they are still encountering other horses, but generally at a slower pace and without the jump element. They also have to leave the other horses to enter the dressage arena but don't have the added pressure of tackling fourteen fences, whilst also dealing with the new experience of competition.
- Showing classes enable you to introduce the young horse to a show environment, often with a lot of other activity going on at local and county show level, again without tackling fences as well.

EXERCISE 94

Flatwork in the Collecting Ring

Aim

The collecting ring is often not all that spacious, and achieving a good warm-up to prepare the horse for your jumping round can be a challenge. These exercises give you some ideas to help address your warm-up on the flat to prepare you and your horse to jump, and some of the techniques covered in Chapter 1 can be used to help you.

In the collecting ring remember to give priority to those working in faster paces and jumping. In normal circumstances the aim is to pass other riders left hand to left hand, but this is not always possible when landing from a fence, for example, so be very aware of the other competitors, especially those whose horses have a red ribbon on their tail (indicating they might kick), on the bridle or forelock (indicating they are horse shy), or a green ribbon (indicating they are novice horses) and a yellow ribbon (indicating they are being ridden by a para rider – which could denote any type of disability, including being deaf or partially sighted as well as other physical disabilities).

How to Ride It

- The goal in your collecting ring warm-up is to allow your horse's muscles to get warmed up, ideally on both reins, and to make sure that you have the rideability you want in the ring for your horse's current level of training.

Stop and go:

- It might sound simple, but ensuring that your horse responds to your aids is key to your warm-up.
- Transitions should not impact too much on the warm-up of other competitors, so check behind you that you aren't about to cause a crash by coming back to halt, for example!
- Ensure that the horse is moving forwards off your leg aids in the upward transitions, and that he is listening to your body position in the downward transitions so you are not having to rely too much on the rein.
- Direct upward transitions – such as halt or walk to canter – are useful for sharpening up backward-thinking horses, and direct downward transitions can be helpful for the stronger, more forward-going horse.
- Working on lengthening and shortening the stride within the canter without losing impulsion is also a useful exercise to do in the warm-up, particularly as the horse steps up the levels and is competing round more technical tracks.

Working suppleness:

- Working suppleness in a small collecting ring can be a challenge as there is not often room to circle safely, so in this circumstance lateral work can be useful (*see* Chapter 1).
- To ensure the horse is listening to your lateral aids and to improve hind-leg suppleness and engagement, use leg yield to and from the track, so long as other riders will not be impeded by you. You can do this in walk, trot and canter if needed.
- To work suppleness and engagement, you can also ride shoulder fore or shoulder in, travers (quarters in) and renvers (quarters out). The latter is particularly helpful if you are limited in terms of riding a change of rein, as it allows you to work a different bend without changing direction. Shoulder fore and shoulder in can be ridden in canter relatively easily, and can also help lighten the forehand if the horse is getting heavy.
- To improve suppleness in the canter, it can sometimes be helpful, if space allows, to ride a small shallow loop in canter, which demands more balance and suppleness of the body than riding a straight line.

Lightening the forehand:

- If your horse is inclined to get strong and a little heavy in the hand by running on to the forehand, then try using some reinback to help engage the hindquarters and lighten the forehand, in addition to some direct transitions up and down the paces.
- If there is space and you can work easily in both directions, turn on the haunches can also be used in a safe part of the arena to help achieve the same aim.

EXERCISE 95

Jumping in the Collecting Ring: The Forward or Excitable Horse

Aim

Warming up a forward-going and excitable horse in an exciting collecting ring can be an interesting experience! The goal is obviously to keep things as calm as possible, but some horses still struggle to cope with the environment, and I have encountered some that may not even jump a fence before going into the main arena! However, there are techniques that you can employ to help make the jumping warm-up a beneficial experience, and some of these are outlined on this page.

How to Ride It

- Unfortunately there is often not room to ride circles in the collecting ring to help settle an excitable horse, but sometimes you can, provided you are very aware of not riding across in front of someone approaching the warm-up fences.
- As an alternative, work on riding a fluent canter round the track until the horse has started to relax and attain a rhythm. From this canter, ride to your warm-up fence, then go back to riding round the track again a few times until you regain a good rhythm. It takes a little longer, but if you just keep riding to the fence without taking a little time in between, the hotter type of horse is likely to anticipate it and become bouncier and less balanced and rhythmical each time you make the turn to the jump.
- Another technique that can be helpful if the horse still rushes to the fence is to ride a halt on the landing side. This can be done progressively on landing as it is not a punishment, more an explanation. Once the horse has halted, pat him, and then repeat the exercise as needed. The idea is that the horse will begin to approach the fence anticipating the transition afterwards and so will not rush in to the same degree. This also helps emphasise the half-halt aid for when you are in the ring.
- Another option is to ride wide to the fence and leg yield back in to it to stop the horse locking on and rushing (though be aware that another rider might be coming in on the straight line approach and doesn't realise your intention). You can practise moving the horse off the lateral aids on the flat in the warm-up before repeating this in your approach to the fence if this technique is helpful to you.

TIPS ON PREPARING TO GO INTO THE RING

Some horses benefit from a little walk and chill time between warm-up and going into the ring so they do not become too overwhelmed, whereas others need the adrenaline rush to stay bold and perform well. This is something that is very individual, so you may need to experiment with both approaches to discover which is the best solution.

EXERCISE 96

Jumping in the Collecting Ring: The Laid-Back Horse

Aim

This exercise outlines some ideas to help motivate the more laid-back horse in your jumping preparation in the collecting ring, where a confined space and the stop-start nature of a warm-up can mean that the canter loses quality and momentum.

How to Ride It

- As with an excitable horse, it can be beneficial to ride several circuits of the warm-up arena in canter before approaching the fence each time, although in this instance for a very different reason. Collecting rings can be quite 'stop start', as riders will often stop after jumping a fence and wait for it to be raised before starting again, and it can be difficult sometimes to keep moving forwards when there is limited room on the track. However, this can cause a laid-back horse to switch off more and lack energy for the approach to the fence. By riding the canter round the outside until you have established the quality you want and then riding to the warm-up fence, you give yourself time to motivate the horse forwards and maintain the flow. If you time it right, you can keep riding round to the fence without riding a downward transition (other riders and horses permitting) until you change from the vertical to the oxer, or are ready to head into the competition ring; this can help keep the horse focused and stop him switching off.
- If you find the horse is either decelerating to the warm-up fence, or loses power on the last strides, a useful technique is to ride him away positively forwards on landing. Try to avoid riding a downward transition (even if that is your intention) until you have had a good response to your forward aids. This trains the horse to anticipate accelerating away after the fence, and therefore hopefully encourages him to maintain the forward pace on the approach.
- If the horse lights up a bit more with a jump-off feeling, then if there is space to do so you can try making an approach off the other rein to the warm-up fence, with a pivot back on the tighter approach (*see* Exercise 97).

EXERCISE 97

Jumping in the Collecting Ring: The Jump-Off

Aim

Although many national classes in the UK are either single or two-phase competitions, which means that the jump-off is included within one round, there are still other classes, particularly those qualifying for championships, that have a separate jump-off. If you are looking to be competitive in the jump-off, you might include some of the following exercises to help prepare for this in the collecting ring.

How to Ride It

- Once you have jumped a fence as normal in your jump-off warm-up, you can ride wide to the fence next time and approach it on the angle (*see* Chapter 9), being aware of where other competitors are, as your line is likely to encroach on the outside track, but possibly also on the line to the other warm-up fence.
- You can also try turning to the fence from a shorter approach, or approach the fence off a tight turn off the other rein. To do the latter, in most collecting rings it will be quite a restricted space to approach from, so using a pivot turn to help keep the straightness and engagement through the turnback can be helpful, and will also sharpen up the horse to the outside aids for the tighter jump-off turns you might want to try.
- You can also practise turning quickly away from the fence on landing, provided you are not about to wipe out another competitor by doing so, including by turning back in the opposite direction of travel if space and other riders allow.

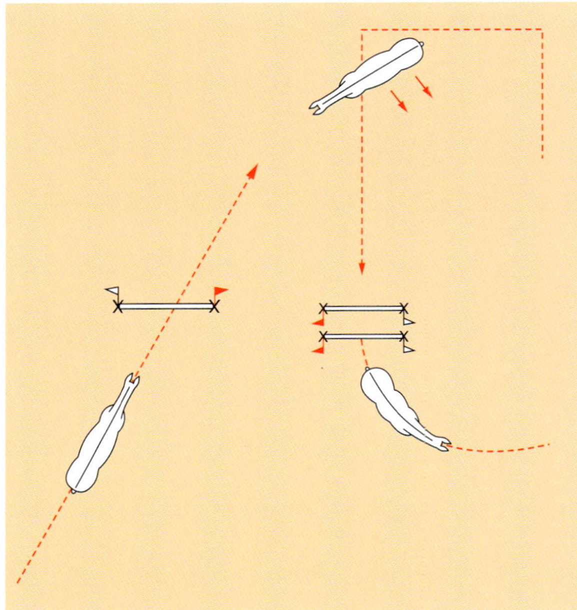

Riding a fence on the angle or turning back off the opposite rein through a pivot turn, or turning tightly on landing, can all be used to prepare your horse for the jump-off if this is helpful to him, but beware of the location of other riders if you are doing this so that you don't impede them in doing so.

TIPS ON PRACTISING JUMP-OFF TECHNIQUE

As the first round and the jump-off are combined in single- and two-phase classes, I would advise not to practise jump-off techniques in the warm-up for these unless you were trying to wake up a lazy horse.

Ensure that you have practised the exercises in Chapter 9 before attempting these in a collecting ring or in the competition itself. You will then know what techniques best suit your horse, and where in the course you might save time, or where you will need to play a little safer in order to accommodate your horse's strengths and weaknesses, as well as his level of experience.

Don't forget that you are also aiming to keep the horse in balance to help him go clear, so ride some standard lines in your warm-up as well.

EXERCISE 98

Walking Distances

Aim

Knowing how many strides the course builder intends you to take between fences helps you to plan your line and how you will ride round a course. Whilst with a young horse this plan may well not happen, because maintaining straightness in a rhythm and with an even stride can be a challenge, as you step up the levels, being aware of the questions the course builder has set in terms of related distances becomes increasingly important.

How to Do It

- Although many Europeans and some British riders measure distances in metres, the easiest calculation to do and therefore, to my mind, the easiest to learn for the purpose of walking distances, is imperial measurements, so yards and feet.
- Courses are built for horses on the assumption of a 4yd stride, with 2yd for take-off at the fence and 2yd for landing, which makes a fairly easy calculation based on multiples of four. So, for example, a one-stride double is 4yd plus 2yd for landing and 2yd for take-off, making it 8yd in total. A three-stride distance is 3 × 4yd plus 2yd for landing and 2yd for take-off, making it 16yd in total. There is a little variation within this, depending on the types of fence and the level of competition, but as a basic principle this works well.
- For ponies it is a little more complicated as the distances have to be adjusted slightly more according to the height of the pony, so there are

Distance Guide

A guide to the measurements used between fences for specific pony height classes and in horse classes.

Number of Strides	128cm Pony (10's)			138cm Pony (10'6"s)			148cm Pony (11's)			Horse (12's)		
	Shorter	Normal	longer	Shorter	Normal	longer	Shorter	Normal	longer	Shorter	Normal	longer
1	19'	20'	21'	21'	22/22'6	23'	23'	23'6"	24'	24ft 6"	25ft 6"	26'6 27'6"
2	29'	30'	31'	31'	32 – 32"6	33'	32' 6"	33'6"	34/34'	35'	36'	37-38'
3	39'	40'	41'	41'	43'	44'	43'	44'	46'	47'	48'	50-51'
4	49'	50'	51'	52'	53'	54'	54'	55'	57/58'	59'	60'	62/63'
5	59'	60'	61'	62'	63'	64'	65'	66'	68/69'	70'	72'	74/75'
6	69'	70'	71'	72f'	73'	74'	76'	77'	79/80'	83'	84'	86/88'

*These distances are for guidance only. Consideration must also be given to site circumstances and material to be used. Distance greater or smaller than those listed above can be used dependant on specific conditions.

distances for 12.2, 13.2 and 14.2hh ponies that are fairly standardised for competition. From a course-walk point of view, mostly a simple formula of 4yd for each stride plus 1yd for take-off and 1yd for landing (instead of 2yd for each) works as a basic guide – except that one-stride doubles can be on anything from 6.3yd to 8yd depending on the pony size.

- The distance for a two-stride double is 29ft or 9.67yd (minimum distance 12.2) to 34ft or 11.3yd (maximum distance 14.2) = 10yd on the above calculation – 8yd for two strides plus one each for take-off and landing.
- A three-stride distance is a minimum of 39ft or 13yd to a maximum of 46ft or 15.3yd = 14yd on the above calculation – 12yd for three canter strides plus 1yd each for take-off and landing.
- A four-stride distance is a minimum of 49ft or 16.3yd to a maximum of 58ft or 19.3yd = 18yd on the above calculation – 16yd for four canter strides plus 1yd each for take-off and landing.

- To practise walking the length of stride correctly, you need to learn to feel what that yard-long stride is for you, as everyone is different. A good way of doing this at home is to measure out one yard on some concrete and stick tape at each end of the distance. Then every time you walk in that direction, practise taking the one pace guided by the tape. If you have space you can always create your own related distance with a sequence of marked-out one-yard strides!
- Another way to do it, for example when walking the course, is to walk the length of a pole to check your stride length. Long poles are exactly the same as a canter stride – that is, 12ft or 4yd long, so should be the same as four of your strides. The shorter version (except stile-type poles) are usually 10ft long (3yd and 1ft), so would be three of your strides plus 1ft. Walking the length of the pole is a quick and easy check on your stride length if you are not sure you are walking the distances correctly.
- The diagram outlines the basic distances that British Showjumping course builders work to.

EXERCISE 99

Walking the Course

Aim

Walking a course and formulating a plan for how you intend to ride it helps you not only to ride it well, but to build your confidence by giving you a process to follow, which can help you to control any nerves before you go into the ring. This page gives you some tips to make sure that you get the most out of your course walk.

How to Do It

- Firstly, it is often useful to have a look at the course plan for the class you are competing in. In Britain, the course plan is available beside the collecting ring before the class starts, and it is often now also available online on the British Showjumping website.
- On the course plan you will be able to confirm the class type – whether it is single phase, A7, and so on – and if the competition is two rounds, it will also have the numbers for the jump-off section listed. The entrance/exit will also be marked, as will the location of the start and finish, which can help you to link the map to the jumps in the arena. Looking at the plan in advance of the course walk gives you a little extra time to learn the course, as sometimes the time allowed to walk the course can be quite tight.

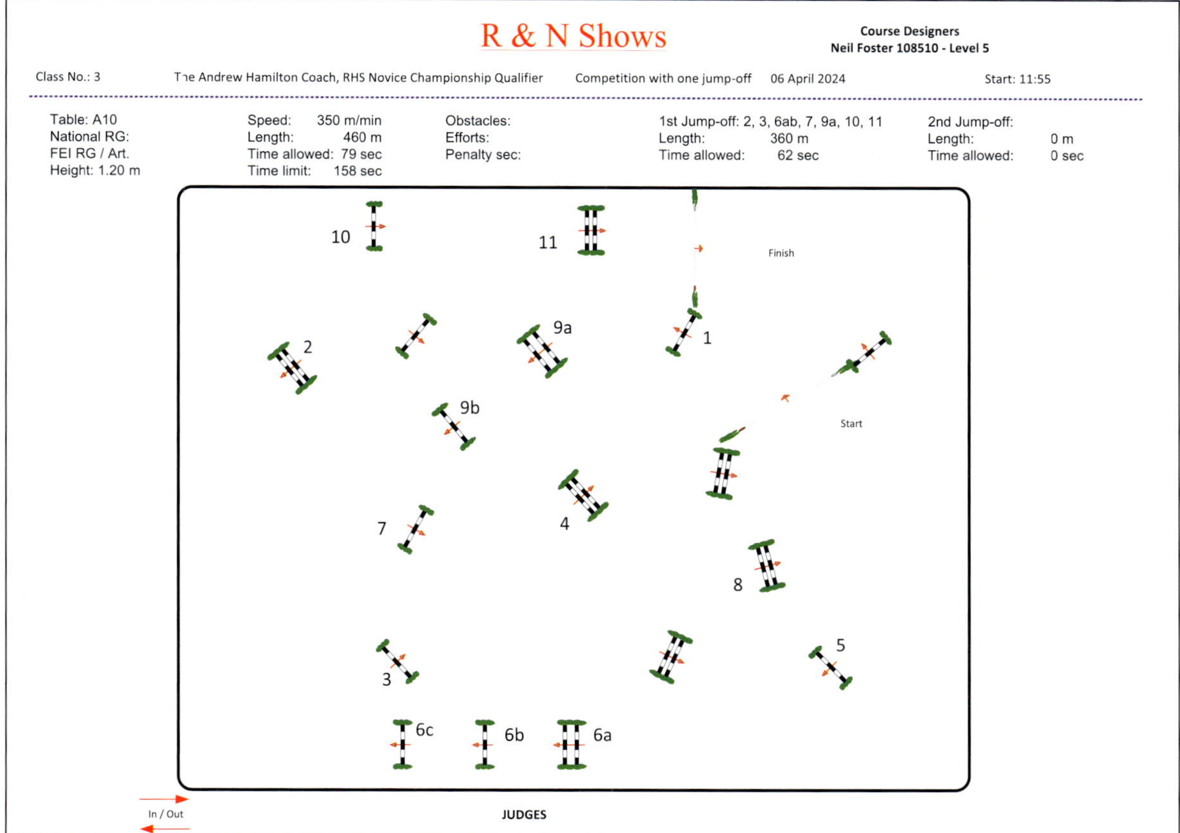

This course plan, supplied by Level 5 course builder Neil Foster, demonstrates the format of a course plan, including class type (table A10 in this instance), fence height, the speed at which the course needs to be ridden (350mpm) and time allowed, plus the second-round jump-off track for those that jump clear in the first round.

- Once you are permitted to walk the course, try to walk the line the course builder intended, including pacing the related distances from middle to middle, as this is where you hope you will be riding them! That also allows you to see where there are other elements to the arena or line that might impact on the ride to or from a fence, such as arena decoration that the course builder might have placed to help (or hinder!) the line, and notice where there is a clear line to the next fence and where your horse might need clear aids to be sure which fence he is approaching.
- With horses whose strides get bigger or faster round a course, you might also look for places where you can add a little leg yield to a fence, for example if there is a long straight run to one that might be a challenge if ridden straight the whole way, or where you might add in a pivot turn to help get them back on their hocks and address straightness and control.
- For horses that can lack impulsion, make a plan for areas where you can ride forwards between fences if needed, and notice where fence locations, such as after a rollback turn, might cause your horse's power to drop off if you are not prepared for it and have a plan to address it in the round.
- If you are competing in a single- or two-phase competition, you also need to notice where the start beam is for the second phase. In single-phase classes you will carry on to the finish even if you have had faults in the first phase, whereas in two-phase classes, faults incurred in the first phase mean the judges will ring the bell to indicate that you cannot continue into the jump-off section.
- In these types of class you will also need to decide whether you are seeking a smooth round and just achieving a double clear, or whether you are going to be competitive and look for faster lines where you might be able to ride tighter turns in the second section of the course. Sometimes what looks like a faster line by turning tightly actually requires too much of a break in your horse's rhythm to achieve it and so is slower than not riding that particular turn – but that is where the art of riding a successful jump-off comes into play!
- For classes with a separate jump-off, it is worth noting which fences are in the jump-off, as sometimes an extra fence is included – this will have a number on it but placed in the middle in front of the fence rather than to the side for the first round, and is a higher number than the last fence on the first round course – for example 14. Also you might want to look at what lines you would take if you were to jump clear, as there is usually no opportunity to go into the ring and walk the jump-off course between the first and second rounds – so otherwise you would only be able to look at the course and plan your route from the sidelines.

TIPS ON HOW TO REMEMBER THE COURSE

Try to pay attention to fence colours and the pattern of the lines within the course, as this can be a way of helping you to remember it. Go back through your plan in your head whilst you are still beside the ring, and make sure you can remember where your fences are in relation to each other whilst you are able to look at the course and check it!

Although watching one or two riders go round the course can be helpful for memorising it, don't forget that your plan is tailored to your horse, and don't be too distracted by how many strides someone else takes between the fences or any issues they might have – stick to your plan!

EXERCISE 100

International Competition

Aim

Showjumping competitions run under FEI (International Equestrian Federation) rules take place in many countries around the world and range from 1* to 5* level, including classes for young horses, amateurs and veterans. Whilst competing overseas is a great experience, those who can't travel to Europe or further afield with their horses can still experience an international competition in Britain. To do so there are a few differences that are outlined below, while a key difference from national events is the trot-up.

How to Do It

- If you are intending to compete in an FEI competition in Britain at 2* level or under, you need to obtain authorisation from British Showjumping's Performance Department; this is generally given provided you are planning to compete at the same height at which you are competing nationally. International amateur classes can have a minimum height of 1.00m, and veteran classes can start at 1.10m, for example.
- If you are a UK national you do not need a full FEI rider registration and FEI horse passport for events in Britain at 2* and under, so you can compete under UK event registration and FEI horse registration, which is a simpler process!
- Once registered, you can apply to enter international shows in the UK, which you can do through British Showjumping, as well as directly with the show centre for some shows.
- The key differences for international shows are as follows:
  - You are required to take your horse's temperature before and during the show and keep records accordingly for disease prevention.
  - You will need to attend the venue the day before jumping starts so that you can present your horse for inspection and perform a trot-up (*see* below).
  - You will need to present your horse's passport, which is then held by the show for the duration.
  - Your horse will be required to wear a bridle number at all times when outside his stable at the show, and is not allowed to leave the designated area for the duration of the competition, so you are required to stable on site. Although you are given a bridle number on arrival, it can be useful to have some spare sets with you so that you can put one on your horse's headcollar, for example, and this will avoid having to keep moving one number between different pieces of kit.
- The trot-up takes place with FEI vets, who assess your horse's health and soundness. You need to present your horse in either a snaffle or a double bridle. Usually a snaffle bridle is sufficient, although I prefer to use a lead rope with a double clip and chain so that you have control evenly on both sides of the bit. You must remove all boots, bandages and rugs for the inspection, so if you need them in the lead-up to this then make sure you have someone who can help you remove them before you present your horse.
- Showjumping trot-ups usually take place in one of the arenas, and the vet will ask you to trot away a set distance that is marked out, and then trot back in a straight line.
- To save embarrassment it is definitely worth practising this with your horse before the event to be sure that he will know what you are asking him to do! Using a voice command when you are practising can be helpful if the horse has a laid-back temperament, so that he understands to go forwards and you don't end up trying to drag him along beside you.
- When practising with a laid-back horse, you can hold a dressage whip in your left hand with the horse on your right-hand side. Give the voice command you want to use to move into trot, and if he doesn't move off appropriately, indicate behind you with your whip towards his quarters to help motivate him forwards (it is not easy to

make contact, but usually you wouldn't need to, as the movement of the whip is mostly sufficient). He may move his quarters away, but usually he will also break into trot at this point. Practising this a couple of times should help him to associate the voice command with trot and remove the need for the whip.

- When you ask him to trot forwards you should be able to keep pace beside his shoulder, ideally with some slack in the lead rope near his head. At the end of the straight line, come back to walk and turn the horse away from you to then face back towards the vet. Again step into trot and trot in a straight line back to the starting point, where you will halt and wait for any further instructions.

If your horse has not trotted up correctly – he might have been dancing about in excitement or not wanting to go into trot – it is likely you will be asked to do it again so that the vet is happy to give you clearance to compete.

CONCLUSION

The preceding chapters have laid out a broad spectrum of exercises that can be used with a variety of horse and rider combinations in different scenarios. In this final chapter I have tried to outline a few routes for linked exercises that could be utilised to develop horse and rider for different goals.

Before I offer the linked exercises, however, I would ask you to consider how the challenges we face as a rider or coach can be approached.

A Strengths-Based Approach

Think about a situation at school, at home or at work, when you have put a huge amount of effort into a particular task for someone. Now imagine that this person comes to look at your hard work and their first response is to spot something you have missed or not done to perfection and to comment on that. How does that make you feel?

Now imagine that, instead of that response, this person comes to look at your efforts and they are thrilled with the hard work you've put in, and recognise your efforts and (hopefully) are pleased with the results too. If there is still something to do to improve it further this might get discussed, but only after the good things you have done and the acknowledgement of your hard work and tremendous effort has been recognised. Not surprisingly you might feel more encouraged about this scenario.

I would suggest that most of us have been in both of these situations at one time or another, and I would guess that most of us had a better sense of wellbeing after the second outcome.

Most horses also try hard to please their human, and respond well to praise. Therefore, if your horse is trying hard to perform one of these exercises and is achieving it in part, even if not yet fully, then praise him for his effort and for making progress in the right direction: this is a far better approach than punishing him for not yet achieving the complete goal.

In terms of training both yourself and your horse, it is far easier to identify where things are going wrong in either our own riding or our horse's way of going. Any time I ask a rider how an exercise went, the first response is nearly always to tell me what they did badly!

If we want to be better riders and to progress our horses more quickly, a more positive, strengths-based framework can be challenging to start with, because it may go against a natural tendency to focus on what went wrong, but it can be hugely effective at developing you as a rider and creating a more positive and enjoyable training environment for the horse.

This is not about completely ignoring the things that aren't going to plan or could be better, but it starts from a basis of finding out what is going well. If you don't know what you and the horse already do well, how can you build on those strengths? If you are doing an exercise, part of performing that exercise should be around identifying which parts of it went well and then trying to identify why they went well: what was it you were doing that made it work, and what was your horse doing well, and why?

By breaking it down and identifying the strengths of each performance, you may find that you and your coach can then use those strengths to help improve other areas of the performance.

As a basic example, you may notice that the horse's canter down the long side of the arena is powerful and rhythmical, but something happens round the turn so that the rhythm and power are no longer there. Ride the canter down the long side again, and assuming it feels as good, notice in detail how the horse is moving (what is he doing well?) and what you are doing to help achieve that good performance: how is your contact, what are you doing with your legs, how are you sitting, where is your upper body? This is where having good eyes on the ground, such as a coach, can help you to identify what is working well. Now see if you can maintain that feeling and those actions through the turn, and notice if the canter improves or whether one of the elements drops off. Use the skills you and your horse are good at down the long side to keep working to achieve the same quality through the turn. This is the basis of a strengths-based approach.

As you work through some of the exercises in this book, whether as a coach or a rider, try experimenting with a strengths-based focus in your training and see if this provides a better relationship with your horse and a more positive tone and outcome to the training sessions.

Visualisation

Another tool to aid performance that links in very well to a strengths-based approach is visualisation. Visualisation before riding a round or performing an exercise can help you to mentally rehearse a physical performance. The really clever part about this is that – or so I am told – if you visualise a performance really well, the brain cannot differentiate it from a real performance. This is really useful from a showjumping perspective as most of us don't get to jump several rounds in the same class, where professional riders might – but if we can ride the round in our heads a few times, we have replicated the effect of actually riding it a few times, with the added bonus that all the rounds were on the same horse! When I have asked riders in a training session to visualise the course before they ride it, it is noticeable how much calmer and more focused they often are when they set off.

A good way to learn how to do visualisation well is to try first using a technique called 'reverse visualisation'. This is where your ability to identify what went well in a performance, using the strengths-based approach outlined above, will be useful.

First of all, notice when a performance went well. It might be a round of showjumps, or performing an exercise well in training. Now try to remember the details. See if you can shut your eyes and be back in that moment riding your horse. Notice the feeling of the canter and the jumps, notice the colours, the sounds, as much detail as possible. And remember how good it felt when it was going so well, how you felt emotionally as well as the physical feelings in your body during the performance.

Ideally all visualisation should be done in real time – in other words, if you took 73 seconds to complete a round of showjumps, your time to visualise it again should be 73 seconds (or longer). If it is taking less time, it is likely that you are not adding enough detail and perhaps not riding every stride of that canter. You can relive those moments of good performance as often as you like – the more you relive it by riding it in your head again, the more you reinforce all the good neural pathways in your brain that helped you achieve that good performance.

Once you are able to do reverse visualisation well, you will have the knowledge of how a good performance feels so you can then use it to help visualisation before a performance.

For this, usually you will need to walk the course first so that you can see each fence, and walk your lines – walk the line you will ride, and don't cut the corners. Once you have memorised the course, take your time and ride it in your head, visualising the full round. There isn't always a lot of time after the course walk until you need to warm up, but a round is often only just over a minute long, so most of us have time for that one minute before we need to get on our horse.

Remember how your good performance feels, and bring that feeling into the round you are about to ride – notice the colour of the fences, remember how your horse's quality canter and jump feel, and apply it to this course. Try to add emotional as well as physical elements to how it feels when it is going well so that you have a complete picture – and remember to breathe while you are doing it!

One useful extra tool to use if needed is the 'rewind' function. It can happen that when you are happily visualising a good round, an inner voice tells you that a certain fence won't go well. If this happens, mentally press rewind and go back to the point in the course before the fence. Now continue to play the round forwards with lots of colour and a positive focus on good performance, and usually the inner voice disappears.

Don't forget to use reverse visualisation for any good performances to keep topping up those positive neural pathways that help to keep developing our strengths. Use this technique any time you need a confidence boost too, as it can help remind us of the good feelings that are associated with a good performance.

Using Linked Exercises

This next section is designed to give you a few ideas for exercises in this book that can be used for the horse in different circumstances.

Young Horse Beginning his Ridden Career

For young horses beginning to learn the basics around ridden work, their balance is likely to be on the forehand and the canter can take a while to develop, depending on factors such as their type, temperament and conformation. In this situation, referring to the Scales of Training outlined in Chapter 1, Exercise 1 is particularly helpful so that you can keep monitoring his development and progress whilst ensuring that the fundamental principles of rhythm, tempo and relaxation are at the centre of your work.

In addition to this, within Chapter 1, Exercise 2 The Half Halt is key to aiding your horse to develop his balance. Also I begin to introduce a basic leg yield (Exercise 4) very early in the horse's education so that he understands that a lateral aid is different from a forward aid: this can greatly help steering as the horse develops.

To begin the introduction to poles and jumping, Exercise 14 in Chapter 2 begins the process, and can be helped by Exercise 15 if the horse requires help with straightness. Once the horse is confident with this, you could also introduce Exercise 21 using angled poles in trot to help develop the strength of the hind leg. If you have begun to establish a basic leg yield, you could also try working through Exercise 27, which incorporates a trot-pole serpentine and a leg-yield exercise as a follow-on; try the leg yield in walk first.

Chapter 3 then provides a basic guide to introducing the horse to jumping. The first exercise (31) is suitable for very novice horses, then progress to Exercise 32 once you feel ready to start jumping.

Veteran Horses

Older horses will almost certainly require a longer warm-up in walk before commencing harder work, and they can benefit from some of the following exercises to help maintain suppleness and range of movement.

Leg yield in Exercises 5 and 6 can be helpful to work on the suppleness of the hind leg, particularly with more experienced horses that are familiar with a straight-line leg yield but may have learnt how to cheat a little in doing so!

Travers and renvers (Exercises 8 and 9) are also useful flatwork exercises for suppleness of the body and hind leg, as in these it is difficult for the horse to evade correct movement if he is ridden well.

Polework (Chapter 2) is also useful for maintaining suppleness and range of movement.

Exercises 18 and 19 are good examples of polework exercises that work suppleness through the turn enhanced by the location of the poles.

Exercises 27 and 28 using serpentines and leg yield are also useful pole exercises for the veteran horse, whilst Exercise 29 is a good one for core strength and also movement in the pelvis, as it uses poles to help control straightness in the reinback.

From a jumping perspective, using leg yield to a fence as outlined in Exercise 84, is another good suppling exercise, while the cavaletti curve from Exercise 86 is useful to help engage the hind leg and create a little more movement in the body.

Horses Lacking Suppleness

Key to developing a horse's suppleness is improving the ride on the flat, so suppling exercises such as leg yield (Chapter 1, Exercises 4 to 6) will be useful, as will shoulder in, travers and renvers (Exercises 7 to 9), as these will require the horse to create movement through both sides of his body.

The canter shallow loop in Exercise 12 of this chapter is also a useful suppling exercise for a more experienced horse.

As with veteran horses, polework (Chapter 2) is very helpful to improve suppleness.

Exercises where the curve incorporates poles are the most helpful, such as Exercises 19 and 20, and angled poles (Exercise 21) can be used raised either to the outside or the inside, depending on what area of suppleness you need to work on.

Linked in to this, Chapter 5, which incorporates jumps and poles, has exercises that will aid the development of the horse's suppleness, including the Egg Timer (Exercise 43), or for smaller arenas the Canter Curve (Exercise 55 in Chapter 6) works on the same principles.

Horses Lacking Straightness

Improving a horse's suppleness on both reins often helps straightness as well, so although the exercises above may be beneficial, to address straightness specifically it is helpful to include poles in the exercise.

Exercise 15 is a very basic straightening exercise using poles, and Exercise 21, using angled poles, but with the poles in a straight line and raised on alternate sides, can be helpful. Exercise 56 uses pivot turns and tramlines to aid straightness.

Gridwork (Chapter 4) is another area of training that can specifically help straightness, and the bounce grid in Exercise 39 uses cross-poles to this end.

Other specific straightness exercises include Exercise 42, which incorporates poles and jumps, while Exercise 89 explains how to use an A-frame of poles to best effect.

Group Lessons

Coaching group lessons and having exercises for polework and jumping that can have several horses working at the same time so that everyone keeps active (at least during the first part of the session) can be a challenge!

In terms of a flatwork warm-up, Chapter 1 Exercise 3, which is lengthening and shortening strides, can be useful in that it can be ridden at the same time by multiple riders, as can leg yield in a straight line (Exercise 4). If you can control the ride to be able to observe each rider without them impeding the view of the next, then shoulder in, travers and renvers can also be worked on (Exercises 7 to 9), as can the canter shallow loop (Exercise 12).

The basic polework exercise (Exercise 14) can be worked easily with multiple riders, provided they are able to keep some distance between each other, as can the shallow loop in Exercise 16 and the angled poles in Exercise 21, plus the canter half circle in Exercise 22.

The serpentine and leg yield exercise (27) can also work well provided you only work the serpentine in one direction (as in ride down the long side to restart at the same place rather than continuing back down the serpentine to the beginning), and make sure the riders know who has priority – so the person riding the serpentine has priority to continue over the person riding down the long side, to avoid crashes! Ensure the poles are secured properly, and be ready to reinstate them if they get knocked.

In Chapter 5 there are several exercises that suit group sessions, including Exercise 42, working on straightness and control, and Exercise 46, the Centipede, particularly if you start by working over poles and use the centre line and the two curving end lines for your warm-up.

Chapter 6 has several configurations that work well in small spaces, and has multiple exercises to warm up over that can be used in group sessions: Exercises 57, 58 and 59.

And Finally...

I hope that you enjoy working through some of these exercises as much as I have enjoyed creating some of them for my clients at home, as well as experimenting with them on my own horses!

Happy jumping!

ACKNOWLEDGEMENTS

There are many people to thank for the creation of this book, and so apologies if I have missed anyone out.

Huge thanks must go firstly to J.A. Allen for giving me the opportunity to try to put 25 years of coaching into written form. Then to my long-suffering husband Anthony, and the rest of my family, for supporting me through this process. And to all the incredible coaches I have had the opportunity to learn from and work with, particularly Susie Gibson, who has been a fantastic coach and mentor to me for many years and has encouraged me through the coaching process. Also to Matt Lanni, who gave me new ways of working with my horses; to Jane Bartle-Wilson and Christopher Bartle, who together transformed my thinking around coaching when I worked for them at Yorkshire Riding Centre; and to Lorna Moore, who first educated me in the art of riding, rather than just galloping over the moors!

For the book content, huge thanks must go to Claire of Claire Hirst Photography for her unending patience, good humour and skills in providing most of the images for this book; and to the models: Michelle, Sophie, Molly, Michelle and Zoe. Thanks also to ATG Photography for the cover shot, 1st Class Images for the photo of para showjumper Claire Pope for Chapter 8, Equipics for the image supplied for Chapter 9, and Majestic Photography for the image for the Conclusion.

And finally, thanks to Michael Bainbridge, British Showjumping's Head of Officials and FEI course designer, for supplying the official British Showjumping distances chart for Chapter 12; and to Level 5 course designer, Neil Foster, for supplying a diagram of one of his courses for the same chapter.

Thanks must also go to Molly Yeulet, for holding the fort on the yard and exercising horses in freezing temperatures with good humour and a smile despite everything, while I sweated over a computer screen trying to complete this book; and to Zoe Ward for the same on weekends. And to Jane and Dickie Jeffreys of Kimmerston Riding Centre, who gave me the opportunity to ride and love their horses when I was a child – I'm sure I must have often driven them demented with my attempts to 'help' on the yard. Finally to British Showjumping for all the opportunities I have been given to learn and develop as a coach.

And last, but by no means least, thank you to all the special horses I have had the opportunity to learn from, but especially Reiver, the horse I owe everything to – I wouldn't have got here without him.

First published in 2025 by J.A. Allen, an imprint of
The Crowood Press Ltd
Ramsbury, Marlborough
Wiltshire SN8 2HR

enquiries@crowood.com
www.crowood.com

British Library Cataloguing-in-Publication Data
A catalogue record for this book is available from the British Library.

ISBN 978 0 7198 3509 4

Typeset by Chennai Publishing Services

Cover design by Blue Sunflower Creative

Printed and bound in India by Thomson Press (India) Limited

RELATED TITLES